Return on Investment in Training and Performance Improvement Programs

Second Edition

**IMPROVING
HUMAN
PERFORMANCE
SERIES**

Return on Investment in Training and Performance Improvement Programs

Second Edition

Jack J. Phillips, Ph.D.

An Imprint of Elsevier Science

Amsterdam Boston Heidelberg London New York Oxford Paris
San Diego San Francisco Singapore Sydney Tokyo

Butterworth–Heinemann is an imprint of Elsevier Science.

∞ Recognizing the importance of preserving what has been written, Elsevier Science prints its books on acid-free paper whenever possible.

Library of Congress Cataloging-in-Publication Data

Phillips, Jack J., 1945–
   Return on investment in training and performance improvement programs / Jack J. Phillips.—2nd ed.
      p. cm.
   Includes bibliographical references and index.
   ISBN 0-7506-7601-9 (alk. paper)
      1. Employees—Training of—Evaluation—Handbooks, manuals, etc.
   2. Rate of return—Handbooks, manuals, etc.   I. Title.

   HF5549.5.T7P434 2003
   658.3′124–dc21

                                                                     2003045312

British Library Cataloguing-in-Publication Data
A catalogue record for this book is available from the British Library.

The publisher offers special discounts on bulk orders of this book.
For information, please contact:

Manager of Special Sales
Elsevier Science
200 Wheeler Road
Burlington, MA 01803
Tel: 781-313-4700
Fax: 781-313-4882

For information on all Butterworth–Heinemann publications available, contact our World Wide Web home page at: http://www.bh.com

10 9 8 7 6 5 4 3 2 1

Printed in the United States of America

Contents

v

Preface

THE USE OF ROI IS EXPLODING

Return on investment (ROI) has become one of the most challenging and intriguing issues facing the human resources development (HRD) and performance improvement field. The interest in ROI has been phenomenal. The topic appears on almost every HRD conference and convention agenda. Articles on ROI appear regularly in HRD practitioner and research journals. Several books have been developed on the topic, and consulting firms have been developed to tackle this critical and important issue.

Several issues are driving the increased interest in ROI. Pressure from clients and senior managers to show the return on their training investment is probably the most influential driver. Competitive economic pressures are causing intense scrutiny of all expenditures, including all training and development costs. Total quality management, reengineering, and Six Sigma have created a renewed interest in measurement and evaluation, including measuring the effectiveness of training. The general trend toward accountability with all staff support groups is causing some HRD departments to measure their contribution. These and other factors have created an unprecedented wave of applications of the ROI process.

NEEDED: AN EFFECTIVE ROI METHODOLOGY

The challenging aspect of ROI is the nature and accuracy of its development. The process often seems very confusing, surrounded by models,

formulas, and statistics that often frighten the most capable practitioners. Coupled with this concern are misunderstandings about the process
and the gross misuse of ROI techniques in some organizations. These
issues sometimes leave practitioners with distaste for ROI. Unfortunately,
ROI cannot be ignored. To admit to clients and senior managers that
the impact of training or performance improvement cannot be measured
is to admit that training does not add value or that HRD should not
be subjected to accountability requirements. In practice, ROI must be
explored, considered, and ultimately implemented in most organizations.

What is needed is a rational, logical approach that can be simplified
and implemented within the current budget constraints and resources of
the organization. This book presents a proven ROI methodology, based
on almost 20 years of development and improvement. It is a process that
is rich in tradition and refined to meet the demands facing training and
performance improvement programs.

The ROI methodology described in this book meets the requirements
of three very important groups. First, the practitioners who have used
this model and have implemented the ROI process in their organizations
continue to report their satisfaction with the process and the success that
it has achieved. The ROI methodology presented here is user-friendly,
easy to understand, and has been proven to pay for itself time and time
again. A second important group, the clients and senior managers who
must approve training and performance improvement budgets, want
measurable results, preferably expressed as a return on investment. The
ROI methodology presented here has fared well with these groups.
Senior managers view the process as credible, logical, practical, and easy
to understand from their perspective. More importantly, it has their buy-
in, which is critical for their future support. The third important group
is the evaluation researchers who develop, explore, and analyze new
processes and techniques. When exposed to this methodology in a two-
day or one-week workshop, the researchers, without exception, give
this process very high marks. They often applaud the techniques for
isolating the effects of training and the techniques for converting data
to monetary values. Unanimously, they characterize the process as an
important—and needed—contribution to the field.

WHY THIS BOOK AT THIS TIME?

Since this book was first published, several ROI related books have been
developed. When examining current publications, there is still no other
book providing a comprehensive, practical presentation on ROI that

uses a process that meets the demands of the three groups previously described. Most models and representations of the ROI process ignore, or provide very little insight into, the two key elements essential to developing the ROI: isolating the effects of training and converting data to monetary values. Recognizing that there are many other factors that will have an influence on output results, this edition provides nine techniques to isolate the effects of training with an example of each technique, far more than any other presentation on the topic. Not enough attention has been provided to the issue of assigning monetary values to the benefits derived from training. This edition also presents ten techniques for converting data to monetary values with an example of each technique.

The wide scale implementation of the ROI methodology has significantly added to the ROI literature. Hundreds of papers, articles, cases, and research reports have been developed and published. This new edition captures the latest thinking on the use of ROI. Our consulting group has also assisted hundreds of clients with the ROI methodology. We have learned much from these assignments and have reflected the experiences in this new edition.

The first edition of this book was developed at the request of many clients and colleagues who have asked for a simplified, concise description of the ROI process, presented in a step-by-step approach. A new edition has been requested and supported by clients and colleagues who want the latest information on ROI. While the original book provided a sound reference, this new edition provides expanded coverage of many topics and issues important to the development and use of ROI. The original book has become a standard reference in the HRD field and a widely used workshop companion. This new edition should surpass the previous success as it presents a model that is rational, feasible, and understandable to the typical practitioner.

TARGET AUDIENCE

The primary audience for this book are managers and professionals involved in training, development, and performance improvement. Whether an individual is involved in needs assessment, instructional design, delivery, or evaluation, this book will be an indispensable reference. Individuals in training and HRD leadership positions (i.e., managers, supervisors, team leaders, directors, and vice presidents) will find it to be a helpful guide to ROI. With its step-by-step approach and case presentations, it will also be useful as a self-study guide, particularly when used with the ROI field book.

A second audience is the management group. Because of the tremendous interest from the management team and clients involved in ROI studies, this book should be a very useful reference for them. In a simple, easy-to-understand approach, it shows how the ROI is developed in language that managers understand.

A third audience are those individuals involved in the design and implementation of change programs other than training, development, and performance improvement. Because the ROI process is appropriate for all change efforts, this book should be a useful reference for HR managers, change agents, quality managers, reengineering coordinators, and information technology specialists. The ROI process described in this book has been used to measure the impact of a variety of human resources programs, reengineering initiatives, and technology implementation situations, as well as in changes of procedures, practices, and policies. Any time change is implemented, this process will capture the return on investment.

The fourth target audience are consultants, researchers, and seminar presenters who find this process to be an effective way to measure the impact of their programs. It provides a workable model for consultants to evaluate change initiatives or consulting interventions. The book provides researchers with a sound tool for evaluating a variety of programs. Seminar presenters will find this book to be a helpful tool to measure the success of their workshops. The ROI process has been applied effectively in measuring the impact of public seminars.

Finally, professors and educators will find this book extremely useful for evaluating education and training. Also, with this group, the book should be a useful textbook or supplemental book for a course on evaluation. Its content should stimulate thought and debate on how the ROI is developed for the educational field.

FEATURES OF THE SECOND EDITION

To make the second edition a more valuable tool, several changes have been made:

1. The introduction is updated to reflect the current material on trends and issues.
2. A new detailed ROI case study on the evaluation of leadership development is included, which contains ten parts. Leadership is one of the most common applications of the ROI methodology.

3. The most recent version of the ROI model is presented.

4. Data collection is expanded to include collection for measuring reaction (Level 1) and learning (Level 2) as well as measuring application (Level 3) and impact (Level 4).

5. A chapter on ROI forecasting is added to reflect the use of the ROI methodology to justify new programs.

6. The guiding principles are prominently displayed and described in their first use.

7. The chapter on isolating the effects of programs has been enhanced and includes the specific steps for participant's estimation, an interpretation of estimation, and the credibility and reliability of the process.

8. The chapter on converting data to monetary values is expanded to include more detail on how and when to convert intangible to monetary values.

9. The chapter on costs has been expanded to show an actual example of a fully loaded cost calculation.

10. The chapter on ROI is significantly expanded to include more information on the interpretation, use, and abuse of ROI.

11. More examples are included to reflect a variety of different types of programs and settings.

12. The references are updated, including those from all types of processes, with 90% of the references after the year 2000.

13. All forms and templates have been updated.

14. A new chapter on communicating results is included to bring attention to this important issue.

15. The chapter on intangible measures has been expanded to include material on intellectual and human capital.

16. Additional resources are included at the end of the book. Also, the book contains links to websites, software, casebooks, and a newly developed ROI field book.

In all, these changes have made this second edition an absolute requirement for the library of anyone interested in training and development and performance improvement.

STRUCTURE OF THE BOOK

This book has two unique features that make it a very useful guide. First, it presents the ROI model in a step-by-step process. A chapter is devoted to each major part of the model as the pieces of the ROI puzzle are methodically put together. At the conclusion, the reader has a clear understanding of the overall ROI process.

The second unique feature is an application of the model in a detailed case that is based on an actual situation. The case is divided into ten parts. One part is included at the end of each chapter, beginning with Chapter 2. Readers can work through the case, step-by-step, exploring the issues uncovered in the chapter and learn how to apply them to their own organizations. The results of each part are presented in the next chapter where a new issue is addressed. This case presentation is a proven learning tool to understanding the ROI process.

CHAPTER DESCRIPTIONS

Chapter 1: Measuring the Return on Investment: Key Issues and Trends

This chapter describes how the ROI process has evolved in recent years and describes how organizations are tackling this important issue. Key issues and trends are briefly described. Various ROI criteria and requirements are presented to build a foundation for the remainder of the book.

Chapter 2: ROI Model

Initially conceived in the late 1970s, the model has been developed, changed, and refined in the past 25 years to arrive at what users characterize as the most logical, rational, and credible approach to the ROI. This chapter presents a brief summary of the model for those who are being introduced to the methodology for the first time.

Chapter 3: Collecting Data

This chapter presents a variety of approaches to one of the most fundamental issues. Ranging from conducting surveys to monitoring performance data, the most common ways to collect data at all levels are described in this chapter. Useful tips and techniques to help select the appropriate method for a specific situation are presented.

Chapter 4: Isolating the Effects of Training

This chapter presents what is perhaps the most important aspect of the ROI process. Ranging from the use of a control group arrangement to obtaining estimates directly from participants, the most useful techniques are presented for determining the amount of improvement directly linked to the training program. The premise of this chapter is that there are many influences on business performance measures with training being only one of them.

Chapter 5: Converting Data to Monetary Benefits

This chapter presents an essential step for developing an economic benefit from training. Ranging from determining the profit contribution of an increased output to using expert opinion to assign a value to data, the most useful techniques to convert both hard and soft data to monetary values are presented, along with many examples.

Chapter 6: Tabulating Program Costs

This chapter details specifically what types of costs should be included in the ROI formula. Different categories and classifications of costs are explored in this chapter with the goal for developing a fully loaded cost profile for each ROI impact study.

Chapter 7: Calculating the Return

This chapter describes the actual ROI calculation and presents several issues surrounding its development, calculation, use, and abuse. The most accepted ROI formulas are presented, along with examples to illustrate the calculation. Common ROI myths are dispelled.

Chapter 8: Identifying Intangible Measures

This is a brief chapter that focuses on nonmonetary benefits from the program. Recognizing that not all of the measures can or should be converted to monetary values, this chapter shows how the intangible measures should be identified, monitored, and reported. Over twenty-five common intangible measures are examined.

Chapter 9: ROI Forecasting

This chapter shows how the return on investment can be used to forecast the payoff of a program before it is implemented. Several examples are presented to highlight each concept. This chapter underscores the range of possibilities available for calculating the ROI at different time frames, using different types of data.

Chapter 10: How to Communicate Results

This chapter provides best-practice approaches to communicate the results of impact studies. The chapter details how to plan for communications, select audiences and media, develop impact studies, and address typical issues that surface during communication.

Chapter 11: Implementation Issues

This concluding chapter addresses a variety of implementation issues. To implement the ROI process effectively requires following logical steps and overcoming several hurdles. This chapter identifies the important issues that must be tackled for the ROI process to become a productive, useful, and long-lasting process.

Acknowledgments

In no way has developing this book been a single-handed effort. Many individuals have helped shape the content and issues contained in each chapter. Much appreciation goes to our clients who provide us the opportunity to continue to experiment with the ROI process. We have had the opportunity to work with hundreds of excellent organizations and individuals.

Special thanks go to the ASTD ROI Network Board for their unwavering support for our ROI methodology: Merrill Anderson, Gwen Berthiez, Tim Bothell, Holly Burkett, Jim Chatt, Toni Hodges, Brian Howard, Don Jacklich, Dan McLinden, Brenda Sayres, Connie Schmidt, Lynn Schmidt, Mike Sullivan, Uichi Tsutsumi, Kyoko Watanabe, and Deb Wharff.

I would like to thank Francine Hawkins for her patience, persistence, and long hours of work to make this manuscript a reality. Joyce Alff stepped up to a challenging assignment and has provided excellent leadership for our publishing programs. She is an excellent editor who contributes a unique professional approach.

I must also acknowledge the important work and contribution of my spouse, business partner, and friend, Patti Phillips, who has applied this process regularly and made significant progress. Patti provided numerous suggestions for the book and reviewed the manuscript. Without her continued support, this book would not be possible.

CHAPTER 1

Measuring the Return on Investment: Key Issues and Trends

Measuring the return on investment (ROI) in training and development and performance improvement has consistently earned a place among the critical issues in the Human Resource Development (HRD) field. The topic appears routinely on conference agendas and at professional meetings. Journals and newsletters regularly embrace the concept with increasing print space. A professional organization has been developed to exchange information on ROI. At least a dozen books provide significant coverage of the topic. Even top executives have stepped up their appetite for ROI information.

Measuring ROI is a topic of much debate. It is rare for any topic to stir up emotions to the degree the ROI issue does. Return on investment is characterized as flawed and inappropriate by some, while others describe it as the only answer to their accountability concerns. The truth probably lies somewhere in between. Understanding the drivers for the ROI process and the inherent weaknesses and advantages of ROI makes it possible to take a rational approach to the issue and implement an appropriate mix of evaluation strategies that includes ROI. This chapter presents the basic issues and trends concerning ROI measurement.

Although the interest in the topic has heightened and much progress has been made, it is still an issue that challenges even the most sophisticated and progressive HRD departments. While some professionals argue that it is not possible to calculate the ROI, others quietly and deliberately proceed to develop measures and ROI calculations. The latter group is gaining tremendous support from the senior management team. Regardless of the position taken on the issue, the reasons for measuring the return still exist. Almost all HRD professionals share a concern that they must eventually show a return on their training investment; otherwise, training funds may be reduced or the HRD department may not be able to maintain or enhance its present status and influence in the organization.

The dilemma surrounding the ROI process is a source of frustration with many senior executives—even within the HRD field itself. Most executives realize that training is a basic necessity when organizations are experiencing significant growth or increased competition. In those cases, training can provide employees with the required skills while fine-tuning skills needed to meet competitive challenges. Training is also important during business restructuring and rapid change where employees must learn new skills and often find themselves doing much more work in a dramatically downsized workforce.

Most executives recognize the need for training and intuitively feel that there is value in training. They can logically conclude that training can pay off in important bottom-line measures such as productivity improvements, quality enhancements, cost reductions, and time savings. They also believe that training can enhance customer satisfaction, improve morale, and build teamwork. Yet, the frustration comes from the lack of evidence to show that the process is really working. While the payoffs are assumed to exist and training appears to be needed, more evidence is needed, or training funds may not be allocated in the future. The ROI methodology represents the most promising way to show this accountability in a logical, rational approach, and is fully described in this book.

ROI PROGRESS AND STATUS

Global Measurement Trends

Before examining the progress of ROI, a few global trends about measurement and evaluation in both private and public sector organizations should be examined. The following measurement trends have been identified in our research and are slowly evolving across organizations and cultures in more than 35 countries (Phillips and Guadet, 2003). Collectively, these eleven important trends have significant impact on the way accountability is addressed:

☐ Evaluation is an integral part of the design, development, delivery, and implementation of programs.

☐ A shift from a reactive approach to a more proactive approach is developing, with evaluation addressed early in the cycle.

☐ Measurement and evaluation processes are systematic and methodical, often built into the delivery process.

☐ Technology is significantly enhancing the measurement and evaluation process, enabling large amounts of data to be collected, processed, analyzed, and integrated across programs.

☐ Evaluation planning is becoming a critical part of the measurement and evaluation cycle.

☐ The implementation of a comprehensive measurement and evaluation process usually leads to increased emphasis on the initial needs analysis.

☐ Organizations without comprehensive measurement and evaluation have reduced or eliminated their program budgets.

☐ Organizations with comprehensive measurement and evaluation have enhanced their program budgets.

☐ The use of ROI is emerging as an essential part of the measurement and evaluation mix.

☐ Many successful examples of comprehensive measurement and evaluation applications are available.

☐ A comprehensive measurement and evaluation process, including ROI, can be implemented for about 4 or 5% of the direct program budget.

Progression of ROI across Sectors

The ROI methodology described in this book had its beginnings in the 1970s when it was applied to the development of a return on investment for a supervisory training program. Since then it has been developed, modified, and refined to represent the process reported here and expanded in all types of situations, applications, and sectors. Figure 1-1 shows how the process has evolved within the different sectors. Applications began in the manufacturing sector, where the process is easily developed. It migrated to the service sector, as major service firms such as banks and telecommunications companies used the ROI process to show the value of various programs. Applications evolved into the health care arena as the industry sought ways to improve educational services, human resources, quality, risk management, and case management. Nonprofit applications began to emerge as these organizations were seeking ways to reduce costs and generate efficiencies. Finally, applications in the public sector began to appear in a variety of types of

Movement within the Sectors

Figure 1-1. Progression of ROI implementation.

government organizations. Public sector implementation has intensified in recent years. An outgrowth of public sector applications includes the use of the process in the educational field where it is now being applied in different settings. The implementation is spreading and all types of organizations and settings are now enjoying application of the ROI methodology.

Typical Applications

The specific types of program applications vary significantly. Table 1-1 shows a full range of current applications representing programs from training and development, education, human resources, change, and technology. Published cases exist in all of these areas. The process is flexible, versatile, and adaptable to almost any type of setting and environment.

Case Studies

The status of the ROI process among practitioners in the field is difficult to pinpoint. Senior HRD managers are reluctant to disclose internal practices and, even in the most progressive organizations, confess

Table 1-1. ROI Applications

A Variety of Applications Are Possible

☐ Executive Education	☐ Retention Strategies
☐ Leadership	☐ Competency Systems
☐ Executive Coaching	☐ Career Development Programs
☐ Diversity Programs	☐ Recruiting Strategies
☐ Wellness/Fitness Initiatives	☐ Orientation Systems
☐ Total Quality Management	☐ Associate Relations Programs
☐ Self-Directed Teams	☐ Gainsharing Programs
☐ Skill-Based/Knowledge-Based Compensation	☐ Technology Implementation
	☐ Safety and Health Programs
☐ Organization Development	☐ e-Learning

that too little progress has been made. Until recently, it was difficult to find cases in the literature that show how an organization has attempted to measure the return on investment in HRD. Recognizing this void as an opportunity, the American Society for Training and Development (ASTD) undertook an ambitious project to develop a collection of cases that represent real life examples of measuring the return on investment. To find cases, more than 2000 individuals were contacted for the initial volume, including practitioners, authors, researchers, consultants, and conference presenters. The response was very encouraging. Ultimately, 18 cases were selected for publication in Volume 1 of *In Action: Measuring Return on Investment* (Phillips, 1994). This publication has become the all-time best seller at ASTD from over 250 of the society's titles sold through catalogs, bookstores, and conferences. Because of the reaction and response, Volume 2 was developed and published three years later (Phillips, 1997). This volume has become the number 2 best seller. With that success, and continuing demand, Volume 3 was published four years later (Phillips, 2001).

Surveys and Research

The various studies indicate the use of, and interest in, the ROI methodology continue to show promise. For example, the American Society for Training and Development (ASTD) concluded in the 2002 industry report that the number one global trend and issue facing human resource development practitioners is developing the return on investment in training (Van Buren, 2002). The trend and issue was number two the

Table 1-2. ROI Opportunies

Metric	Percentage of organizations rating metric as important or very important (wish list)	Percentage of organizations indicating utilization of metric (doing list)
ROI in Training	78%	11%
ROI in Development	62%	2%
Impact of Training Experiences on Performance	88%	27%

year before, underscoring its continuing dominance of the issue, but a growing trend as well.

Research studies are continuously conducted to show the progress of ROI as well as the dilemmas concerning ROI. Perhaps one of the most comprehensive studies was conducted by the Corporate Leadership Council involving 278 organizations showing the tremendous interest in ROI (Drimmer, 2002). This study attempted to understand the variety of metrics desired and utilized by training and development practitioners. Although several metrics were explored, Table 1-2 shows the status of ROI and business impact as training and development metrics. As the table shows, 78% of the organizations have ROI on their wish list, rating it either important or very important as a desired metric. However, those same organizations currently indicate that 11% of them are using ROI. The same comparison is presented for ROI in development (which are the nontraining types of programs) as well as the business impact measure (where the impact of training experiences on performance is developed). Two important issues evolve from this study. First, the use of ROI continues to grow. A total of 13% of organizations are using ROI in training and development. This is up from previous reports of utilization. Second, there is tremendous interest in ROI, showing that almost 80% of the organizations are pursuing it. This creates a significant dilemma for organizations and underscores the lack of understanding for ROI, the misconceptions of the methodology, and the difficulty in making it work in certain situations. Nevertheless, it outlines a tremendous opportunity (instead of problem) as organizations strive to bring more accountability through the use of the ROI methodology.

Another major study attempted to determine how organizations measure the impact of corporate universities (Phillips, 2000). A detailed benchmarking study examined how major corporate universities are dealing with the accountability issue and, in particular, ROI. Among the conclusions are that best-practice corporate universities are moving up the levels of evaluation, up to and including business impact and ROI. These same corporate universities also want to use ROI, but are struggling with how to calculate it and what to do with the results.

These and other studies indicate two important conclusions.

1. There is a tremendous and growing interest in the ROI methodology as a training and development evaluation tool all around the globe.
2. While progress has been made, there is much more progress to be made to reach the desired level of utilization.

The ASTD ROI Network

Perhaps one of the most visible signs of the acceptance of ROI methodology is the ASTD ROI Network. Founded in 1996, the ROI Network was formed by a group of practitioners involved in implementing the ROI process. The purpose of the organization is to promote the science and practice of individual and organizational measurement and accountability. The network established three strategic goals:

1. To leverage the knowledge, skills, and experience of practitioners and sponsors.
2. To reinforce and support practitioner knowledge, skills, and experience.
3. To promote innovative ROI measurement and evaluation practices.

Through websites, list servers, newsletters, research grants, and conferences, the network has routinely exchanged information around the ROI process. Membership is global as are the ROI Network board members. In 2002, the network was acquired by the American Society for Training and Development and now operates as the ASTD ROI Network, initially with 400 members. Membership in the network is an option available to all ASTD members under one of its classic membership options (www.ASTD.org).

Conferences

Sometimes the best way to judge a trend and interest in a topic is to observe the conference offered by the variety of conference providers. The International Quality and Productivity Center (IQPC) routinely offers ROI conferences, sometimes as many as four or five per year, not only in the United States, but also in Europe, southeast Asia, and Australia. These conferences are designed to explore the issues surrounding ROI, particularly implementation and utilization. The ASTD ROI Network has offered conferences each year with its sixth annual conference conducted in December 2002.

ASTD, recognizing the increased importance of ROI, established a "Conference within a Conference" at its International Conference and Exposition. This practice began in 2000 and continues. It provides a cohesive and coordinated track of programs designed to focus directly on the ROI process. From a practical point of view, an individual could attend an entire conference on ROI while attending the International Conference and Exposition.

The American Productivity and Quality Center (APQC) has also offered conferences on ROI, as has the Institute for Industrial Relations (IIR). IIR, based in Europe, has offered conferences in Europe, Canada, and the United States.

Global Expansion

Measuring the return on investment is becoming a truly global issue. Organizations from all over the world are concerned about the accountability of training and are exploring ways and techniques to measure the results of training. In a survey of 35 members of the International Federation of Training and Development Organizations, measuring return on investment was consistently rated the hottest topic among members of those organizations (Phillips, 1999). Whether the economy is mature or developing, the accountability of training is still a critical issue.

Many professional associations in different countries have offered workshops, seminars, and dedicated conferences to the measurement issue, including ROI. Some associations have sponsored individual workshops on ROI. The formal ROI presentations have been made in over 50 countries with implementation organized and coordinated in at least 35 countries. Two examples underscore the role of these organizations in implementing ROI in their respective countries. Enterprise

Ireland, an Ireland government agency, sponsored workshops on ROI for training and development professionals, followed by workshops for executives. The agency took the lead in coordinating and introducing ROI to organizations in Ireland.

Japan Management Association (JMA), an organization of medium to large business organizations in Japan, introduced the ROI process to its member organizations. JMA translated one of the major books on ROI and sponsored workshops and other learning activities around the ROI process. JMA is coordinating the implementation of the ROI methodology in Japan. Part of this implementation was the development of a special publication, *Measurement of Training Evaluation*. This publication featured case studies from Texas Instruments, Verizon Communications, Apple Computers, Motorola, Arthur Andersen, Cisco Systems, AT&T, and the U.S. Office of Personnel Management. The purpose of the publication was to show Japanese business and industry how other organizations are using the ROI process.

These two examples illustrate how associations, conferences, and publications are being utilized around the globe to introduce a variety of organizations to the ROI process.

Paradigm Shift

The progress with ROI underscores the need for training and performance improvement to shift from an activity-based process to a results-based process. As depicted in Table 1-3, a significant paradigm shift has occurred in recent years that will have a dramatic effect on the accountability of training, education, and development programs. Organizations have moved from training for activity to training with a focus on bottom-line results, and this shift is evident from the beginning to the end of the process. The shift has often occurred because of the forces described in this chapter. In some cases, the shift has occurred because progressive HRD departments have recognized the need for ROI and have been persistent in making progress on this issue.

ROI Is Here to Stay

One thing is certain in the ROI debate—it is not a fad. As long as there is a need for accountability of training expenditures and the concept of an investment payoff is desired, ROI will be utilized to evaluate major investments in training and performance improvement.

A "fad" is a new idea or approach or a new spin on an old approach. The concept of ROI has been used for centuries. The 75th anniversary

Table 1-3. Paradigm Shift in Training and Performance Improvement

Activity Based	Results Based
Characterized by:	Characterized by:
☐ no business need for the program	☐ program linked to specific business needs
☐ no assessment of performance issues	☐ assessment of performance effectiveness
☐ no specific measurable objectives for application and impact	☐ specific objectives for application and impact
☐ no effort to prepare program participants to achieve results	☐ results expectations communicated to participants
☐ no effort to prepare the work environment to support application	☐ environment prepared to support transfer of learning
☐ no efforts to build partnerships with key managers	☐ partnerships established with key managers and clients
☐ no measurement of results or cost benefit analysis	☐ measurement of results and cost benefit analysis
☐ planning and reporting is input-focused	☐ planning and reporting is output-focused

issue of *Harvard Business Review* (HBR) traced the tools used to measure results in organizations (Sibbet, 1997). In the early issues of HBR, during the 1920s, ROI was the emerging tool to place a value on the payoff of investments. With increased adoption and use, it appears that ROI is here to stay. Today, hundreds of organizations are routinely developing ROI calculations for training and performance improvement programs.

Its status has grown significantly and the rate of implementation has been phenomenal. The number of organizations and individuals involved with the process underscores the magnitude of ROI implementation. Table 1-4 presents a summary of the current status. With this much evidence of the growing interest, the ROI process is now becoming a standard tool for program evaluation.

WHY ROI?

There are good reasons why return on investment has gained acceptance. Although the viewpoints and explanations may vary, some things are very clear. The key issues are outlined here.

Table 1-4. ROI by the Numbers

☐ The ROI methodology has been refined over a 25-year period.
☐ The ROI methodology has been adopted by hundreds of organizations in manufacturing, service, nonprofit, and government settings.
☐ Thousands of studies are developed each year using the ROI methodology.
☐ A hundred case studies are published on the ROI methodology.
☐ Two thousand individuals have been certified to implement the ROI methodology in their organizations.
☐ Organizations in 35 countries have implemented the ROI methodology.
☐ Fourteen books have been developed to support the process.
☐ A 400-member professional network has been formed to share information.
☐ The ROI methodology can be implemented for 4–5% of the HRD budget.

Increased Budgets

Most training and development budgets have continued to grow year after year. In the United States alone, the cumulative average growth rate of training expenditures in the last decade was 5% (Industry Report, 2002). According to a survey by the American Society for Training and Development, training grew 10% between 2000 and 2001, and expenditures for 2002 continued at the same pace. The report on the state of corporate training found that increased spending occurred primarily among small- and medium-sized firms; industries such as finance, insurance, real estate, transportation, public utilities, and technology spend the most on training; e-learning is more popular than ever; and outsourced training is increasing. "The continued growth in training is encouraging," says Tina Sung, president and CEO of ASTD. "It illustrates that companies understand the importance of investing in their people . . . even in an economic turndown" (Kleiman, 2002).

As organizations recognize the importance and necessity for training and development, budgets continue to increase annually by organization, industry, and country. Many organizations and countries see training as an investment instead of a cost. Consequently, senior managers are willing to invest because they can anticipate a payoff for their investments.

In developing countries, increased training is needed as new jobs are created and new plants and processes are established. Skill upgrading is

Table 1-5. Definitions of Evaluation Levels

Level	Brief Description
1. Reaction and Planned Action	Measures participant's reaction to the program and outlines specific plans for implementation.
2. Learning	Measures skills, knowledge, or attitude changes.
3. Application and Implementation	Measures changes in behavior on-the-job and specific application and implementation.
4. Business Impact	Measures business impact of the program.
5. Return on Investment	Compares the monetary value of the results with the costs for the program, usually expressed as a percentage.

necessary to develop core competencies needed to maintain a productive labor force. In some countries, the governments require minimum levels of funding for training to ensure that skills are developed.

The learning organization concept continues to be implemented in many organizations, requiring additional focus on learning and training. In addition, the concern about intellectual capital and human capital has created a desire to invest more heavily in learning activities and formal training.

As expenditures grow, accountability becomes a more critical issue. A growing budget creates a larger target for internal critics, often prompting the development of an ROI process. The function, department, or process showing the most value will likely receive the largest budget increase.

The Ultimate Level of Evaluation

The ROI process adds a fifth level to the four levels of evaluation, which were developed almost 40 years ago (Kirkpatrick, 1975). Table 1-5 shows the five-level framework used in this book. At Level 1, Reaction and Planned Action, satisfaction from program participants is measured, along with a listing of how they planned to apply what they have learned. At Level 2, Learning, measurements focus on what participants learned during the program using tests, skill practices, role plays, simulations, group evaluations, and other assessment tools. At Level 3, Application and Implementation, a variety of follow-up methods are used to determine if participants applied on the job what they learned. At Level 4, Business Impact, the measurement focuses on the changes in the impact measures linked to the program. Typical Level 4 measures include output, quality, costs, time, and customer satisfaction. At Level 5, Return on Investment (the ultimate level of evaluation), the measurement compares the program's monetary benefits with the program costs. The evaluation cycle is not complete until the Level 5 evaluation is conducted.

Change, Quality, and Reengineering

ROI applications have increased because of the growing interest in a variety of organizational improvement, quality, and change programs, which have dominated in organizations, particularly in North America, Europe, and Asia. Organizations have embraced almost any trend or fad that has appeared on the horizon. Unfortunately, many of these change efforts have not been successful and have turned out to be passing fads embraced in attempts to improve the organizations. The training and development function is often caught in the middle of this activity, either by supporting the process with programs or actually coordinating the new process in these organizations. While the ROI process is an effective way to measure the accountability of training, it has rarely been used in the past. A complete implementation of the process requires thorough needs assessment and significant planning before an ROI program is implemented. If these two elements are in place, unnecessary passing fads, doomed for failure, can be avoided. With the ROI process in place, a new change program that does not produce results will be exposed. Management will be aware of it early so that adjustments can be made.

Total Quality Management, Continuous Process Improvement, and Six Sigma have brought increased attention to measurement issues. Today, organizations measure processes and outputs that were not previously measured, monitored, and reported. This focus has placed increased pressure on the training and development function to develop measures of program success.

Restructuring and reengineering initiatives and the threat of outsourcing have caused training executives to focus more directly on bottom-line issues. Many training processes have been reengineered to align programs more closely with business needs, and obtain maximum efficiencies in the training cycle. These change processes have brought increased attention to evaluation issues and have resulted in measuring the contribution of specific programs, including ROI.

Business Mindset of Training Managers

The business management mindset of many current education and training managers causes them to place more emphasis on economic issues within the function. Today's education and training manager is more aware of bottom-line issues in the organization and more knowledgeable of operational and financial concerns. This new "enlightened" manager often takes a business approach to training and development, with ROI as part of the strategy (Van Adelsberg and Trolley, 1999).

ROI is a familiar term and concept for business managers, particularly those with business administration and management degrees. They have studied the ROI process in their academic preparation where ROI is to evaluate the purchase of equipment, building a new facility, or buying a new company. Consequently, they understand and appreciate ROI and are pleased to see the ROI methodology applied to the evaluation of training and performance improvement.

Accountability Trend

There has been a persistent trend of accountability in organizations all over the globe. Every support function is attempting to show its worth by capturing the value that it adds to the organization. From the accountability perspective, the training and development function should be no different from the other functions—it must show its contribution to the organization.

This accountability trend has developed a variety of different types of measurement processes, sometimes leaving much confusion to the potential user of the processes. As Figure 1-2 shows, there are a variety of measurement possibilities developed in recent years and offered to organizations as a recommended measurement of the process or scheme. While this has created much confusion, many organizations have migrated to the proven acceptance of ROI. Used for hundreds of years, and for the reasons outlined in this section, ROI has become a preferred choice for training and development practitioners to show the monetary payoff of training.

Figure 1-2. A variety of measurement possibilities.

Top Executive Requirement

ROI is now taking on increased interest in the executive suite. Top executives who watched their training budgets continue to grow without the appropriate accountability measures have become frustrated and, in an attempt to respond to the situation, have turned to ROI. Top executives are now demanding return on investment calculations from departments and functions where they were not previously required. For years, training and development managers convinced top executives that training couldn't be measured, at least at the monetary contribution level. Yet, many of the executives are now aware that it can and is being measured in many organizations. Top executives are subsequently demanding the same accountability from their training and development functions.

The payoff of training is becoming a conversation topic in top executive circles. An initial illustration of this trend occurred in 1995 when the *William & Mary Business Review* selected the topic, "Corporate Training: Does It Pay Off?," as the theme of its summer issue. Each year the *William & Mary Business Review* focuses on an important issue facing corporate executives to stimulate intellectual and practical debate of prevailing management issues. According to the editor of the special issue, "A company's training investment is most likely to pay off when training is held accountable for results. Lacking such data, senior management budgets money for training based on blind faith that it will do *some* good. Then business turn sour, CEOs lose their faith, and training suffers the biggest budget cuts" (White, 1995). This special issue was distributed to top corporate leaders and executives. Since that publication, the ROI topic has been covered in all types of publications such as *Fortune, USA Today, Business Week, Harvard Business Review, The Wall Street Journal,* and *The Financial Times.* Executives have a never-ending desire to explore ROI for learning applications. It is not unusual for the majority of participants in an ROI workshop to attend because of the requirement from the top executives, even in Europe, Africa, and Asia (Virzi, 2002).

THE CONCERNS WITH ROI

Although much progress has been made, the ROI process is not without its share of problems and concerns. The mere presence of the process creates a dilemma for many organizations. When an organization embraces the concept and implements the process, the management team is usually anxiously waiting for results, only to be disappointed when they are not readily available. For an ROI process to be useful, it must balance many issues such as feasibility, simplicity, credibility, and soundness. More specifically, three major audiences must be pleased with the ROI process to accept and use it:

☐ Practitioners who design, develop, and delivery programs.
☐ Senior managers, sponsors, and clients who initiate and support programs.
☐ Researchers who need a credible process.

HRD Practitioners

For years, HRD practitioners have assumed that ROI could not be measured. When they examined a typical process, they found long formulas, complicated equations, and complex models that made the ROI process appear too confusing. With this perceived complexity, HRD managers could visualize the tremendous efforts required for data collection and analysis, and more importantly, the increased cost necessary to make the process work. Because of these concerns, HRD practitioners are seeking an ROI process that is simple and easy to understand so that they can easily implement the steps and strategies. They also need a process that will not take an excessive time frame to implement and will not consume too much precious staff time. Finally, practitioners need a process that is not too expensive. With competition for financial resources, they need a process that will require only a small portion of the HRD budget. In summary, the ROI process, from the perspective of the HRD practitioner, must be user friendly, save time, and be cost efficient.

Senior Managers/Sponsors/Clients

Managers who must approve HRD budgets, request HRD programs, or live with the results of programs, have a strong interest in developing the ROI in training. They want a process that provides quantifiable results, using a method similar to the ROI formula applied to other types of investments. Senior managers have a never-ending desire to have it all come down to an ROI calculation, reflected as a percentage. And, as do HRD practitioners, they also want a process that is simple and easy to understand. The assumptions made in the calculations and the methodology used in the process should reflect their point of reference, background, and level of understanding. They do not want, or need, a string of formulas, charts, and complicated models. Instead, they need a process that they can explain to others, if necessary. More important, they need a process with which they can identify, one that is sound and realistic enough to earn their confidence.

Researchers

Finally, researchers will only support a process that measures up to their close examination. Researchers usually insist that models, formulas, assumptions, and theories are sound and based on commonly accepted practices. They also want a process that produces accurate values and consistent outcomes. If estimates are necessary, researchers want a process that provides the most accuracy within the constraints of the situation, recognizing that adjustments need to be made when there is uncertainty in the process. The challenge is to develop acceptable requirements for an ROI process that will satisfy researchers and, at the same time, please practitioners and senior managers. Sound impossible? Maybe not.

Criteria for an Effective ROI Process

To satisfy the needs of the three critical groups described above, the ROI process must meet several requirements. Eleven essential criteria for an effective ROI process follow.

1. The ROI process must be **simple**, void of complex formulas, lengthy equations, and complicated methodologies. Most ROI attempts have failed with this requirement. In an attempt to obtain statistical perfection and use too many theories, some ROI models have become too complex to understand and use. Consequently, they have not been implemented.

2. The ROI process must be **economical** and must be implemented easily. The process should become a routine part of training and development without requiring significant additional resources. Sampling for ROI calculations and early planning for ROI are often necessary to make progress without adding new staff.

3. The assumptions, methodology, and techniques must be **credible**. Logical, methodical steps are needed to earn the respect of practitioners, senior managers, and researchers. This requires a very practical approach for the process.

4. From a research perspective, the ROI process must be **theoretically sound** and based on generally accepted practices. Unfortunately, this requirement can lead to an extensive, complicated process. Ideally, the process must strike a balance between maintaining a practical and sensible approach *and* a sound and theoretical basis for the process. This is perhaps one of the greatest challenges to those who have developed models for the ROI process.

5. The ROI process must **account for other factors** that have influenced output variables. One of the most often overlooked issues, isolating the influence of the HRD program, is necessary to build credibility and accuracy within the process. The ROI process should pinpoint the contribution of the training program when compared to the other influences.

6. The ROI process must be appropriate with a **variety of HRD programs**. Some models apply to only a small number of programs such as sales or productivity training. Ideally, the process must be applicable to all types of training and other HRD programs such as career development, organization development, and major change initiatives.

7. The ROI process must have the **flexibility** to be applied on a pre-program basis as well as a postprogram basis. In some situations, an estimate of the ROI is required before the actual program is developed. Ideally, the process should be able to adjust to a range of potential time frames.

8. The ROI process must be **applicable with all types of data**, including hard data, which are typically represented as output, quality, costs, and time; *and* soft data, which include job satisfaction, customer satisfaction, absenteeism, turnover, grievances, and complaints.

9. The ROI process must **include the costs of the program**. The ultimate level of evaluation is to compare the benefits with costs. Although the term ROI has been loosely used to express any benefit of training, an acceptable ROI formula must include costs. Omitting or underestimating costs will only destroy the credibility of the ROI values.

10. The actual calculation must use an **acceptable ROI formula**. This is often the benefits/cost ratio (BCR) or the ROI calculation, expressed as a percent. These formulas compare the actual expenditure for the program with the monetary benefits driven from the program. While other financial terms can be substituted, it is important to use a standard financial calculation in the ROI process.

11. Finally, the ROI process must have a successful **track record** in a variety of applications. In far too many situations, models are created but never successfully applied. An effective ROI process should withstand the wear and tear of implementation and should get the results expected.

Because these criteria are considered essential, an ROI methodology should meet the vast majority, if not all criteria. The bad news is that most ROI processes do not meet these criteria. The good news is that the ROI process presented in this book meets all of the criteria.

Definitions and Formulas

Although definitions and formulas are presented throughout this book, several issues need defining early in the book. The term human resource development is used throughout the book to refer to training, education, and development. This terminology, accepted throughout the United States and many other countries, reflects the pioneering work of

Table 1-6. Human Resource Development Definition

	Focus	Time for Payback	Risk for Payback
Training	Job Related Skills	Short	Low
Education	Preparation for Next Job	Medium	Moderate
Development	Cultural Change	Long	High

Nadler (Nadler and Wiggs, 1986). In this context, training focuses directly on job-related skills and has a short time frame for payback. Consequently, it represents a low-risk investment. Education, on the other hand, focuses primarily on preparation for the next job. It has a medium time frame for payback and represents a moderate risk for payback. Development represents more of a cultural change and has a long time frame for payback. Consequently, the risks for payback are quite high. This definition, illustrated in Table 1-6, shows why many organizations place emphasis directly on training where the risk is low and the payback is quick. This definition also explains some of the difficulties of applying the ROI process. The return on investment for short-term training programs is easier to capture with the ROI process. It is more difficult to attain the ROI in educational programs because of the increased time for payback and because other intervening variables may enter the process. Developmental programs are the most difficult for ROI application because of the long-term focus and the full range of variables that may enter the process and complicate the linkage with the performance change. The good news is that successful ROI studies have been conducted for programs in all three categories, including development.

The term *learning solution* is sometimes used in lieu of *training* to underscore the point that there are many solutions to performance problems or performance opportunities. This term is becoming more prevalent among organizations that have characterized themselves as learning organizations.

The term *program* is used to reflect learning solution, seminar, workshop, on-the-job training, or other interventions in which learning takes place. In reality, training is a process and not a one-time event or program. However, because of the common use of the term, *program* will be used throughout the book to reflect the specific intervention, whether it is off the job or on the job.

The term *participant* is used to refer to the individual involved in the training program or learning solution. It replaces the term *trainee* or *student* and is more commonly used than *stakeholder.*

The term *sponsor* is the individual or group who initiates, approves, and supports the program or impact study. Usually a part of senior management, this individual cares about the outcome of the ROI evaluation and is sometimes labeled the *client.*

Finally, the term *CEO* is used to refer to the top executive at a specific organizational entity. The CEO could be chief administrator, managing director, division president, major operations executive, or other top official, and often reflects the most senior management in the organizational entity where the program is implemented.

A final definition offered in this chapter is the basic definition of return on investment. Two common formulas are offered: Benefits/Costs Ratio (BCR) and ROI:

$$BCR = \frac{\text{Program Benefits}}{\text{Program Costs}}$$

$$ROI\ (\%) = \frac{\text{Net Program Benefits}}{\text{Program Costs}} \times 100$$

The BCR uses the total benefits and costs. In the ROI formula, the costs are subtracted from the total benefits to produce net benefits which are then divided by the costs. For example, a telemarketing sales training program at Hewlett-Packard Company produced benefits of $3,296,977 with a cost of $1,116,291 (Seagraves, 2001). Therefore, the benefits/costs ratio is:

$$BCR = \frac{\$3,296,977}{\$1,116,291} = 2.95\ (\text{or } 2.95{:}1)$$

As this calculation shows, for every $1 invested, $2.95 in benefits are returned. In this example, net benefits are $3,296,977 − $1,116,291 = $2,180,616. Thus, the ROI is:

$$ROI\ (\%) = \frac{\$2,180,616}{\$1,116,291} \times 100 = 195\%$$

This means that for each $1 invested in the program, there is a return of $1.95 in *net* benefits, after costs are covered. The benefits are usually expressed as annual benefits, representing the amount saved or gained for a complete year after program completion. While the benefits may continue after the first year if the program has long-term effects, the impact usually diminishes and is omitted from calculations. This conservative approach is used throughout the application of the ROI process in this book. The values for return on investment are usually quite large, in the range of 25 to 500%, which illustrates the potential impact of successful programs.

BARRIERS TO ROI IMPLEMENTATION

Although progress has been made in the implementation of ROI, significant barriers inhibit the implementation of the concept. Some of these barriers are realistic while others are actually myths based on false perceptions. Each barrier is briefly described in this following sections.

Costs and Time

The ROI process will add some additional costs and time to the evaluation process of programs, although the added amount will not be excessive. It is possible this barrier alone stops many ROI implementations early in the process. A comprehensive ROI process can be implemented for 3–5% to the overall training budget. The additional investment in ROI could perhaps be offset by the additional results achieved from these programs and the elimination of unproductive or unprofitable programs.

Lack of Skills and Orientation for HRD Staff

Many training and performance improvement staff members do not understand ROI nor do they have the basic skills necessary to apply the process within their scope of responsibilities. Measurement and evaluation is not usually part of the preparation for the job. Also, the typical training program does not focus on results, but more on learning outcomes. Staff members attempt to measure results by measuring learning. Consequently, a tremendous barrier to implementation is the change needed for the overall orientation, attitude, and skills of the HRD staff. As Pogo, the cartoon character, once said, "We have met the enemy and he is us." This certainly applies to the ROI implementation.

Faulty Needs Assessment

Many of the current HRD programs do not have an adequate needs assessment. Some of these programs have been implemented for the wrong reasons based on management requests or efforts to chase a popular fad or trend in the industry. If the program is not needed, the benefits from the program will be minimal. An ROI calculation for an unnecessary program will likely yield a negative value. This is a realistic barrier for many programs.

Fear

Some HRD departments do not pursue ROI because of fear of failure or fear of the unknown. Fear of failure appears in many ways. Designers, developers, facilitators, and program owners may be concerned about the consequence of negative ROI. They fear that ROI will be a performance evaluation tool instead of a process improvement tool. The ROI process will also stir up the traditional fear of change. This fear, often based on unrealistic assumptions and a lack of knowledge of the process, becomes a realistic barrier to many ROI implementations.

Discipline and Planning

A successful ROI implementation requires much planning and a disciplined approach to keep the process on track. Implementation schedules, evaluation targets, ROI analysis plans, measurement and evaluation policies, and follow-up schedules are required. The HRD staff may not have enough discipline and determination to stay on course. This becomes a barrier, particularly when there are no immediate pressures to measure the return. If the current senior management group is not requiring ROI, the HRD staff may not allocate time for planning and coordination. Other pressures and priorities also often eat into the time necessary for ROI implementation. Only carefully planned implementation will be successful.

False Assumptions

Many HRD staff members have false assumptions about the ROI process, that keep them from attempting ROI. Typical of these assumptions are the following:

☐ The impact of a training program cannot be accurately calculated.

☐ Managers do not want to see the results of training and development expressed in monetary values.

☐ If the CEO does not ask for the ROI, he or she is not expecting it.

☐ "I have a professional, competent staff. Therefore, I do not have to justify the effectiveness of our programs."

☐ The training process is a complex, but necessary activity. Therefore, it should not be subjected to an accountability process.

These false assumptions form realistic barriers that impede the progress of ROI implementation.

BENEFITS OF ROI

Although the benefits of adopting the ROI process may appear to be obvious, several distinct and important benefits can be derived from the implementation of ROI in an organization.

These key benefits, inherent with almost any type of impact evaluation process, make the ROI process an attractive challenge for the human resource development function.

Measure Contribution

It is the most accurate, credible, and widely used process to show the impact of training. The HRD staff will know the specific contribution from a select number of programs. The ROI will determine if the benefits of the program, expressed in monetary values, have outweighed the costs. It will determine if the program made a contribution to the organization and if it was, indeed, a good investment.

Set Priorities

Calculating ROI in different areas will determine which programs contribute the most to the organization, allowing priorities to be established for high impact training. Successful programs can be expanded into other areas—if the same need is there—ahead of other programs. Inefficient programs can be designed and redeployed. Ineffective programs may be discontinued.

Focus on Results

The ROI process is a results-based process that brings a focus on results with all programs, even for those not targeted for an ROI calculation. The process requires instructional designers, facilitators, participants, and support groups to concentrate on measurable objectives: what the program is attempting to accomplish. Thus, this process has the added benefit of improving the effectiveness of all training programs.

Earn Respect of Senior Executives and Sponsor

Developing the ROI information is one of the best ways to earn the respect of the senior management team and the sponsor (the person who really cares about the program). Senior executives have a never-ending desire to see ROI. They will appreciate the efforts to connect training to business impact and show the actual monetary value. It makes them feel comfortable with the process and makes their decisions much easier. Sponsors who often support, approve, or initiate training and development, and performance improvement programs see the ROI as a breath of fresh air. They actually see the value of the training, building confidence about the initial decision to go with the process.

Alter Management Perceptions of Training

The ROI process, when applied consistently and comprehensively, can convince the management group that training is an investment and not an expense. Managers will see training as making a viable contribution to their objectives, thus increasing the respect for the function. This is an important step in building a partnership with management and increasing management support for training.

ROI BEST PRACTICES

The continuing progress with ROI implementation has provided an opportunity to determine if specific strategies are common among organizations pursuing the ROI process. Several common strategies that are considered to be the best practices for measurement and evaluation have emerged. Whether they meet the test to be labeled "best practice" will never be known, since it is risky to label any practice as a best practice. Although the following strategies are presented as a comprehensive framework, few organizations have adopted all of them. However, parts

Table 1-7. Evaluation Targets for a Large Telecommunication Company

Level	Percent of Courses
Level 1 Participant Satisfaction	100%
Level 2 Learning	60%
Level 3 Application (Behavior)	30%
Level 4 Business Impact	10%
Level 5 Return on Investment	5%

of the strategy exist in one way or another in each of the several hundred organizations involved in ROI certification, described in Chapter 11, *Implementation Issues*.

Evaluation Targets

Recognizing the complexity of moving up the chain of evaluation levels, as described in Table 1-4, some organizations attempt to manage the process by setting targets for each level. A target for an evaluation level is the percentage of HRD programs measured at that level. Repeat sessions of the same program are counted in the total. For example, at Level 1, where it is easy to measure reaction, organizations achieve a high level of activity, with many organizations requiring 100% evaluation. In these situations, a generic questionnaire is administered at the end of each program. Level 2, Learning, is another relatively easy area to measure and the target is high, usually in the 50–70% range. This target depends on the organization, based on the nature and type of programs. At Level 3, Application, the percentage drops because of the time and expense of conducting follow-up evaluations. Targets in the range of 25–35% are common. Targets for Level 4, Business Impact, and Level 5, ROI, are relatively small, reflecting the challenge of comprehending any new process. Common targets are 10% for Levels 4 and 5% for Level 5. An example of evaluation targets established for a large telecommunications company is shown in Table 1-7. In this example, half of Level 4 evaluations are taken to Level 5, the ROI.

Establishing evaluation targets has two major advantages. First, the process provides objectives for the HRD staff to clearly measure accountability progress for all programs or any segment of the HRD process. Second, adopting targets also focuses more attention on the accountability process, communicating a strong message about the extent of commitment to measurement and evaluation.

Micro-Level Evaluation Is Credible

It is difficult to evaluate an entire HRD function such as management development, career development, executive education, or technical training. The ROI process is more effective when applied to one program that can be linked to a direct payoff. In situations where a series of courses with common objectives must be completed before the objectives can be met, an evaluation of the series of courses may be appropriate. For this reason, ROI evaluation should be considered as a micro-level activity that will usually focus on a single program or a few tightly integrated programs. This decision to evaluate several programs—or just one program—should include consideration of objectives of the program, timing of the programs, and cohesiveness of the series. Attempting to evaluate a group of programs conducted over a long period becomes quite difficult. The cause and effect relationship becomes more confusing and complex.

Variety of Data Collection Methods

Best practice companies use a variety of approaches to collect evaluation data. They do not become aligned with one or two practices that dominate data collection, regardless of the situation. They recognize that each program, setting, and situation is different and, consequently, different techniques are needed to collect the data. Interviews, focus groups, and questionnaires work quite well in some situations. In others, action plans, performance contracts, and performance monitoring are needed to determine the specific impact of the program. These organizations deliberately match the data collection method with the program, following a set of criteria developed internally.

Isolating the Effects of Training

One of the most critical elements of the ROI process is attempting to isolate the impact of the training program from other influences that may have occurred during the same time period. Best practice organizations recognize that many influences affect business results measures. Although training is implemented in harmony with other systems and processes, sometimes there is a need to know the contribution of training, particularly when there are different process owners. Consequently, after a program is conducted, training must share only a part of the credit for improved performance. When an ROI calculation is planned, these organizations attempt to use one or more methods to isolate the effects of training. They go beyond the typical use of a control group arrangement, which has set the standard for this process for many years. They explore the use of a variety of other techniques to arrive at a realistic estimate of training's impact on output measures.

Sampling for ROI Calculations

Because of the resources required for the process, most training programs do not include ROI calculations. Therefore, organizations must determine the appropriate level of ROI evaluation. There is no prescribed formula, and the number of ROI impact studies depends on many variables, including:

- [ ] staff expertise on evaluation,
- [ ] the nature and type of HRD programs,
- [ ] resources that can be allocated to the process,
- [ ] the support from management for training and development,
- [ ] the organization's commitment to measurement and evaluation, and
- [ ] pressure from others to show ROI calculations.

Other variables specific to the organization may enter the process. It is rare for organizations to use statistical sampling when selecting sample programs that target ROI calculations. For most, this approach represents far too many calculations and too much analysis. Using a practical approach, most organizations settle on evaluating one or two sessions of their most popular programs. For example, Apple Computer developed an ROI calculation for their program, Process Improvement Teams (Burkett, 2001). Still others select a program from each of its major training segments. For example, in a large bank, with six academies, a program is selected each year from each academy for an ROI calculation. For organizations implementing the ROI concept for the first time, it is recommended that only one or two courses be selected for an initial calculation as a learning process.

While it is important to be statistically sound in the approach to sampling, it is more important to consider a trade-off between resources available and the level of activity management is willing to accept for

ROI calculations. The primary objective of an ROI calculation is not only to convince the HRD staff that the process works, but to show others (usually senior management) that HRD does make a difference. Therefore, it is important that the sampling plan be developed with the input and approval of senior management. In the final analysis, the selection process should yield a level of sampling in which senior management is comfortable in its accountability assessment of the HRD function.

Converting Program Results to Monetary Values

Because the specific return on investment is needed, business impact data must be converted to monetary benefits. Best practice organizations are not content to show that a program improved productivity, enhanced quality, reduced employee turnover, decreased absenteeism, or increased customer satisfaction. They convert these data items to monetary units so that the benefits can be compared to costs, which in turn leads to an ROI calculation. These organizations take an extra step to develop a realistic value for these data items. For hard data items such as productivity, quality, and time, the process is relatively easy. However, for soft data items such as customer satisfaction, employee turnover, employee absenteeism, and job satisfaction, the process is more difficult. Yet, techniques are available, and are utilized, to make these conversions reasonably accurate.

FINAL THOUGHTS

While there is almost universal agreement that more attention is needed on ROI, it is promising to note the tremendous success of ROI. Its use is expanding. Its payoff is huge. The process is not very difficult or impossible. The approaches, strategies, and techniques are not overly complex and can be useful in a variety of settings. The combined and persistent efforts of practitioners and researchers will continue to refine the techniques and create successful applications.

REFERENCES

Burkett, H. "Program Process Improvement Teams," *In Action: Measuring Return on Investment*, vol. 3. Alexandria, VA: American Society for Training and Development 2001.

Drimmer, Alan. *Reframing the Measurement Debate: Moving Beyond Program Analysis in the Learning Function.* Washington DC: Corporate Executive Board, 2002.

Industry Report 2002 (October 2002). *Training,* 34(10), pp. 33–75.

Kirkpatrick, D.L. "Techniques for Evaluating Training Programs," *Evaluating Training Programs.* Alexandria, VA: American Society for Training and Development, 1975, pp. 1–17.

Kleiman, Carol, "Smart Bosses Leave Training on the Budget." *Chicago Tribune,* July 28, 2002, p. C5.

Nadler, L., and G.D. Wiggs. *Managing Human Resource Development.* San Francisco, CA: Jossey-Boss, Inc., 1986.

Pfau, Bruce N., and Ira T. Kay. *The Human Capital Edge: 21 People Management Practices Your Company Must Implement (or Avoid) to Maximize Shareholder Value.* New York, NY: McGraw Hill, 2002.

Phillips, J.J. (Ed.). *In Action: Measuring Return on Investment,* vol. 1. Alexandria, VA: American Society for Training and Development, 1994.

Phillips, J.J. "Measuring Training's ROI: It Can Be Done!" *William & Mary Business Review,* Summer 1995, pp. 6–10.

Phillips, J.J. (Ed.). *In Action: Measuring Return on Investment,* vol. 2. Alexandria, VA: American Society for Training and Development, 1997.

Phillips, J.J. *HRD Trends Worldwide: Shared Solutions to Compete in a Global Economy.* Boston, MA, Butterworth–Heinemann, 1999.

Phillips, J.J. *The Corporate University: Measuring the Impact of Learning.* Houston, TX: American Productivity & Quality Center, 2000.

Phillips, J.J., and C. Gaudet. *HRD Trends Worldwide: Shared Solutions to Compete in a Global Economy,* 2nd ed. Boston, MA: Butterworth–Heinemann (In press) 2003.

Phillips, P.P. (Ed.). *In Action: Measuring Return on Investment,* vol. 3. Alexandria, VA: American Society for Training and Development, 2001.

Seagraves, T.L. "Mission Possible: Selling Complex Services Over the Phone." *In Action: Measuring Return on Investment,* vol. 3. Alexandria, VA: American Society for Training and Development, 2001.

Sibbet, D. "75 Years of Management Ideas and Practice, 1922–1997." *Harvard Business Review,* Supplement, 1997.

Van Adelsberg, David, and Edward A. Trolley. *Running Training Like a Business: Delivering Unmistakable Value.* San Francisco, CA: Berrett-Koehler Publishers, Inc., 1999.

Van Buren, Mark E. *State of the Industry.* Alexandria, VA: American Society for Training and Development, 2002.

Virzi, Anna Maria, "Calculating Return on Investment: Learning to Measure Learning." *Baseline,* May 2002, p. 91.

White, Mark W. "Confessions of a Former Training Manager." *William & Mary Business Review,* Summer 1995, pp. 3–5.

CHAPTER 2

ROI Model

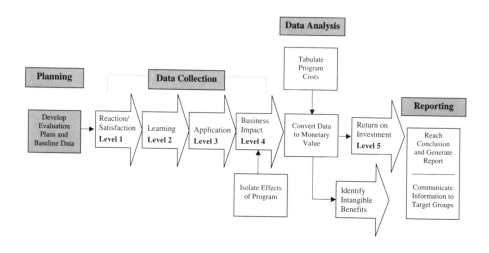

THE ROI MODEL

The calculation of the return on investment follows the basic model illustrated above, where a potentially complicated process can be simplified with sequential steps. The ROI model provides a systematic approach to ROI calculations. A step-by-step approach keeps the process manageable so that users can tackle one issue at a time. The model also emphasizes that this is a logical, systematic process that flows from one step to another. Applying the model provides consistency from one ROI calculation to another. This chapter describes the development of the complete ROI methodology and then briefly discusses each step of the model.

BUILDING THE ROI METHODOLOGY

Building a comprehensive measurement and evaluation process is like a puzzle where the pieces are developed and put in place over time. Figure 2-1 depicts this puzzle and the pieces necessary to build a comprehensive measurement and evaluation process. The building block is the selection of *an evaluation framework*, which is a categorization of data. The balanced scorecard process (Kaplan and Norton, 1996) or the four levels of evaluation developed by Kirkpatrick (1975) offers the beginning point for such a framework. The framework selected for the process presented here is a modification of Kirkpatrick's four levels and includes a fifth level—return on investment.

A major building block, the ROI process model, is necessary to show how data are collected, processed, analyzed, and reported to various target audiences. This process model ensures that appropriate techniques and procedures are consistently used to address almost any situation.

A third building block is the development of operating standards. These standards help ensure that the results of the study are stable and not influenced by the individual conducting the study. Replication is critical for the credibility of an evaluation process. The use of operating standards allows for replication, so that if more than one individual evaluates a specific program, the results are the same. In the ROI methodology, the operating standards are labeled as guiding principles.

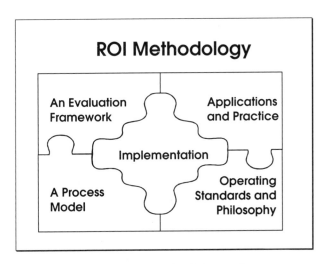

Figure 2-1. ROI methodology elements.

Next, appropriate attention must be given to implementation issues, as the ROI process becomes a routine part of training and performance. Several issues must be addressed involving skills, communication, roles, responsibilities, plans, and strategies.

Finally, there must be successful applications and practice describing the implementation of the process within the organization, the value a comprehensive measurement and evaluation process brings to the organization, and the impact the specific program evaluated has on the organization. While it is helpful to refer to studies developed by other organizations, it is more useful and convincing to have studies developed directly within the organization.

The remainder of this chapter focuses on the individual building blocks of the comprehensive ROI methodology.

AN EVALUATION FRAMEWORK

The concept of different levels of evaluation is both helpful and instructive to understanding how the return on investment is calculated. Table 2-1 revisits the five levels of evaluation presented in the previous chapter. It serves as the framework for evaluation, defining the types of data collected, the sequence of collection, and the approximate timing.

Level 1, *Reaction, Satisfaction, and Planned Action*, measures satisfaction of program participants, along with their plans to apply what they have learned. Almost all organizations evaluate at Level 1, usually with a generic, end-of-program questionnaire. While this level of evaluation is important as a customer satisfaction measure, a favorable reaction does not ensure that participants have learned new skills or knowledge (Dixon, 1990).

Level 2, *Learning*, focuses on what participants learned during the program, using tests, skill practices, role plays, simulations, group evaluations, and other assessment tools. A learning check is helpful to ensure that participants have absorbed the program material and know how to use it properly. However, a positive measure at this level is no guarantee that what is learned will be applied on the job. The literature is laced with studies showing the failure of learning to be transferred to the job (e.g., Broad, 1997).

At Level 3, *Application and Implementation*, a variety of follow-up methods are used to determine whether participants applied what they learned on the job. The frequency and use of skills are important measures at this level. While Level 3 evaluation is important to gauge the

Table 2-1. Characteristics of Evaluation Levels

Level	Chain of Impact	Measurement Focus	Value of Information	Customer Focus
1	Reaction, Satisfaction, & Planned Action ↓	Measures participants' reaction to and satisfaction with the program and captures planned actions	Low	Consumer
2	Learning ↓	Measures changes in knowledge, skills, and attitudes		
3	Application & Implementation ↓	Measures changes in on-the-job behavior and progress with planned actions		
4	Business Impact ↓	Measures changes in business impact variables	↓	↓
5	Return on Investment	Compares program monetary benefits to the costs of the program	High	Client

Customers: Consumers = The customers who are actively involved in the training process.
Client = The customers who fund, support, and approve the training project.

success of the application of a program, it still does not guarantee that there will be a positive business impact in the organization.

The Level 4, *Business Impact*, measures focuses on the actual results achieved by program participants as they successfully apply what they have learned. Typical Level 4 measures include output, quality, costs, time, and customer satisfaction. Although the program may produce a measurable business impact, there is still a concern that the program may cost too much.

Level 5, *Return on Investment*, the ultimate level of evaluation, compares the monetary benefits from the program with the program costs. Although the ROI can be expressed in several ways, it is usually presented as a percentage or cost/benefit ratio. The evaluation chain of impact, illustrated in Figure 2-1, is not complete until the Level 5, ROI evaluation, is developed.

While almost all training organizations conduct evaluations to measure satisfaction, very few conduct evaluations at the ROI level. Perhaps the best explanation for this situation is that ROI evaluation is often characterized as a difficult and expensive process. When business results and ROI are desired, it is also very important to evaluate the other levels. A chain of impact should occur through the levels as the skills and knowledge learned (Level 2) are applied on the job (Level 3) to produce business impact (Level 4). If measurements are not taken at each level, it is difficult to conclude that the results achieved were actually caused by the program (Alliger and Janak, 1989). Because of this, it is recommended that evaluation be conducted at all levels when a Level 5 evaluation is planned. This is consistent with the practices of benchmarking forum members of the American Society for Training and Development (ASTD) (Van Buren, 2002) and best-practice corporate universities as identified in a study conducted by the American Quality and Productivity Center (Phillips, 2000).

Also, from the perspective of the client, the value of information increases with movement through the chain of impact. The ROI methodology is a client-centered process, meeting the data needs for the individuals who initiate, approve, and sponsor the program.

THE ROI MODEL

The ROI model, presented in Figure 2-2, is a step-by-step approach to develop the ROI calculation and the other measures in the ROI methodology. Each major part of the model is described in this section.

Evaluation Planning

Several pieces of the evaluation puzzle must be explained when developing the evaluation plan for an ROI calculation. Three specific elements are important to evaluation success (purpose, feasibility, and objectives of programs) and are outlined in this section.

PURPOSE

Although evaluation is usually undertaken to improve the HRD process, several distinct purposes can be identified. Evaluation is planned to:

☐ Improve the quality of learning and outcomes
☐ Determine whether a program is accomplishing its objectives

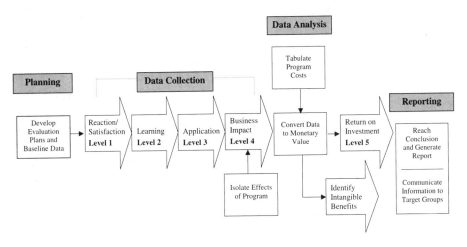

Figure 2-2. The ROI Model.

☐ Identify the strengths and weaknesses in the learning process
☐ Determine the benefits/costs analysis of an HRD program
☐ Assist in marketing HRD programs in the future
☐ Determine whether the program was appropriate for the target audience
☐ Establish a database, which can assist in making decisions about the programs
☐ Establish priorities for funding

Although there are other purposes of evaluation, these are some of the most important purposes (Russ-Eft and Preskill, 2001). Evaluation purposes should be considered prior to developing the evaluation plan because the purposes will often determine the scope of the evaluation, the types of instruments used, and the type of data collected. For example, when an ROI calculation is planned, one of the purposes would be to compare the costs and benefits of the program. This purpose has implications for the type of data collected (hard data), type of data collection method (performance monitoring), type of analysis (thorough), and the communication medium for results (formal evaluation report). For most programs, multiple evaluation purposes are pursued.

FEASIBILITY

An important consideration in planning the ROI impact study is to determine the appropriate levels for evaluation. Some evaluations will stop at Level 3, where a detailed report will determine the extent to which participants are using what they have learned. Others will be evaluated at Level 4, impact, where the consequences of their on-the-job application are monitored. A Level 4 impact study will examine hard and soft data measures directly linked to the program. This type of study will require that the impact of the program be isolated from other influences. Finally, if the ROI calculation is needed, two additional steps are required; the Level 4 impact data must be converted to monetary value and the costs of the program captured so that the ROI can be developed. Only a few programs should be taken to this level of evaluation.

During the planning stage, the feasibility for a Level 4 or 5 impact study should be examined. Relevant questions that need to be addressed are:

☐ What specific measures have been influenced with this program?
☐ Are those measures readily available?
☐ Can the effect of the program on those measures be isolated?
☐ Are the costs of the program readily available?
☐ Will it be practical and feasible to discuss costs?
☐ Can the impact data be converted to monetary value?
☐ Is the actual ROI needed or necessary?

These and other questions are important to examine during the planning process to ensure that the evaluation is appropriate for the program. Each issue will be examined in more detail as the ROI methodology is explained.

OBJECTIVES OF PROGRAMS

Training programs are evaluated at different levels as briefly described earlier. Corresponding to the levels of evaluation are levels of objectives:

☐ Reaction and Satisfaction objectives (1)
☐ Learning objectives (2)
☐ Application objectives (3)
☐ Impact objectives (4)
☐ ROI objectives (5)

Before the ROI evaluation begins, the program objectives must be identified or developed. The objectives form the basis for determining the depth of the evaluation, meaning that they determine what level of evaluation will take place. Historically, learning objectives are routinely developed. Application and impact objectives are not always in place, but are necessary for the proper focus on results.

Program objectives link directly to the front-end analysis. As shown in Figure 2-3, after the business need is determined (4), the needs analysis identifies the job performance (3) necessary to meet the business need. The skills and/or knowledge (2) needed to achieve the desired performance are identified, taking into consideration the preferences (1) for the learning solution to improve skills and knowledge. In the ROI methodology, it is necessary to develop objectives at each level to ensure program success and link those objectives to levels of evaluation. As the figure illustrates, participant satisfaction objectives link to Level 1 evaluation; learning objectives link to Level 2 evaluation; application objectives link to Level 3 evaluation; impact objectives link to Level 4 evaluation; and ROI objectives link to the ROI outcome.

If the application and impact objectives are not available, they have to be developed, using input from several groups such as job incumbents, program developers, facilitators, and on-the-job team leaders.

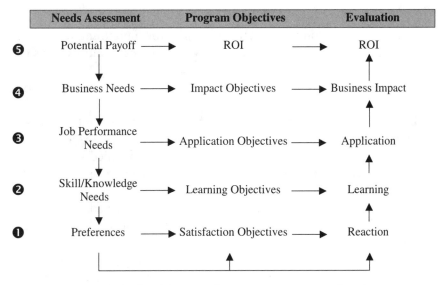

Figure 2-3. Linking needs assessment to evaluation.

Tied very closely to setting objectives is the timing of the data collection. In some cases, preprogram measurements are taken to compare with postprogram measures and, in some cases, multiple measures are taken. In other situations, preprogram measurements are not available and specific follow-ups are still taken after the program. The important issue in this part of the process is to determine the timing for the follow-up evaluation. For example, a major airline initiated data collection for an evaluation three weeks after a customer-service skills training program. In another example, an Indonesian company needed five years to measure the payback for employees attending an MBA program in the United States. For most professional and supervisory training, a follow-up is usually conducted in the range of three to six months.

Evaluation Plans

To complete the planning process, three simple planning documents are developed: the Data Collection Plan, the ROI Analysis Plan, and the Project Plan. These documents should be completed before the evaluation project is implemented—ideally, before the program is designed or developed. Appropriate up-front attention will save much time later when data are actually collected.

DATA COLLECTION PLAN

Figure 2-4 shows a completed data collection form planning for an interactive sales skills program. The three-day training program was designed for retail sales associates in the electronics department of a major store chain (Phillips and Phillips, 2001). An ROI calculation was planned for a pilot of three groups.

This document provides a place for the major elements and issues regarding collecting data for the four evaluation levels. Broad areas for objectives are appropriate for planning. Specific, detailed objectives are developed later, before the program is designed. The "measures" column defines the specific measure; the "method" describes the technique used to collect the data; the "source" of the data is identified; the "timing" indicates when the data are collected; and the "responsibilities" identifies who will collect the data.

The objectives for Level 1 usually include positive reactions to the training program of completed action plans. If it is a new program, another category, *suggested improvements*, may be included. Reaction is

Program: Interactive Sales Training **Responsibility:** P. Phillips _____ **Date:** _____

Level	Broad Program Objectives	Measures	Data Collection Method and Instruments	Data Sources	Timing	Responsibilities
❶	**Reaction, Satisfaction, and Planned Actions** • Positive reaction— four out of five • Action items	• A 1–5 rating on a composite of five measures • Yes or No	• Questionnaire	• Participant (third Day)	• End of Program (third Day)	• Facilitator
❷	**Learning** • Learn to use five simple skills	• Pass or fail on skill practice	• Observation of skill practice by facilitator	• Facilitator	• Second day of program	• Facilitator
❸	**Application and Implementation** • Initial use of five simple skills • At least 50% of participants use all skills with every customer	• Verbal feedback • 5th item checked on a 1 to 5 scale	• Follow-up session • Follow-up questionnaire	• Participant • Participant	• Three weeks after second day • Three months after program	• Facilitator • Store training coordinator
❹	**Business Impact** • Sales Increase	• Weekly average sales per sales associate	• Business performance monitoring	• Company records	• Three months after program	• Store training coordinator
❺	**ROI** • 50%					

Comments: The ROI objective was set at a high value because of the store sample size; the executives wanted convincing data.

Figure 2-4. *Sample data collection form.*

typically measured on a scale, collected by questionnaires directly from participants, and administered by the facilitator.

Level 2 evaluation focuses on the measures of learning. The specific objectives include those areas where participants are expected to change knowledge, skills, or attitudes. The measure is a pass/fail observed by facilitator. The method of assessing learning is the skill practice observed by the facilitator (source). The timing for Level 2 evaluation is usually during or at the end of the program, and the responsibility usually rests with the facilitator.

For Level 3 evaluation, the objectives represent broad areas of program application, including significant on-the-job activities that should follow application. The evaluation method usually includes one of the postprogram methods described later and is usually conducted weeks or months after program completion. Because responsibilities are often shared among several groups, including the training and development staff, division trainers, or local managers, it is important to clarify this issue early in the process.

For Level 4 evaluation, objectives focus on business impact variables influenced by the program. The objectives may include the way in which each item is measured. If not, the measure is defined in the measures column. For example, if one of the objectives were to improve quality, a specific measure would indicate how that quality is actually measured, such as defects per thousand units produced. While the preferred evaluation method is business performance monitoring, other methods such as action planning may be appropriate. The timing depends on how quickly participants can generate a sustained business impact. It is usually a matter of months after training. The participants, supervisors, division training coordinators or perhaps an external evaluator may be responsible for Level 4 data collection in this case.

The ROI objective is established, if appropriate. This value, most commonly expressed as a percent, defines the minimum acceptable rate of return for investing in the program. The program sponsor or the individual requesting the impact study usually provides the value. In this example, the regional store executives set the number at 50%.

The data collection plan is an important part of the evaluation strategy and should be completed prior to moving forward with the training program. For existing training programs, the plan is completed before pursuing the ROI impact study. The plan provides a clear direction of what type of data will be collected, how it will be collected, who will provide the data, when it will be collected, and who will collect it.

ROI ANALYSIS PLAN

Figure 2-5 shows a completed ROI analysis plan for the interactive selling skills program. This planning document is the continuation of the data collection plan presented in Figure 2-4 and captures information on several key items that are necessary to develop the actual ROI calculation. In the first column, significant data items are listed, usually Level 4 business impact data, but in some cases could include Level 3 items. These items will be used in the ROI analysis. The method to isolate the effect of training is listed next to each data item in the second column. For most cases the method will be the same for each data item, but there could be variations. For example, if no historical data are available for one data item, then trend-line analysis is not possible for that item, although it may be appropriate for other items. The method of converting data to monetary values is included in the third column, using one of the ten strategies outlined earlier.

The costs categories that will be captured for the training program are outlined in the fourth column. Instructions about how certain costs should be prorated would be noted here. Normally the cost categories will be consistent from one program to another. However, a specific cost that is unique to the program would also be noted. The intangible benefits expected from this program are outlined in the fifth column. This list is generated from discussions about the program with sponsors and subject-matter experts. Communication targets are outlined in the sixth column. Although there could be many groups that should receive the information, four target groups are always recommended:

1. Senior management group (sponsor)
2. Manager of participants
3. Program participants
4. Training and development staff

All four of these groups need to know about the results of ROI analysis. Finally, other issues or events that might influence program implementation would be highlighted in the last column. Typical items include the capability of participants, the degree of access to data sources, and unique data analysis issues.

The ROI analysis plan, when combined with the data collection plan, provides detailed information on calculating the ROI, illustrating how the process will develop from beginning to end.

Program: Interactive Sales Training **Responsibility:** P. Phillips   **Date:**

Data Items	Methods of Isolating the Effects of the Program	Methods of Converting Data	Cost Categories	Intangible Benefits	Communication Targets	Other Influences and Issues
• Weekly sales per associate	• Control group analysis • Participant estimate	• Direct conversion using profit contribution	• Facilitation fees • Program materials • Meals and refreshments • Facilities • Participant salaries and benefits • Cost of coordination • Evaluation	• Customer satisfaction • Employee satisfaction	• Program participants • Electronics Dept. managers at targeted stores • Store managers at targeted stores • Senior store executives district, region, headquarters • Training staff: instructors, coordinators, designers, and managers	• Must have job coverage during training • No communication with control group • Seasonal fluctuations should be avoided

Figure 2-5. Sample ROI analysis plan.

PROJECT PLAN

The final plan developed for the evaluation planning phase is a project plan. A project plan consists of a description of the program and brief detail about the program, such as duration, target audience, and number of participants. It also shows the time line of the project, beginning with the planning of the study to the last communication of the results. This plan becomes an operational tool to keep the project on track. Sometimes, the end date drives the entire planning process. For example, a senior executive may request that the data surrounding the impact study be developed and presented to the senior team on a particular date. With that ending point, all the other dates are added. Any appropriate project-planning tool can be used to develop the plan.

Collectively, these three planning documents (the data collection plan, the ROI analysis plan, and the project plan) provide the direction necessary for the ROI impact study. Most of the decisions regarding the process are made as these planning tools are developed. The remainder of the project becomes a methodical, systematic process of implementing the plan. This is a crucial step in the ROI methodology, where valuable time allocated to this process will save precious time later.

Collecting Data

Data collection is central to the ROI methodology. Both hard data (representing output, quality, cost, and time) and soft data (including job and customer satisfaction) are collected. Data are collected using a variety of methods including the following:

- [ ] **Surveys** are taken to determine the degrees to which participants are satisfied with the program, have learned skills and knowledge, and have used various aspects of the program. Survey responses are often developed on a sliding scale and usually represent perception data. Surveys are useful for Levels 1, 2, and 3 data.
- [ ] **Questionnaires** are usually more detailed than surveys and can be used to uncover a wide variety of data. Participants provide responses to a variety of open-ended and forced response questions. Questionnaires can be used to capture Levels 1, 2, 3, and 4 data.
- [ ] **Tests** are conducted to measure changes in knowledge and skills (Level 2). Tests come in a wide variety of formal (criterion-referenced tests, performance tests and simulations, and skill practices)

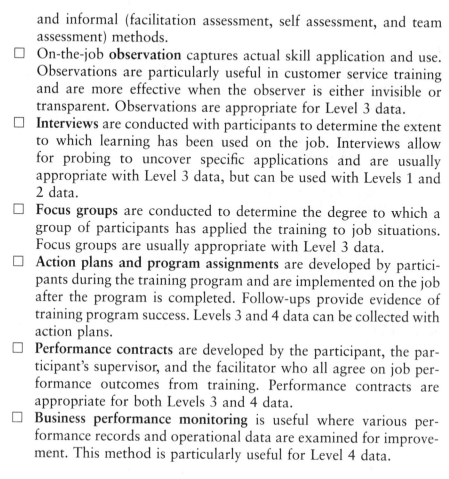

and informal (facilitation assessment, self assessment, and team assessment) methods.

☐ On-the-job **observation** captures actual skill application and use. Observations are particularly useful in customer service training and are more effective when the observer is either invisible or transparent. Observations are appropriate for Level 3 data.

☐ **Interviews** are conducted with participants to determine the extent to which learning has been used on the job. Interviews allow for probing to uncover specific applications and are usually appropriate with Level 3 data, but can be used with Levels 1 and 2 data.

☐ **Focus groups** are conducted to determine the degree to which a group of participants has applied the training to job situations. Focus groups are usually appropriate with Level 3 data.

☐ **Action plans and program assignments** are developed by participants during the training program and are implemented on the job after the program is completed. Follow-ups provide evidence of training program success. Levels 3 and 4 data can be collected with action plans.

☐ **Performance contracts** are developed by the participant, the participant's supervisor, and the facilitator who all agree on job performance outcomes from training. Performance contracts are appropriate for both Levels 3 and 4 data.

☐ **Business performance monitoring** is useful where various performance records and operational data are examined for improvement. This method is particularly useful for Level 4 data.

The important challenge in data collection is to select the method or methods appropriate for the setting and the specific program, within the time and budget constraints of the organization. Data collection methods are covered in more detail in Chapter 3.

Isolating the Effects of Training

An often overlooked issue in most evaluations is the process of isolating the effects of training. In this step of the process, specific strategies are explored that determine the amount of output performance directly related to the program. This step is essential because there are many factors that will influence performance data after training. The specific strategies of this step will pinpoint the amount of improvement directly related to the training program, resulting in increased accuracy and credibility of ROI calculations. The following techniques have been used by organizations to tackle this important issue:

- [ ] A **control group** arrangement is used to isolate training impact. With this strategy, one group receives training, while another similar group does not receive training. The difference in the performance of the two groups is attributed to the training program. When properly set up and implemented, the control group arrangement is the most effective way to isolate the effects of training.
- [ ] **Trend lines** are used to project the values of specific output variables if training had not been undertaken. The projection is compared to the actual data after training, and the difference represents the estimate of the impact of training. Under certain conditions, this strategy can accurately isolate the training impact.
- [ ] When mathematical relationships between input and output variables are known, a **forecasting model** is used to isolate the effects of training. With this approach, the output variable is predicted using the forecasting model with the assumption that no training is conducted. The actual performance of the variable after the training is then compared with the forecasted value, which results in an estimate of the training impact.
- [ ] **Participants** estimate the amount of improvement related to training. With this approach, participants are provided with the total amount of improvement, on a preprogram and postprogram basis, and are asked to indicate the percent of the improvement that is actually related to the training program.
- [ ] **Supervisors of participants** estimate the impact of training on the output variables. With this approach, supervisors of participants are presented with the total amount of improvement and are asked to indicate the percent related to training.
- [ ] **Senior management** estimates the impact of training. In these cases, managers provide an estimate or "adjustment" to reflect the portion of the improvement related to the training program. While perhaps inaccurate, there are some advantages of having senior management involved in this process.
- [ ] **Experts** provide estimates of the impact of training on the performance variable. Because the estimates are based on previous experience, the experts must be familiar with the type of training and the specific situation.

☐ When feasible, **other influencing factors** are identified and the impact estimated or calculated, leaving the remaining, unexplained improvement attributed to training. In this case, the influence of all of the other factors is developed, and training remains the one variable not accounted for in the analysis. The unexplained portion of the output is then attributed to training.

☐ In some situations, **customers** provide input on the extent to which training has influenced their decision to use a product or service. Although this strategy has limited applications, it can be quite useful in customer service and sales training.

Collectively, these techniques provide a comprehensive set of tools to tackle the important and critical issue of isolating the effects of training. Chapter 4 is devoted to this important step in the ROI methodology.

Converting Data to Monetary Values

To calculate the return on investment, data collected in a Level 4 evaluation are converted to monetary values and compared to program costs. This requires a value to be placed on each unit of data connected with the program. A wide variety of techniques are available to convert data to monetary values. The specific techniques selected usually depends on the types of data and the situation:

☐ **Output data** are converted to profit contribution or cost savings. In this strategy, output increases are converted to monetary value based on their unit contribution to profit or the unit of cost reduction. Standard values for these items are readily available in most organizations.

☐ The **cost of quality** is calculated and quality improvements are directly converted to cost savings. Standard values for these items are available in many organizations.

☐ For programs where employee time is saved, the **participants' wages and employee benefits** are used to develop the value for time. Because a variety of programs focuses on improving the time required to complete projects, processes, or daily activities, the value of time becomes an important and necessary issue. This is a standard formula in most organizations.

☐ **Historical costs**, developed from cost statements, are used when they are available for a specific variable. In this case, organizational cost data establishes the specific monetary cost savings of an improvement.

☐ When available, **internal and external experts** may be used to estimate a value for an improvement. In this situation, the credibility of the estimate hinges on the expertise and reputation of the individual.

☐ **External databases** are sometimes available to estimate the value or cost of data items. Research, government, and industry databases can provide important information for these values. The difficulty lies in finding a specific database related to the situation.

☐ **Participants** estimate the value of the data item. For this approach to be effective, participants must be capable of providing a value for the improvement.

☐ **Supervisors and managers** provide estimates when they are both willing and capable of assigning values to the improvement. This approach is especially useful when participants are not fully capable of providing this input or in situations where supervisors need to confirm or adjust the participant's estimate. This approach is particularly helpful to establish values for performance measures that are very important to senior management.

☐ **Soft measures are linked mathematically to other measures** that are easier to measure and value. This approach is particularly helpful when establishing values for measures that are very difficult to convert to monetary values, such as data often considered intangible, like customer satisfaction, employee satisfaction, grievances, and employee complaints.

☐ **HRD staff** estimates may be used to determine a value of an output data item. In these cases, it is essential for the estimates to be provided on an unbiased basis.

This step in the ROI model is very important and absolutely necessary for determining the monetary benefits from a training program. The process is challenging, particularly with soft data, but can be methodically accomplished using one or more of these strategies. Because of its importance, Chapter 5 is devoted to this step in the ROI methodology.

Tabulating Cost of the Program

The other part of the equation on a benefits/costs analysis is the program cost. Tabulating the costs involves monitoring or developing all of the

related costs of the program targeted for the ROI calculation. Among
the cost components that should be included are:

☐ the cost to design and develop the program, possibly prorated over
  the expected life of the program;
☐ the cost of all program materials provided to each participant;
☐ the cost for the instructor/facilitator, including preparation time as
  well as delivery time;
☐ the cost of the facilities for the training program;
☐ travel, lodging, and meal costs for the participants, if applicable;
☐ salaries plus employee benefits of the participants who attend the
  training; and
☐ administrative and overhead costs of the training function, allocated in some convenient way.

In addition, specific costs related to the needs assessment and evaluation should be included, if appropriate. The conservative approach is
to include all of these costs so that the total is fully loaded. Chapter 6
is devoted to this step in the ROI methodology.

Calculating the Return on Investment

The return on investment is calculated using the program benefits and
costs. The benefits/costs ratio (BCR) is the program benefits divided by
cost. In formula form it is:

$$BCR = \frac{Program\ Benefits}{Program\ Costs}$$

Sometimes this ratio is stated as a cost/benefit ratio, although the
formula is the same as BCR.

The return on investment uses the net benefits divided by program
costs. The net benefits are the program benefits minus the costs. In
formula form, the ROI becomes:

$$ROI\ (\%) = \frac{Net\ Program\ Benefits}{Program\ Costs} \times 100$$

This is the same basic formula used in evaluating other investments
where the ROI is traditionally reported as earnings divided by invest-

ment. The ROI from some training programs is high. For example, in sales, supervisory, and managerial training, the ROI can be quite high (frequently over 100%), while the ROI value for technical and operator training may be lower. Chapter 7 is devoted to ROI calculations.

Identifying Intangible Benefits

In addition to tangible, monetary benefits, most training programs will have intangible, nonmonetary benefits. The ROI calculation is based on converting both hard and soft data to monetary values. Intangible benefits include items such as:

- ☐ increased job satisfaction,
- ☐ increased organizational commitment,
- ☐ improved teamwork,
- ☐ improved customer service,
- ☐ reduced complaints, and
- ☐ reduced conflicts.

During data analysis, every attempt is made to convert all data to monetary values. All hard data such as output, quality, and time are converted to monetary values. The conversion of soft data is attempted for each data item. However, if the process used for conversion is too subjective or inaccurate, and the resulting values lose credibility in the process, then the data is listed as an intangible benefit with the appropriate explanation. For some programs, intangible, nonmonetary benefits are extremely valuable, often carrying as much influence as the hard data items. Chapter 8 is devoted to the nonmonetary, intangible benefits.

Reporting

The final step in the ROI model is reporting. This very critical step often lacks the proper attention and planning to ensure that it is successful. This step involves developing appropriate information in the format impact studies and other brief reports. The heart of the step includes the different techniques used to communicate to a wide variety of target audiences. In most ROI studies, several audiences are interested in and need the information. Careful planning to match the communication method with the audience is essential to ensure that the message is understood and appropriate actions follow. Chapter 10 is devoted to this critical step in the process.

OPERATING STANDARDS AND PHILOSOPHY

To ensure consistency and replication of impact studies, operating standards must be developed and applied as the process model is used to develop ROI studies. It is extremely important for the results of a study to stand alone and not vary depending on the individual conducting the study. The operating standards detail how each step and issue of the process will be handled. Table 2-2 shows the guiding principles that form the basis for the operating standards.

The guiding principles not only serve as a way to consistently address each step, but also provide a much-needed conservative approach to the

Table 2-2. Operating Standards

Guiding Principles

1. When a higher-level evaluation is conducted, data must be collected at lower levels.
2. When an evaluation is planned for a higher level, the previous level of evaluation does not have to be comprehensive.
3. When collecting and analyzing data, use only the most credible source.
4. When analyzing data, choose the most conservative among the alternatives.
5. At least one method must be used to isolate the effects of the solution.
6. If no improvement data are available for a population or from a specific source, it is assumed that little or no improvement has occurred.
7. Estimates of improvements should be adjusted (discounted) for the potential error of the estimate.
8. Extreme data items and unsupported claims should not be used in ROI calculations.
9. Only the first year of benefits (annual) should be used in the ROI analysis of short-term solutions.
10. Costs of the solution should be fully loaded for ROI analysis.
11. Intangible measures are defined as measures that are purposely not converted to monetary values.
12. The results from the ROI methodology must be communicated to all key stakeholders.

analysis. A conservative approach may lower the actual ROI calculation, but it will also build credibility with the target audience. In the remaining chapters, each guiding principle is described with an example.

IMPLEMENTATION ISSUES

A variety of environmental issues and events will influence the successful implementation of the ROI process. These issues must be addressed early to ensure that the ROI process is successful. Specific topics or actions include:

- ☐ a policy statement concerning results-based training and development;
- ☐ procedures and guidelines for different elements and techniques of the evaluation process;
- ☐ meetings and formal sessions to develop staff skills with the ROI process;
- ☐ strategies to improve management commitment and support for the ROI process;
- ☐ mechanisms to provide technical support for questionnaire design, data analysis, and evaluation strategy; and
- ☐ specific techniques to place more attention on results.

The ROI process can fail or succeed based on these implementation issues. Chapter 11 is devoted to this important topic.

APPLICATION AND PRACTICE

It is extremely important for the ROI methodology to be utilized in organizations and develop a history of application. The ROI methodology described is rich in tradition, with application in a variety of settings and over 100 published case studies. In addition, thousands of case studies will soon be deposited in a website/database for future use as a research and application tool (Phillips and Burkett, 2003). However, it is more important to obtain success with the ROI process within the organization and document the results as impact studies. Consequently, the HRD staff is encouraged to develop their own impact studies to compare with others. Impact studies within the organization provide the most convincing data to senior management teams that the training and performance improvement is adding significant value and that the six types of data form the basis for actions for improvement. Case studies also provide information needed to improve processes in the different areas of the training function, as part of the continuous improvement process.

FINAL THOUGHTS

This chapter presented the ROI model for calculating the return on investment for a training program. The step-by-step process takes the complicated issue of calculating ROI and breaks it into simple, manageable tasks and steps. The building blocks for the process, the pieces of the puzzle, were examined to show how the ROI methodology has been developed. When the process is thoroughly planned, taking into consideration all potential strategies and techniques, the process becomes manageable and achievable. The remaining chapters focus on the major elements of this model and ways to implement it.

INTRODUCTION TO CASE STUDY

One of the most effective ways to understand the ROI methodology is to examine an actual case study. The following is the beginning of a case that is presented in the remaining chapters of this book. Although it represents an actual situation, a few of the issues and events have been slightly modified at the request of the organization. The case reflects the issues as they are presented in each chapter. To fully understand the case and all the issues, it is recommended that each part of the case be read and the discussion questions addressed before moving to the next part of the case.

CASE STUDY—PART A, LINEAR NETWORK SYSTEMS

Background

Linear Network Systems (LNS) is an important supplier to the telecom industry, producing a variety of network equipment. A publicly held company, LNS has been operating for more than 15 years with manufacturing and support facilities scattered throughout the United States and Canada. The company has been successful and stable.

Although LNS has been a very profitable company, it recently experienced competitive cost and quality pressures that caused some deterioration in sales. Although several factors are related to the decline, senior management is concerned about the ability of the first-level management team to lead today's workforce. The President of LNS asked the Human Resource Development manager, Pam O'Kelly, to provide appropriate training.

For several months, LNS has been attempting to develop these team leaders. Several team building sessions have been conducted. The president felt that the leaders were experiencing some difficulty in making the transition to leadership and that they needed to develop leadership skills to motivate team members to improve productivity.

Situation

O'Kelly contacted a consulting firm to inquire about potential leadership training. The principal consultant suggested that a needs assessment be conducted to determine specific training needs and also to determine if other issues need to be addressed. LNS officials reluctantly agreed to a needs assessment. They were convinced that training was needed and wanted the "standard leadership training" program. After some convincing, the consultant conducted the needs assessment using four methods:

1. reviewing operational performance documents,
2. interviewing a sample of first level managers and middle managers,
3. observing a small sample of first level managers on the job, and
4. administering a questionnaire to all first- and second-level managers.

The assessment identified a lack of skills and a need for significant leadership training. Most of the skills focused on understanding and motivating employees, setting goals, and providing leadership skills.

The Program

A 6-module, 24-hour training program was proposed for one plant as a pilot group. All first-level operating and support managers would be trained at the same time. The program would be conducted in 6 4-hour segments scattered over a 1-month period. Between sessions, participants would be requested to apply the new skills so that there would be transfer of training to the job. Initially, the program was planned to focus on the following areas:

☐ understanding employee needs,
☐ motivating employees for improved performance,
☐ counseling employees,
☐ solving problems with employees,
☐ providing appropriate leadership behavior, and
☐ inspiring teamwork.

The program was labeled "Leadership for Improved Performance" and was planned for all 16 supervisors in the pilot plant. A follow-up evaluation was planned several months after the training was completed. If the program were effective, LNS would offer it throughout their organization.

Discussion Questions

1. How important is the needs assessment for this situation? Is the resistance to a needs assessment typical? At what levels should the needs assessment be conducted?
2. At what levels should this program be evaluated?
3. Should the objectives of the program be modified? If so, how?

REFERENCES

Alliger, G.M., and E.A. Janak. "Kirkpatrick's Levels of Training Criteria: Thirty Years Later," *Personal Psychology*, 1989, vol. 42, pp. 331–342.

Broad, M.L. "Built-In Evaluation," *In Action: Measuring Return on Investment*, vol. 1, J.J. Phillips (Ed.). Alexandria, VA: American Society for Training and Development, 1994, pp. 55–70.

Broad, M.L. (Ed.) *In Action: Transferring Learning to the Workplace*. Alexandria, VA: American Society for Training and Development, 1997.

Broad, M.L., and J.W. Newstrom. *Transfer of Training*. Reading, MA: Addison-Wesley, 1992.

Dixon, N.M. *Evaluation: A Tool for Improving HRD Quality*. San Diego, CA: University Associates, Inc., 1990.

Ford, D. "Three R's in the Workplace," *In Action: Measuring Return on Investment*, vol. 1, J.J. Phillips (Ed.). Alexandria, VA: American Society for Training and Development, 1994, pp. 85–104.

Kaplan, R.S., and D.P. Norton. *Balanced Scorecard*. Boston, MA: Harvard Business School Press, 1996.

Kirkpatrick, D.L. "Techniques for Evaluating Training Programs," *Evaluating Training Programs*. Alexandria, VA: American Society for Training and Development, 1975, pp. 1–17.

Nadler, L., and G.D.Wiggs. *Managing Human Resource Development*. San Francisco, CA: Jossey-Bass, Inc., 1986.

Phillips, J.J. *Handbook of Training Evaluation and Measurement Methods*, 3rd ed. Boston, MA: Butterworth–Heinemann, 1997.

Phillips, J.J. *The Corporate University: Measuring the Impact of Learning*. Houston, TX: American Productivity & Quality Center, 2000.

Phillips, P.P., and H. Burkett. *The ROI Field Book*, Boston, MA: Butterworth–Heinemann (In Press), 2003.

Phillips, P.P., and J.J. Phillips. "Measuring Return on Investment in Interactive Sales Training," *In Action: Measuring Return on Investment*, vol. 3. Alexandria, VA: American Society for Training and Development, 2001, pp. 233–249.

Russ-Eft, D., and H. Preskill. *Evaluation in Organizations*. Cambridge, MA: Perseus Publishing, 2001.

Van Buren, M.E. *State of the Industry*. Alexandria, VA: American Society for Training and Development, 2002.

CHAPTER 3

Collecting Data

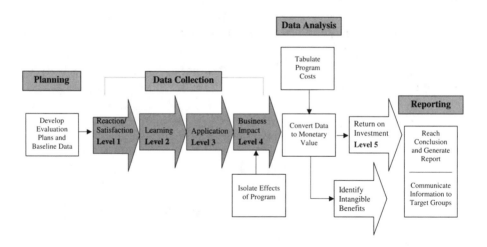

Collecting data during and after the training program has been conducted is the first operational phase of the ROI process, as depicted in the model above. This step is usually the most time consuming of all steps and is also the part of the ROI process that can be the most disruptive to the organization. Fortunately, a variety of methods are available to capture data at the appropriate time after training. This chapter defines the sources of data and outlines the common approaches for collecting postprogram data.

58

SOURCES OF DATA

When considering the possible data sources that will provide input on the success of a training program, six categories are easily defined. These categories are briefly described in the following sections.

Organizational Performance Records

The most useful and credible data source for ROI analysis is from the records and reports of the organization. Whether individualized or group-based, the records reflect performance in a work unit, department, division, region, or organization overall. This source can include all types of measures, which are usually available in abundance throughout the organization. Collecting data from this source is preferred for Level 4 evaluation, since it usually reflects business impact data and it is relatively easy to obtain. However, sloppy record keeping by some organizations may make locating particular reports difficult.

Participants

The most widely used data source for an ROI analysis is the program participants. Participants are frequently asked about reaction and satisfaction, extent of learning, and how skills and knowledge have been applied on the job. Sometimes they are asked to explain the impact of those actions. Participants are a rich source of data for Levels 1, 2, 3, and 4 evaluations. They are very credible because they are the individuals who have been involved in the program and achieved the performance. Also, they are often the most knowledgeable of the processes and other influencing factors. The challenge is to find an effective and efficient way to capture data in a consistent manner.

Managers of Participants

Another important source of data is those individuals who directly supervise or direct program participants. This group will often have a vested interest in the evaluation process, since they approved the participants' attendance at the program. In many situations, they observe the participants as they attempt to use the knowledge and skills acquired in the program. Consequently, they can report on the successes linked to the program as well as the difficulties and problems associated with application. Although supervisor input is usually best for Level 3 data, it can be useful for Level 4. It is important, however, for supervisors to maintain objectivity when assessing the program participants.

Subordinates of Participants

In situations where supervisors and managers are being trained, their direct reports can provide information about the perceived changes in observable behavior that have occurred since the program was conducted. Input from subordinates is appropriate for Level 3 data (behavior) but not Level 4. While collecting data from this source can be very helpful and instructive, it is often avoided because of the potential biases that can enter into the feedback process.

Team/Peer Group

Those individuals who serve as team members with the participant or occupy peer level positions in the organization are another source of data for a few types of programs. In these situations, peer group members provide input on perceived behavioral changes of participants (Level 3 data). This source of data is more appropriate when all team members participate in the program, and consequently, when they report on the collective efforts of the group or behavioral changes of specific individuals. Because of the subjective nature of this process, and the lack of opportunity to fully evaluate the application of skills, this source of data is somewhat limited.

Internal/External Groups

In some situations, internal or external groups, such as the training and development staff, program facilitators, expert observers, or external consultants, may provide input on the success of the individuals when they learn and apply the skills and knowledge covered in the program. Sometimes expert observers or assessors may be used to measure learning (Level 2 data). This source may be useful for on-the-job observation (Level 3 data) after the training program has been completed. Collecting data from this source has limited uses. Because internal groups may have a vested interest in the outcome of evaluation, their input may lose credibility.

Questionnaires and Surveys

Probably the most common form of data collection method is the questionnaire (Alreck and Settle, 1995). Ranging from short reaction forms to detailed follow-up tools, questionnaires can be used to obtain subjective information about participants, as well as to objectively document measurable business results for an ROI analysis. With this versatility and popularity, the questionnaire is the preferred method for capturing Levels 1, 2, 3, and 4 data in some organizations.

Surveys represent a specific type of questionnaire with several applications for measuring training success. Surveys are used in situations where attitudes, beliefs, and opinions are captured only; whereas, a questionnaire has much more flexibility and captures data ranging from attitude to specific improvement statistics. The principles of survey construction and design are similar to questionnaire design. The development of both types of instruments is covered in this section.

Types of Questions

In addition to the types of data sought, the types of questions distinguish surveys from questionnaires. Surveys can have yes or no responses when an absolute agreement or disagreement is required, or a range of responses may be used from strongly disagree to strongly agree. A five-point scale is very common.

A questionnaire may contain any or all of these types of questions:

- ☐ *Open-ended question:* has an unlimited answer. The question is followed by an ample blank space for the response.
- ☐ *Checklist:* provides a list of items where a participant is asked to check those that apply in the situation.
- ☐ *Two-way question:* has alternate responses, a yes/no or other possibilities.
- ☐ *Multiple-choice question:* has several choices, and the participant is asked to select the one most applicable.
- ☐ *Ranking scale:* requires the participant to rank a list of items.

Questionnaire Design Steps

Questionnaire design is a simple and logical process. There is nothing more confusing, frustrating, and potentially embarrassing than a poorly designed or an improperly worded questionnaire. The following steps can ensure that a valid, reliable, and effective instrument is developed (Robson, 2002).

☐ **Determine the specific information needed.** As a first step in questionnaire design, the topics, skills, or attitudes presented in the program are reviewed for potential items for the questionnaire. It is sometimes helpful to develop this information in outline form so that related questions or items can be grouped. Other issues related to the application of the program are explored for inclusion in the questionnaire.

☐ **Involve management in the process.** To the extent possible, management should be involved in this process, either as a client, sponsor, supporter, or interested party. If possible, managers most familiar with the program or process should provide information on specific issues and concerns that often frame the actual questions planned for the questionnaire. In some cases, managers want to provide input on specific issues or items. Not only is manager input helpful and useful in questionnaire design, but it also builds ownership in the measurement and evaluation process.

☐ **Select the type(s) of questions.** Using the previously listed five types of questions, the first step in questionnaire design is to select the type(s) that will best result in the specific data needed. The planned data analysis and variety of data to be collected should be considered when deciding which questions to use.

☐ **Develop the questions.** The next step is to develop the questions based on the type of questions planned and the information needed. Questions should be simple and straightforward to avoid confusion or lead the participant to a desired response. A single question should only address one issue. If multiple issues need to be addressed, separate the questions into multiple parts, or simply, develop a separate question for each issue. Terms or expressions unfamiliar to the participant should be avoided.

☐ **Check the reading level.** To ensure that the questionnaire can be easily understood by the target audience, it is helpful to assess the reading level. Most word processing programs have features that will evaluate the reading difficulty according to grade level. This provides an important check to ensure the perceived reading level of the target audience matches the questionnaire design.

☐ **Test the questions.** Proposed questions should be tested for understanding. Ideally, the questions should be tested on a sample group of participants. If this is not feasible, the sample group of employees should be at approximately the same job level as participants. From this sample group, feedback, critiques, and suggestions are sought to improve questionnaire design.

☐ **Address the anonymity issue.** Participants should feel free to respond openly to questions without fear of reprisal. The confidentiality of their responses is of utmost importance, since there is usually a link between survey anonymity and accuracy. Therefore, surveys should be anonymous unless there are specific reasons why individuals have to be identified. In situations where participants must complete the questionnaire in a captive audience, or submit a completed questionnaire directly to an individual, a neutral third party should collect and process the data, ensuring that the identity is not revealed. In cases where identity must be known (e.g., to compare output data with the previous data or to verify the data), every effort should be made to protect the respondent's identity from those who may be biased in their actions.

☐ **Design for ease of tabulation and analysis.** Each potential question should be considered in terms of data tabulation, data summary, and analysis. If possible, the data analysis process should be outlined and reviewed in mock-up form. This step avoids the problems of inadequate, cumbersome, and lengthy data analysis caused by improper wording or design.

☐ **Develop the completed questionnaire and prepare a data summary.** The questions should be integrated to develop an attractive questionnaire with proper instructions so that it can be administered effectively. In addition, a summary sheet should be developed so that the data can be tabulated quickly for analysis.

Questionnaire Content: During Program

The areas of feedback used on reaction forms depend, to a large extent, on the organization and the purpose of the evaluation. Some forms are simple while others are detailed and require a considerable amount of time to complete. A feedback questionnaire should be designed to supply the information necessary to satisfy the purpose of evaluation. The following is a comprehensive listing of the most common types of feedback solicited:

☐ *Progress with objectives.* To what degree were the objectives met?
☐ *Program content.* Was the content appropriate?

- ☐ *Instructional materials.* Were the materials useful?
- ☐ *Prework materials.* Were the prework materials necessary? Helpful?
- ☐ *Assignments.* Were the out-of-class assignments helpful?
- ☐ *Method of delivery.* Was the method of delivery appropriate for the objectives?
- ☐ *Instructor/facilitator.* Was the facilitator effective?
- ☐ *New information.* How much new information was included?
- ☐ *Motivation to learn.* Were you motivated to learn this content?
- ☐ *Relevance.* Was the program relevant to your needs?
- ☐ *Importance.* How important is this content to the success of your job?
- ☐ *Registration/logistics.* Were the scheduling and registration efficient?
- ☐ *Facilities.* Did the facilities enhance the learning environment?
- ☐ *Potential barriers.* What potential barriers exist for the application of the material?
- ☐ *Planned improvements/use of material.* How will you apply what you have learned?
- ☐ *Recommendations for target audiences.* What is the appropriate audience for this program?
- ☐ *Overall evaluation.* What is your overall rating of the program?

Objective questions covering each of these areas will ensure thorough feedback from participants. This feedback can be extremely useful in making adjustments in a program and/or assist in predicting performance after the program. The instructor/facilitator evaluation deserves additional comments. In some organizations, the primary evaluation centers on the facilitator (a separate form may be used for each facilitator, if there are several), covering a variety of areas such as the following:

- ☐ Preparation for sessions
- ☐ Knowledge of the subject matter, including familiarity with content and depth of understanding
- ☐ Presentation skills, including clarity of the presentation, pacing of material, and eye contact
- ☐ Communication skills, including the use of understandable language, real-life examples, and the promotion of discussion
- ☐ Assessing learner understanding and responding appropriately to learner needs and questions
- ☐ Use of appropriate technology and responding effectively to technical requirements of learners

☐ Encouraging application of learning through the use of real-life examples, job-related discussions, and relevant exercises

In most medium- to large-size organizations where there is significant training and development activity, the Level 1 instrument is usually automated for computerized scanning and reporting. Typical Level 1 questions can easily be developed for a scan sheet and programmed to present reports to help understand and use the data. Some organizations use direct input into a website to develop not only detailed reports, but also to develop databases, allowing feedback data to be compared to other programs or the same program with other facilitators.

Collecting learning data using a questionnaire is very common. Most types of tests, whether formal or informal, are questionnaire-based and are described in more detail in this chapter. However, several questions can be developed to use with the reaction form to gain insight into the extent to which learning took place during the program. For example, some possible areas to explore on a reaction questionnaire, all aimed at measuring the extent of learning, would be:

☐ skill enhancement
☐ knowledge gain
☐ ability
☐ capability
☐ competence
☐ awareness

In addition, other questions can focus in directly on the learning issue, such as:

☐ difficulty of the material
☐ confidence in using what is learned

These questions are developed using a format similar to the reaction part of the questionnaire. They measure the extent to which learning has taken place, usually based on confidence and perception.

Questionnaire Content: Postprogram

The following items represent a comprehensive list of questionnaire content possibilities for capturing follow-up data (Harrell, 2001). Figure 3-1 presents a questionnaire used in a follow-up evaluation of a program on leadership development. The evaluation was designed to capture data

Leadership Development Program Impact Questionnaire

Are you currently in a supervisory or management role/capacity?   Yes ❑   No ❑

1. Listed below are the objectives of the Leadership Program. After reflecting on the program, please indicate your degree of success in achieving these objectives. *Please check the appropriate response beside each item.*

Skill/Behavior	No Success	Very Little Success	Limited Success	Generally Successful	Completely Successful
A. Apply the 11-step goal-setting process	❑	❑	❑	❑	❑
B. Apply the 12-step leadership planning process	❑	❑	❑	❑	❑
C. Identify the 12 core competencies of outstanding leaders	❑	❑	❑	❑	❑
D. Identify 10 ways to create higher levels of employee loyalty and satisfaction	❑	❑	❑	❑	❑
E. Apply the concept of Deferred Judgment in five scenarios	❑	❑	❑	❑	❑
F. Apply the creative problem-solving process to an identified problem	❑	❑	❑	❑	❑
G. Identify the 7 best ways to build positive relationships	❑	❑	❑	❑	❑
H. Given a work setting situation, apply the 4-step approach to deal with errors	❑	❑	❑	❑	❑
I. Practice 6 ways to improve communication effectiveness	❑	❑	❑	❑	❑

2. Did you implement on-the-job action plans as part of the Leadership Development Program? Yes ❑   No ❑

   If yes, complete and return your Action Plans with this questionnaire. If not, please explain why you did not complete your action plans.

   _____

   _____

3. Have you used the written materials since you participated in the program?
   Yes ❑   No ❑
   Please explain. _____

Figure 3-1. Impact questionnaire.

4. For the following skills, please indicate the extent of improvement during the last few months because of your participation in the Leadership Development Program. *Check the appropriate response for each item.*

Skill Area	No Opportunity to Apply	No Change	Some Change	Moderate Change	Significant Change	Very Significant Change
A. ORGANIZING						
1) Prioritizing daily activities	❑	❑	❑	❑	❑	❑
2) Applying creative techniques	❑	❑	❑	❑	❑	❑
3) Organizing daily activities	❑	❑	❑	❑	❑	❑
4) Raising level of performance standards in area of responsibility	❑	❑	❑	❑	❑	❑
B. WORK CLIMATE						
1) Applying coaching	❑	❑	❑	❑	❑	❑
2) Applying techniques/initiatives that influence motivational climate	❑	❑	❑	❑	❑	❑
3) Implementing actions that influenced retaining people	❑	❑	❑	❑	❑	❑
4) Implementing job enrichment opportunities for valued associates	❑	❑	❑	❑	❑	❑
5) Implementing better control and monitoring systems	❑	❑	❑	❑	❑	❑
6) Applying techniques that influenced better teamwork	❑	❑	❑	❑	❑	❑
7) Improving written communications	❑	❑	❑	❑	❑	❑
8) Improving oral communications	❑	❑	❑	❑	❑	❑
9) Implementing personal leadership plan	❑	❑	❑	❑	❑	❑

5. List the three (3) behaviors or skills from the above list that you have used most frequently as a result of the program.

A) _____

B) _____

C) _____

Figure 3-1. Continued.

6. What has changed about you or your work as a result of your participation in this program? (Specific behavior change such as: increased delegation to employees, improved communication with employees, employee participation in decision making, improved problem solving, etc.)

_____

_____

_____

7. How has your organization benefited from your participation in the program? Please identify specific business accomplishments or improvements that you believe are linked to participation in this program. Think about how the improvements actually resulted in influencing business measures such as: increased revenue, increased overall shipments, improved customer satisfaction, improved employee satisfaction, decreased costs, saved time, etc.

_____

_____

_____

_____

8. Reflect on your specific business accomplishments/improvements as stated above and think of specific ways that you can convert your accomplishments into a monetary value. Along with the monetary value, please indicate your basis for the calculations.

Estimated monetary amount $ _____

Indicate if above amount is weekly, monthly, quarterly, or annually.

❏   Weekly   ❏   Monthly   ❏   Quarterly   ❏   Annually

What is your basis for your estimates? (What influenced the benefits/savings and how did you arrive at the value above?) _____

_____

_____

_____

_____

_____

9. What percentage of the improvement above was actually influenced by the application of knowledge and skills from the *Leadership Development Program*?

☞ _____ % (0% = None and 100% = All)

10. What level of confidence do you place on the above estimations?

☞ _____ % *Confidence* (0% = No Confidence and 100% = Certainty)

11. Do you think this *Leadership Development Program* represented an appropriate investment for the company?

Yes ❏   **No** ❏

Please explain. _____

_____

Figure 3-1. Continued.

12. Indicate the extent to which you think your application of knowledge, skills, and behavior learned in the *Leadership Development Program* had a positive influence on the following business measures in your own work or your work unit. *Please check the appropriate response beside each measure.*

Business Measure	Not Applicable	Applies But No Influence	Some Influence	Moderate Influence	Significant Influence	Very Significant Influence
A. Work output	❑	❑	❑	❑	❑	❑
B. Quality	❑	❑	❑	❑	❑	❑
C. Cost control	❑	❑	❑	❑	❑	❑
D. Efficiency	❑	❑	❑	❑	❑	❑
E. Response time to customers	❑	❑	❑	❑	❑	❑
F. Cycle time of products	❑	❑	❑	❑	❑	❑
G. Sales	❑	❑	❑	❑	❑	❑
H. Employee turnover	❑	❑	❑	❑	❑	❑
I. Employee absenteeism	❑	❑	❑	❑	❑	❑
J. Employee satisfaction	❑	❑	❑	❑	❑	❑
K. Employee complaints	❑	❑	❑	❑	❑	❑
L. Customer satisfaction	❑	❑	❑	❑	❑	❑
M. Customer complaints	❑	❑	❑	❑	❑	❑
N. Other (please specify)	❑	❑	❑	❑	❑	❑

Please cite specific examples or provide more details: _____

_____
_____
_____
_____

13. What barriers, if any, have you encountered that have prevented you from using skills/behaviors gained in the *Leadership Development Program*? *Check all that apply.*

❑ I have had no opportunity to use the skills
❑ I have not had enough time to apply the skills

Figure 3-1. Continued.

❑ My work environment does not support the use of these skills/behaviors
❑ My supervisor does not support this type of program
❑ This material does not apply to my job situation
❑ Other (please specify): _____

If any of the above are checked, please explain if possible. _____

_____

_____

14. What enablers, if any, are present to help you use the skills or knowledge gained from this program? Please explain.

_____

_____

15. What additional support could be provided by management that would influence your ability to apply the skills and knowledge learned from the program? _____

_____

16. What additional benefits have been derived from this program? _____

_____

_____

17. What additional solutions do you recommend that would help to achieve the same business results that the *Leadership Development Program* has influenced? _____

_____

_____

18. Would you recommend the *Leadership Development Program* to others?   **Yes** ❑   **No** ❑
Please explain. If no, why not. If yes, what groups/jobs and why? _____

_____

_____

19. What specific suggestions do you have for improving this program? _____

_____

_____

20. Other Comments:

_____

_____

Figure 3-1. Continued.

for an ROI analysis, the primary method of data collection being this questionnaire. This example will be used to illustrate many of the issues involving potential content items for questionnaire design with emphasis on application (Level 3) and Impact (Level 4).

Progress with objectives. Sometimes it is helpful to assess progress with the objectives in the follow-up evaluation as is illustrated in question 1 in Figure 3-1. While this issue is usually assessed during the program (because it is Level 1 data), it can be helpful to revisit the objectives after the participants have had an opportunity to apply what has been learned.

Action plan implementation. If an action plan is required in the program, the questionnaire should reference the plan and determine the extent to which it has been implemented. If the action plan requirement is very low-key, perhaps only one question would be devoted to the follow-up on the action plan, as illustrated in question 2 in Figure 3-1. If the action plan is very comprehensive and contains an abundance of Levels 3 and 4 data, then the questionnaire takes a secondary role and most of the data collection process will focus directly on the status of the completed action plan.

Use of program materials and handouts. If participants are provided with materials to use on the job, it may be helpful to determine the extent to which these materials are used. This is particularly helpful when operating manuals, reference books, and job aids have been distributed and explained in the program and are expected to be used on the job. Question 3 in Figure 3-1 focuses on this issue.

Application of knowledge/skills. As shown in question 4 in Figure 3-1, it is helpful to determine the level of improvement in skills directly linked to the program. A more detailed variation of this question is to list each skill and indicate the frequency of use and the effectiveness of use of these skills. For many skills, it is important to experience frequent use quickly after acquisition so that the skills become internalized. In this example, question 5 addresses the skill frequency issue.

Changes with work. Sometimes it is helpful to determine what specific activities or processes have changed about participants' work as a result of the program. As question 6 in Figure 3-1 illustrates, the participant explores how the skill applications (listed previously) have actually changed work habits, processes, and output.

Improvements/accomplishments. Question 7 in Figure 3-1 begins a series of four impact questions that are appropriate for most follow-up questionnaires. This question seeks specific accomplishments and improvements directly linked to the program and focuses on specific measurable successes that can be easily identified by the participants. Since this question is an open-ended question, it can be helpful to provide examples that indicate the nature and range of responses requested. However, examples can also be constraining in nature and may actually limit the responses.

Monetary impact. Perhaps the most difficult question (number 8 in Figure 3-1) asks participants to provide monetary values for the improvements identified in question 7. Only the first year improvement is sought. Participants are asked to specify net improvements so that the actual monetary values will represent gains from the program. An important part of the question is the basis for the calculation, where participants specify the steps taken to develop the annual net value and the assumptions made in the analysis. It is very important for the basis to be completed with enough detail to understand the process.

Improvements linked with program. The next question in the impact series (question 9 in Figure 3-1) isolates the effects of the training. Participants indicate the percent of the improvement that is directly related to the program. As an alternative, participants may be provided with the various factors that have influenced the results and are asked to allocate the percentages to each factor.

Confidence level. To adjust for the uncertainty of the data provided in questions 8 and 9, participants were asked to offer a level of confidence for the estimation, expressed as a percentage with a range of 0–100%, as shown in question 10 in Figure 3-1. This input allows participants to reflect their level of uncertainty with this process.

Investment perception. The value of the program, from the viewpoint of the participant, can be useful information. As illustrated in question 11 in Figure 3-1, participants are asked if they perceive this program to represent an appropriate investment. Another option for this question is to present the actual cost of the program so that participants can respond more accurately from the investment perspective. It may be useful to express the cost as a per participant cost. Also, the question can be divided into two parts—one reflecting the investment of funds by the company and the other an investment in the participants time in the program.

Linkage with output measures. Sometimes it is helpful to determine the degree to which the program has influenced certain output measures, as shown in question 12 in Figure 3-1. In some situations, a detailed analysis may reveal specifically which measures this program has influenced. However, when this issue is uncertain, it may be helpful to list the potential business performance measures influenced by the program and seek input from the participants. The question should be worded so that the frame of reference is for the time period after the program was conducted.

Barriers. A variety of barriers can influence the successful application of the skills and knowledge learned in the training program. Question 13 in Figure 3-1 identifies these barriers. As an alternative, the perceived barriers are listed and participants check all that apply. Still another variation is to list the barriers with a range of responses, indicating the extent to which the barrier inhibited results.

Enablers. Just as important as barriers are the enablers, those issues, events, or situations which enable the process to be applied successfully on the job. Question 14 provides an open-ended question for enablers. The same options are available with this question as in the question on barriers.

Management support. For most programs, management support is critical to the successful application of newly acquired skills. At least one question should be included on the degree of management support, such as question 15 in Figure 3-1. Sometimes this question is structured so that various descriptions of management support are detailed, and participants check the one that applies to their situation. This information is very beneficial to help remove or minimize barriers.

Other benefits. In most programs, additional benefits will begin to emerge, particularly in the intangible area. Participants should be asked to detail any benefits not presented elsewhere. In this example, question 16 shows the open-ended question for additional benefits.

Other solutions. A training program is only one of many potential solutions to a performance problem. If the needs assessment is faulty or if there are alternative approaches to developing the desired skills or knowledge, other potential solutions could be more effective and achieve the same success. In question 17 the participant is asked to identify other solutions that could have been effective in obtaining the same or similar results. This information can be particularly helpful as the training and development function continues to shift to a performance improvement function.

Target audience recommendations. Sometimes it is helpful to solicit input about the most appropriate target audience for this program. In question 18, the participants are asked to indicate which groups of employees would benefit the most from attending this program.

Suggestions for improvement. As a final wrap-up question, participants are asked to provide suggestions for improving any part of the program or process. As illustrated in question 19, the open-ended structure is intended to solicit qualitative responses to be used to make improvements.

Improving the Response Rate for Questionnaires and Surveys

The content items represent a wide range of potential issues to explore in a follow-up questionnaire or survey. Obviously, asking all of the questions could cause the response rate to be reduced considerably. The challenge, therefore, is to tackle questionnaire design and administration for maximum response rate. This is a critical issue when the questionnaire is the primary data collection method and most of the evaluation hinges on questionnaire results. The following actions can be taken to increase response rate.

Provide advance communication. If appropriate and feasible, participants should receive advance communications about the requirement to complete a questionnaire. This minimizes some of the resistance to the process, provides an opportunity to explain in more detail the circumstances surrounding the evaluation, and positions the follow-up evaluation as an integral part of the program, not an add-on activity.

Communicate the purpose. Participants should understand the reason for the questionnaire, including who or what has initiated this specific evaluation. Participants should know if the evaluation is part of a systematic process or a special request for this program.

Explain who will see the data. It is important for participants to know who will see the data and the results of the questionnaire. If the questionnaire is anonymous, it should clearly be communicated to participants what steps will be taken to ensure anonymity. Participants should know if senior executives will see the combined results of the study.

Describe the data integration process. Participants should understand how the questionnaire results will be combined with other data, if applicable. The questionnaire may be only one of the data collection methods used. Participants should know how the data is weighted and integrated in the final report.

Keep the questionnaire as simple as possible. While a simple questionnaire does not always provide the full scope of data necessary for an ROI analysis, the simplified approach should always be a goal. When questions are developed, and the total scope of the questionnaire is finalized, every effort should be made to keep it as simple and brief as possible.

Simplify the response process. To the extent possible, it should be easy to respond to the questionnaire. If appropriate, a self-addressed stamped envelope should be included. Perhaps the e-mail system could be used for response, if it is easier. In still other situations, a response box is provided near the workstation.

Utilize local manager support. Management involvement at the local level is critical to response rate success. Managers can distribute the questionnaires themselves, make reference to the questionnaire in staff meetings, follow-up to see if questionnaires have been completed, and generally show the support for completing the questionnaire. This direct supervisor support will cause some participants to respond with usable data.

Let the participants know they are part of the sample. If appropriate, participants should know that they are part of a carefully selected sample and that their input will be used to make decisions regarding a much larger target audience. This action often appeals to a sense of responsibility for participants to provide usable, accurate data for the questionnaire.

Consider incentives. A variety of different types of incentives can be offered and they usually fall into three categories. First, an incentive is provided in exchange for the completed questionnaire. For example, if participants return the questionnaire personally or through the mail, they will receive a small gift, such as a mouse pad or coffee mug. If identity is an issue, a neutral third party can provide the incentive. In the second category, the incentive is provided to make participants feel guilty about not responding. Examples are a dollar bill (or equivalent currency) clipped to the questionnaire or a pen enclosed in the envelope. Participants are asked to "take the money, buy a beverage, and fill out the questionnaire," or "please use this pen to complete the questionnaire." A third group of incentives is designed to obtain a quick response. This approach is based on the assumption that a quick response will ensure a greater response rate. If an individual puts off completing the questionnaire, the odds of completing it diminish considerably. The initial group of participants may receive a more expensive gift or they may be part of a drawing for an incentive. For example, in one study involving 75 participants, the first 25 returned questionnaires were placed in a drawing for a $500 credit card gift certificate. The next 25 were added to the first 25 for another drawing. After the first 50, there is no incentive. The longer a participant waits, the lower the odds for winning.

Have an executive sign the introductory letter. Participants are always interested in who sent the letter with the questionnaire. For maximum effectiveness, a senior executive who is responsible for a major area where the participants work should sign the letter. Employees may be more willing to respond to a senior executive when compared to situations where a member of the training and development staff signs a letter.

Use follow-up reminders. A follow-up reminder should be sent one week after the questionnaire is received and another sent two weeks after it is received. Depending on the questionnaire and the situation, these times could be adjusted. In some situations, a third follow-up is recommended. Sometimes the follow-up should be sent in different media. For example, a questionnaire may be sent through regular mail, whereas, the first follow-up reminder is from the immediate supervisor and a second follow-up reminder is sent through e-mail.

Send a copy of the results to the participants. Even if it is an abbreviated form, participants should see the results of the study. More importantly, participants should understand that they will receive a copy of the study when they are asked to provide the data. This promise will often increase the response rate, as some individuals want to see the results of the entire group along with their particular input.

Review the questionnaire in the session. It is critical for participants to understand the questionnaire as much as possible. It is very helpful for them to see a copy in advance of data collection. Ideally, the questionnaire should be distributed and reviewed during the session. Each question should be briefly discussed and any issues or concerns about the questions need to be clarified. Ideally, a commitment to provide data is secured from the participate. This not only helps the response rate, but also improves the quality and quantity of data.

Consider a captive audience. The best way to have an extremely high response rate is to consider a captive audience. In a follow-up session, a routine meeting, or a session designed to collect data, participants meet and provide input, usually in the first few minutes of the meeting. Sometimes a routine meeting (such as a sales, technology, or management meeting) provides ample setting to collect the data. This approach is ideal in a major program with a series of the different courses. Each subsequent course is an opportunity to collect data about the previous course.

Communicate the timing of data flow. Participants should be provided with specific deadlines for providing the data. They also need to know when they will receive results. The best approach is to provide the exact date when the last questionnaires will be allowed, the date when the analysis is complete, the date that they will receive the results of the study, and the date the sponsor will receive the results. The specific timing builds respect for the entire process.

Select the appropriate media. The medium for the survey (whether paper-based, web-based, or e-mail) should match the culture of the group, and not necessarily selected for the convenience of the evaluator. Sometimes an optional response media will be allowed. The important thing is to make it fit the audience.

Consider having the input to be anonymous. Anonymous data is often more objective, and sometimes more free flowing. If participants believe that their input is anonymous, they will be more constructive and candid in their feedback and their response rates will generally be higher.

Treat data with confidence. Confidentiality is an important part of the process. A confidentiality statement should be included, indicating that participants' names will not be revealed to anyone other than the data collectors and those involved in analyzing the data. In some cases, it may be appropriate to indicate specifically who will actually see the raw data. Also, specific steps taken to ensure the confidentiality of the data are detailed.

Use a pilot test. Consider using a pilot test on a sample of the target audience. This is one of the best ways to ensure that the questionnaire is designed properly and the questions flow adequately. Pilot testing can be accomplished quickly with a very small sample size and can be very revealing.

Explain how long it will take to complete the questionnaire. Although this appears to be a trivial issue, participants need to have a realistic understanding of how long it will take them to provide the data. There is nothing more frustrating than to grossly underestimate how much time it will take to complete the questionnaire. The pilot test should provide the information needed to adequately allocate time for the response.

Personalize the process, if possible. Participants will respond to personal messages and requests. If possible, the letter with the questionnaire should be personalized. Also, if it is possible, a personal phone call is a helpful follow-up reminder. The personal touch brings appropriate sincerity and responsibility to the process.

Provide an update. In some cases it may be appropriate to provide an update on current response total and the progress on the entire project. It is helpful for individuals to understand how others are doing. Sometimes this creates a subtle pressure and reminder to provide data.

Collectively, these items help boost response rates of follow-up questionnaires. Using all of these strategies can result in a 60–80% response rate, even with lengthy questionnaires that might take 45 minutes to complete.

TESTS

Testing is important for measuring learning in program evaluations. Pre- and postcourse comparisons using tests are very common. An improvement in test scores shows the change in skill, knowledge, or attitude attributed to the program. The principles of test development are similar to those for the design and development of questionnaires and attitude surveys. This section presents additional information on types of tests and test construction (Westgaard, 1999).

Types of Tests

Several types of tests, which can be classified in three ways, are used in HRD. The first is based upon the medium used for administering the test.

NORM-REFERENCED TEST

Norm-referenced tests compare participants with each other or to other groups rather than to specific instructional objectives. They are characterized by using data to compare the participants to the "norm" or average. Although norm-referenced tests have only limited use in some HRD evaluations, they may be useful in programs involving large numbers of participants in which average scores and relative rankings are important. In some situations, participants who score highest on the exams are given special recognition or awards or made eligible for other special activities.

CRITERION-REFERENCED TEST

The criterion-referenced test (CRT) is an objective test with a predetermined cut-off score. The CRT is a measure against carefully written objectives for the HRD program. In a CRT, the interest lies in whether or not participants meet the desired minimum standards, not how that participant ranks with others. The primary concern is to measure, report, and analyze participant performance as it relates to the instructional objectives.

Criterion-referenced testing is a popular measurement instrument in HRD (Shrock and Coscarelli, 2000). Its use is becoming widespread and is frequently used in e-learning. It has the advantage of being objective-based, precise, and relatively easy to administer. It does require programs with clearly defined objectives that can be measured by tests.

PERFORMANCE TESTING

Performance testing allows the participant to exhibit a skill (and occasionally knowledge or attitudes) that has been learned in an HRD program. The skill can be manual, verbal, analytical, or a combination of the three. Performance testing is used frequently in job-related training where the participants are allowed to demonstrate what they have learned. In supervisory and management training, performance testing comes in the form of skill practices or role-plays. Participants are asked to demonstrate discussion or problem-solving skills they have acquired.

For a performance test to be effective, the following steps are recommended for its design and administration.

- ☐ The test should be a representative sample of the HRD program, and should allow the participant to demonstrate as many skills as possible that are taught in the program.
- ☐ Every phase of the test should be thoroughly planned, including the time, the preparation of the participant, the collection of necessary materials and tools, and the evaluation of results.
- ☐ Thorough and consistent instructions are necessary. As with other tests, the quality of the instructions can influence the outcome of a performance test. All participants should be provided the same instructions.
- ☐ Acceptable standards must be developed for a performance test so that employees know in advance what has to be accomplished to be considered satisfactory and acceptable for test completion.
- ☐ Information that may lead participants astray should not be included.

With these general guidelines, performance tests can be developed into effective tools for program evaluation. Although more costly than written tests, performance tests are essential in situations where a high degree of fidelity is required between work and test conditions.

Simulations

Another technique to measure learning is job simulations. This method involves the construction and application of a procedure or task that simulates or models the activity for which the HRD program is being conducted. The simulation is designed to represent, as closely as possible, the actual job situation. Simulation may be used as an integral part of the HRD program as well as for evaluation. In evaluation, participants are provided an opportunity to try out their performance in the simulated activity and have it evaluated based on how well the task was accomplished. Simulations may be used during the program, at the end of the program, or as part of the follow-up evaluation.

There are a variety of simulation techniques used to evaluate program results.

☐ **Electrical/mechanical simulation.** This technique uses a combination of electronics and mechanical devices to simulate real-life situations, and is used in conjunction with programs to develop operational and diagnostic skills.

☐ **Task simulation.** This approach involves the performance of a simulated task as part of an evaluation.

☐ **Business games.** Business games have grown in popularity in recent years. They represent simulations of part or all of a business enterprise in which participants change the variables of the business and observe the effect of those changes. The game not only reflects the real-world situation but also represents the synopsis of the HRD program of which it is a part.

☐ **In-basket.** The in-basket is particularly useful in supervisory and management training programs. Portions of a supervisor's job are simulated through a series of items that normally appear in the in-basket. These items are typically memos, notes, letters, and reports, which create realistic conditions facing the supervisor. The participant's performance in the in-basket represents an evaluation of the program.

☐ **Case study.** A possibly less effective, but still popular, technique is a case study. A case study gives a detailed description of a problem and usually contains a list of several questions. The participant is asked to analyze the case and determine the best course of action.

☐ **Role playing.** In role playing, sometimes referred to as skill practice, participants practice a newly learned skill as they are observed by other individuals. Participants are given their assigned role with specific instructions, which sometimes include an ultimate course of action. The participant then practices the skill with other individuals to accomplish the desired objectives.

In summary, simulations come in a wide variety. They offer an opportunity for participants to practice what is being taught in an HRD program and have their performance observed in a simulated job condition. They can provide extremely accurate evaluations if the performance in the simulation is objective and can be clearly measured.

Informal Tests

In some situations, it is important to have an informal check of learning that provides some assurance that participants have acquired skills, knowledge, or perhaps some changes in attitudes. This approach is appropriate when other levels of evaluation are pursued. For example, if a Level 3 on-the-job application evaluation is planned, it might not be critical to have a comprehensive Level 2. An informal assessment of learning may be sufficient. After all, resources are scarce and a comprehensive evaluation at all levels becomes quite expensive. The following are some alternative approaches to measuring learning that might suffice when inexpensive, low-key, informal assessments are needed.

EXERCISES/PROBLEMS/ACTIVITIES

Many HRD programs contain specific activities, exercises, or problems that must be explored, developed, or solved during the program. Some of these are constructed in terms of involvement exercises, while others require individual problem-solving skills. When these are integrated into the program, there are several specific ways in which to measure learning.

☐ The results of the exercise can be submitted for review and evaluated by the facilitator.
☐ The results can be discussed in a group with a comparison of various approaches and solutions. The group can reach an assessment of how much each individual has learned.

☐ The solutions to the problem or exercises can be shared with the group and the participant and provide a self-assessment indicating the degree to which skills and/or knowledge have been obtained from the exercise.

☐ The facilitator can review the individual progress or success of each participant to determine the relative success.

SELF-ASSESSMENT

In many applications, a self-assessment may be appropriate. Participants are provided an opportunity to assess the extent of skills and knowledge acquisition. This is particularly applicable when Levels 3, 4, and 5 evaluations are planned, and it is important to know if learning has improved. A few techniques can ensure that the process is effective.

☐ The self-assessment should be made on an anonymous basis so that individuals feel free to express a realistic and accurate assessment of what they have learned.

☐ The purpose of the self-assessment should be explained, along with the plans for the data. Specifically, if there are implications for course design or individual retesting this should be discussed.

☐ If there has been no improvement or the self-assessment is unsatisfactory, there should be some explanation as to what that means and what the implications will be. This will help to ensure that accurate and credible information is provided.

FACILITATOR ASSESSMENT

Another technique is for facilitators to provide an assessment of the learning that has taken place. Although this approach is very subjective, it may be appropriate when a Level 3, 4, or 5 evaluation is planned. One of the most effective ways to accomplish this is to provide a checklist of the specific skills that need to be acquired in the course. Facilitators can then check off their assessment of the skills individually. Also, if there is a particular body of knowledge that needs to be acquired, the categories could be listed with a checklist for assurance that the individual has a good understanding of those items.

INTERVIEWS

Another helpful collection method is the interview, although it is not used in evaluation as frequently as questionnaires. The HRD staff, the participant's supervisor, or an outside third party can conduct interviews. Interviews can secure data not available in performance records, or data difficult to obtain through written responses or observations (Kvale, 1996). Also, interviews can uncover success stories that can be useful in communicating evaluation results. Participants may be reluctant to describe their results in a questionnaire, but will volunteer the information to a skillful interviewer who uses probing techniques. While the interview process uncovers reaction, Learning, and Impact, it is primarily used with Application data. A major disadvantage of the interview is that it is time consuming and requires interviewer preparation to ensure that the process is consistent.

Types of Interviews

Interviews usually fall into two basic types: (1) structured and (2) unstructured. A structured interview is much like a questionnaire. Specific questions are asked with little room to deviate from the desired responses. The primary advantages of the structured interview over the questionnaire are that the interview process can ensure that the questionnaire is completed and the interviewer understands the responses supplied by the participant.

The unstructured interview allows for probing for additional information. This type of interview uses a few general questions, which can lead into more detailed information as important data are uncovered. The interviewer must be skilled in the probing process.

Interview Guidelines

The design issues and steps for interviews are similar to those of the questionnaire. A few key issues need emphasis:

- [ ] **Develop questions to be asked.** After the type of interview is determined, specific questions need to be developed. Questions should be brief, precise, and designed for easy response.
- [ ] **Try out the interview.** The interview should be tested on a small number of participants. If possible, the interviews should be conducted as part of the trial run of the HRD program. The responses should be analyzed and the interview revised, if necessary.
- [ ] **Prepare the interviewers.** The interviewer should have the appropriate level of core skills, including active listening, asking probing questions, and collecting and summarizing information into a meaningful form.

☐ **Provide clear instructions to the participant.** The participant should understand the purpose of the interview and know how the information will be used. Expectations, conditions, and rules of the interview should be thoroughly discussed. For example, the participant should know if statements would be kept confidential.

☐ **Administer the interviews according to a scheduled plan.** As with the other evaluation instruments, interviews need to be conducted according to a predetermined plan. The timing of the interview, the individual who conducts the interview, and the location of the interview are all issues that become relevant when developing a plan. For a large number of participants, a sampling plan may be necessary to save time and reduce the evaluation cost.

FOCUS GROUPS

An extension of the interview, focus groups, are particularly helpful when in-depth feedback is needed for a Level 3 evaluation. The focus group involves a small group discussion conducted by an experienced facilitator. It is designed to solicit qualitative judgments on a planned topic or issue. Group members are all required to provide their input, as individual input builds on group input (Subramony, et al., 2002).

When compared with questionnaires, surveys, tests, or interviews, the focus group strategy has several advantages. The basic premise of using focus groups is that when quality judgments are subjective, several individual judgments are better than one. The group process, where participants stimulate ideas in others, is an effective method for generating qualitative data. It is inexpensive and can be quickly planned and conducted. Its flexibility makes it possible to explore a training program's unexpected outcomes or applications.

Applications for Evaluation

The focus group is particularly helpful when qualitative information is needed about the success of a training program. For example, the focus group can be used in the following situations:

☐ to evaluate the reactions to specific exercises, cases, simulations, or other components of a training program;

☐ to assess the overall effectiveness of program application; and

☐ to assess the impact of the program in a follow-up evaluation after the program is completed.

Essentially, focus groups are helpful when evaluation information is needed but cannot be collected adequately with questionnaires, interviews, or quantitative methods.

Guidelines

While there are no set rules on how to use focus groups for evaluation, the following guidelines are helpful:

☐ **Ensure that management buys into the focus group process.** Because this is a relatively new process for evaluation, it might be unknown to management. Managers need to understand focus groups and their advantages. This should raise their level of confidence in the information obtained from group sessions.

☐ **Plan topics, questions, and strategy carefully.** As with any evaluation instrument, planning is critical. The specific topics, questions, and issues to be discussed must be carefully planned and sequenced. This enhances the comparison of results from one group to another and ensures that the group process is effective and stays on track.

☐ **Keep the group size small.** While there is no magic group size, a range of 8 to 12 seems to be appropriate for most focus group applications. A group has to be large enough to ensure different points of view, but small enough to provide every participant a chance to freely exchange comments.

☐ **Use a representative sample of the target population.** If possible, groups should be selected to represent the target population. The group should be homogeneous in experience, rank, and job level in the organization.

☐ **Facilitators must have appropriate expertise.** The success of a focus group rests with the facilitator who must be skilled in the focus group process. Facilitators must know how to control aggressive members of the group and diffuse the input from those who want to dominate the group. Also, facilitators must be able to create an environment in which participants feel comfortable in offering comments freely and openly. Because of this, some organizations use external facilitators.

In summary, the focus group is an inexpensive and quick way to determine the strengths and weaknesses of training programs, particularly with management and supervisory training. However, for a complete evaluation, focus group information should be combined with data from other instruments.

OBSERVATIONS

Another potentially useful data collection method is observing participants and recording any changes in their behavior. The observer may be a member of the HRD staff, the participant's supervisor, a member of a peer group, or an external party. The most common observer, and probably the most practical, is a member of the HRD staff.

Guidelines for Effective Observation

Observation is often misused or misapplied to evaluation situations, leaving some to abandon the process. The effectiveness of observation can be improved with the following guidelines.

☐ **The observations should be systematic.** The observation process must be planned so that it is executed effectively without any surprises. The persons observed should know in advance about the observation and why they are being observed unless the observation is planned to be invisible. The timing of observations should be a part of the plan. There are right times to observe a participant, and there are wrong times. If a participant is observed when times are not normal (i.e., in a crisis), the data collected may be useless.

☐ **The observer's should know how to interpret and report what they see.** Observations involve judgment decisions. The observer must analyze which behaviors are being displayed and what actions the participants are taking. Observers should know how to summarize behavior and report results in a meaningful manner.

☐ **The observer's influence should be minimized.** Except for mystery observers and electronic observations, it is impossible to completely isolate the overall effect of an observer. Participants may display the behavior they think is appropriate, and they will usually be at their best. The presence of the observer must be minimized. To the extent possible, the observer should blend into the work environment or extend the observation period.

☐ **Select observers carefully.** Observers are usually independent of the participants, typically a member of the HRD staff. The independent observer is usually more skilled at recording behavior and making interpretations of behavior. They are usually unbiased in these interpretations. Using them enables the HRD department to bypass training observers and relieves the line organization of that responsibility. On the other hand, the HRD staff observer has the appearance of an outsider checking the work of others. There may be a tendency for participants to overreact and possibly resent this kind of observer. Sometimes it might be more plausible to recruit observers from outside the organization. This approach has an advantage of neutralizing the prejudicial feelings entering the decisions.

☐ **Observers must be fully prepared.** Observers must fully understand what information is needed and what skills are covered in the program. They must be trained for the assignment and provided a chance to practice observation skills.

Observation Methods

Five methods of observation are utilized, depending on the circumstances surrounding the type of information needed. Each method is described briefly.

BEHAVIOR CHECKLIST AND CODES

A behavior checklist can be useful for recording the presence, absence, frequency, or duration of a participant's behavior as it occurs. A checklist will not usually provide information on the quality, intensity, or possibly the circumstances surrounding the behavior observed. The checklist is useful because an observer can identify exactly which behaviors should or should not occur. Measuring the duration of a behavior may be more difficult and requires a stopwatch and a place on the form to record the time interval. This factor is usually not as important when compared to whether or not a particular behavior was observed and how often. The number of behaviors listed in the checklist should be small and listed in a logical sequence, if they normally occur in a sequence. A variation of this approach involves a coding of behaviors on a form. This method is less time consuming because the code is entered that identifies a specific behavior.

DELAYED REPORT METHOD

With a delayed report method, the observer does not use any forms or written materials during the observation. The information is either recorded after the observation is completed or at particular time intervals during an observation. The observer attempts to reconstruct what has been observed during the observation period. The advantage of this approach is that the observer is not as noticeable, and there are no forms being completed or notes being taken during the observation. The observer can blend into the situation and be less distracting. An obvious disadvantage is that the information written may not be as accurate and reliable as the information collected at the time it occurred. A variation of this approach is the 360-degree feedback process in which surveys are completed on other individuals based on observations within a specific time frame.

VIDEO RECORDING

A video camera records behavior in every detail, an obvious advantage. However, this intrusion may be awkward and cumbersome, and the participants may be unnecessarily nervous or self-conscious when they are being videotaped. If the camera is concealed, the privacy of the participant may be invaded. Because of this, video recording of on-the-job behavior is not frequently used.

AUDIO MONITORING

Monitoring conversations of participants who are using the skills taught in the training program is an effective observation technique. For example, in a large communication company's telemarketing department, sales representatives are trained to sell equipment by telephone. To determine if employees are using the skills properly, telephone conversations are monitored on a selected and sometimes random basis. While this approach may stir some controversy, it is an effective way to determine if skills are being applied consistently and effectively. For it to work smoothly it must be fully explained and the rules clearly communicated.

COMPUTER MONITORING

For employees who work regularly with a keyboard, computer monitoring is becoming an effective way to "observe" participants as they perform job tasks. The computer monitors times, sequence of steps, and other activities to determine if the participant is performing the work according to what was learned in the training program. As technology continues to be a significant part of jobs, computer monitoring holds promise of monitoring actual applications on the job. This is particularly helpful for Level 3 data.

BUSINESS PERFORMANCE MONITORING

Data are available in every organization to measure performance. Monitoring performance data enables management to measure performance in terms of output, quality, costs, and time. In determining the use of data in the evaluation, the first consideration should be existing databases and reports. In most organizations, performance data suitable for measuring the improvement resulting from an HRD program are available (Mondschein, 1999). If not, additional record-keeping systems will have to be developed for measurement and analysis. At this point, as with many other points in the process, the question of economics enters. Is it economical to develop the record-keeping system necessary to evaluate an HRD program? If the costs are greater than the expected return for the entire program, then it is meaningless to develop them.

Using Current Measures

The recommended approach is to use existing performance measures, if available. Specific guidelines are recommended to ensure that current measurement systems are easily developed.

Identify appropriate measures. Performance measures should be reviewed to identify the items related to the proposed objectives of the program. Sometimes, an organization will have several performance measures related to the same item. For example, the efficiency of a production unit can be measured in a variety of ways:

- ☐ number of units produced per hour
- ☐ number of on-schedule production units
- ☐ percent utilization of the equipment
- ☐ percent of equipment downtime
- ☐ labor cost per unit of production
- ☐ overtime required per piece of production
- ☐ total unit cost

Each of these, in its own way, measures the efficiency or effectiveness of the production unit. All related measures should be reviewed to determine those most relevant to the HRD program.

Convert current measures to usable ones. Occasionally, existing performance measures are integrated with other data and it may be difficult to keep them isolated from unrelated data. In this situation, all existing related measures should be extracted and retabulated to be more appropriate for comparison in the evaluation. At times, conversion factors may be necessary. For example, the average number of new sales orders per month may be presented regularly in the performance measures for the sales department. In addition, the sales costs per sales representative are also presented. However, in the evaluation of an HRD program, the average cost per new sale is needed. The two existing performance records are required to develop the data necessary for comparison.

Develop a collection plan. A data-collection plan defines the data to be collected, the source of the data, when data are collected, who will collect it, and where it will be collected. A blank copy of the plan is shown in Figure 3-3. This plan should contain provisions for the evaluator to secure copies of performance reports in a timely manner so that the items can be recorded and available for analysis.

Developing New Measures

In some cases, data are not available for the information needed to measure the effectiveness of an HRD program. The HRD staff must work with the participating organization to develop record-keeping systems, if this is economically feasible. In one organization, a new employee orientation system was implemented on a company-wide basis. Several measures were planned, including early turnover representing the percentage of employees who left the company in the first six months of their employment. An improved employee orientation program should influence this measure. At the time of the program's inception, this measure was not available. When the program was implemented, the organization began collecting early turnover figures for comparison. Typical questions when creating new measures:

☐ Which department will develop the measurement system?
☐ Who will record and monitor the data?
☐ Where will it be recorded?
☐ Will forms be used?

These questions will usually involve other departments or a management decision that extends beyond the scope of the HRD department. Possibly the administration division, the HR department, or information technology section will be instrumental in helping determine if new measures are needed and, if so, how they will be collected.

ACTION PLANNING AND FOLLOW-UP ASSIGNMENTS

In some cases, follow-up assignments can develop Level 3 and Level 4 data. In a typical follow-up assignment, the participant is instructed to meet a goal or complete a particular task or project by the determined follow-up date. A summary of the results of these completed assignments provides further evidence of the impact of the program.

The action plan is the most common type of follow-up assignment and is fully described in this section. With this approach, participants are required to develop action plans as part of the program. Action plans contain detailed steps to accomplish specific objectives related to the program. The plan is typically prepared on a printed form such as the one shown in Figure 3-2. The action plan shows what is to be done, by

---

Name: _____ Instructor Signature _____ Follow-Up Date: _____

Objective: _____ Evaluation Period _____ to _____

Improvement Measure: _____ Current Performance _____ Target Performance _____

Action Steps	Analysis
1.	A. What is the unit of measure? _____
2.	B. What is the value (cost) of one unit? $ _____
3.	C. How did you arrive at this value?
4.	
5.	
6.	D. How much did the measure change during the evaluation period (monthly value)? _____
7.	E. What percent of this change was actually caused by this program? _____ %
Intangible Benefits:	F. What level of confidence do you place on the above information (100%=Certainty and 0%=No Confidence)? _____ %

Comments: _____

_____

Figure 3-2. Action plan.

whom, and the date by which the objectives should be accomplished. The action plan approach is a straightforward, easy-to-use method for determining how participants will change their behavior on the job and achieve success with training. The approach produces data answers with such questions as:

- ☐ What steps or action items have been accomplished and when?
- ☐ What on-the-job improvements or accomplishments have been realized since the program was conducted?
- ☐ How much of the improvements are linked to the program?
- ☐ What may have prevented participants from accomplishing specific action items?
- ☐ What is the monetary value of the improvement?

With this information, HRD professionals can decide if a program should be modified and in what ways, while managers can assess the findings to evaluate the worth of the program.

Developing the Action Plan

The development of the action plan requires two tasks: (1) determining the areas for action and (2) writing the action items. Both tasks should be completed during the program. The areas or measures for action should originate from the need for the program, the content of the program and, at the same time, be related to on-the-job activities. Participants can independently develop a list of potential areas for action or a list may be generated in group discussions. The list may include a measure needing improvement or represent an opportunity for increased performance. Typical categories are:

- ☐ Productivity
- ☐ Sales, Revenue
- ☐ Quality/Process Improvement
- ☐ Efficiency
- ☐ Time Savings
- ☐ Cost Savings
- ☐ Complaints
- ☐ Job Satisfaction
- ☐ Work Habits
- ☐ Customer Satisfaction
- ☐ Customer Service

The specific action items support the business measure and are usually more difficult to write than the identification of the action areas. The most important characteristic of an action item is that it is written so that everyone involved will know when it occurs. One way to help achieve this goal is to use specific action verbs. Some examples of action items are:

- ☐ *Learn* how to operate the new RC-105 drill press machine in the adjacent department, by *(date)*.
- ☐ *Identify* and *secure* a new customer account, by *(date)*.
- ☐ *Handle* every piece of paper only once to improve my personal time management, by *(date)*.
- ☐ *Learn* to talk with my employers directly about a problem that arises rather than avoiding a confrontation, by *(date)*.

Typical questions when developing action steps:

- ☐ How much time will this action take?
- ☐ Are the skills for accomplishing this action item available?
- ☐ Who has the authority to implement the action plan?
- ☐ Will this action have an effect on other individuals?
- ☐ Are there any organizational constraints for accomplishing this action item?

If appropriate, each action item should have a date for completion and indicate other individuals or resources required for completion. Also, planned behavior changes should be observable. It should be obvious to the participant and others when it happens. Action plans, as used in this context, do not require the prior approval or input from the participant's supervisor, although it may be helpful.

Using Action Plans Successfully

The action plan process should be an integral part of the program and not an add-on or optional activity. To gain maximum effectiveness from action plans and to collect data for ROI calculations, the following steps should be implemented.

Communicate the action plan requirement early. One of the most negative reactions to action plans is the surprise factor often inherent in the way in which the process is introduced. When program participants realize that they must develop an unexpected detailed action plan, there is often immediate, built-in resistance. Communicating to participants in advance, where the process is shown to be an integral part of the program, will often minimize resistance. When participants fully realize the benefits before they attend the first session, they take the process more seriously and usually perform the extra steps to make it more successful. In this scenario, the action plan is positioned as an application tool—not an evaluation tool.

Describe the action planning process at the beginning of the program. At the first session, action plan requirements are discussed, including an explanation of the purpose of the process, why it is necessary, and the basic requirements during and after the program. Some facilitators furnish a separate notepad for participants to collect ideas and useful techniques for their action plan. This is a productive way to focus more attention and effort on the process.

Teach the action planning process. An important prerequisite for action plan success is an understanding of how it works and how specific action plans are developed. A portion of the program's agenda is allocated to teaching participants how to develop plans. In this session, the requirements are outlined, special forms and procedures are discussed, and a completed example is distributed and reviewed. Sometimes an entire program module is allocated to this process so that participants will fully understand it and use it. Any available support tools, such as key measures, charts, graphs, suggested topics, and sample calculations should be used in this session to help facilitate the plan's development.

Allow time to develop the plan. When action plans are used to collect data for an ROI calculation, it is important to allow participants time to develop plans during the program. Sometimes it is helpful to have participants work in teams so they can share ideas as they develop specific plans. In these sessions, facilitators often monitor the progress of individuals or teams to keep the process on track and to answer questions. In some management and executive development programs, action plans are developed in an evening session, as a scheduled part of the program.

Have the facilitator approve the action plans. It is essential for the action plan to be related to program objectives and, at the same time, represent an important accomplishment for the organization when it is completed. It is easy for participants to stray from the intent and purposes of action planning and not give it the attention that it deserves. Consequently, it is helpful to have the facilitator or program director actually sign off on the action plan, ensuring that the plan reflects all of the requirements and is appropriate for the program. In some cases, a space is provided for the facilitator's signature on the action plan document.

Require participants to assign a monetary value for each improvement. Participants are asked to determine, calculate, or estimate the monetary value for each improvement outlined in the plan. When the actual improvement has occurred, participants will use these values to capture the annual monetary benefits of the plan. For this step to be effective, it may be helpful to provide examples of typical ways in which values can be assigned to the actual data (Phillips and Phillips, 2001).

Ask participants to isolate the effects of the program. Although the action plan is initiated because of the training program, the actual improvements reported on the action plan may be influenced by other factors. Thus, the action planning process should not take full credit for the improvement. For example, an action plan to reduce employee turnover in an agency could take only partial credit for an improvement, because of the other variables that influenced the turnover rate (Phillips and Phillips, 2002). While there are at least nine ways to isolate the effects of training, participant estimation is usually more appropriate in the action planning process. Consequently, the participants are asked to estimate the percent of the improvement actually related to this particular program. This question can be asked on the action plan form or on a follow-up questionnaire.

Ask participants to provide a confidence level for estimates. Since the process to convert data to monetary values may not be exact and the amount of the improvement directly related to the program may not be precise, participants are asked to indicate their level of confidence in those two values, collectively. On a scale of 0 to 100%, where 0% means no confidence and 100% means complete confidence, this value provides participants a mechanism to express their uneasiness with their ability to be exact with the process.

Require action plans to be presented to the group, if possible. There is no better way to secure commitment and ownership of the action planning process than to have a participant describe his or her action plan in front of fellow participants. Presenting the action plan helps to ensure that the process is thoroughly developed and will be implemented on the job. Sometimes the process spurns competition among the group. If the number of participants is too large for individual presentations, perhaps one participant can be selected from the team (if the plans are developed in teams). Under these circumstances, the team will usually select the best action plan for presentation to the group, raising the bar for others.

Explain the follow-up mechanism. Participants must leave the session with a clear understanding of the timing of the action plan implementation and the planned follow-up. The method in which the data will be collected, analyzed, and reported should be openly discussed. Five options are common:

1. The group is reconvened to discuss the progress on the plans.
2. Participants meet with their immediate manager and discuss the success of the plan. A copy is forwarded to the HRD department.
3. A meeting is held with the program evaluator, the participant, and the participant's manager to discuss the plan and the information contained in it.
4. Participants send the plan to the evaluator and it is discussed in a conference call.
5. Participants send the plan directly to the evaluation with no meetings or discussions. This is the most common option.

While there are other ways to collect the data, it is important to select a mechanism that fits the culture, requirements, and constraints of the organization.

Collect action plans at the predetermined follow-up time. Because it is critical to have an excellent response rate, several steps may be necessary to ensure that the action plans are completed and the data are returned to the appropriate individual or group for analysis. Some organizations use follow-up reminders by mail or e-mail. Others call participants to check progress. Still others offer assistance in developing the final plan. These steps may require additional resources, which have to be weighed against the importance of having more data. When the action plan process is implemented as outlined in this chapter, the response rates will normally be very high in the 60–90% range. Usually participants will see the importance of the process and will develop their plans in detail before leaving the program.

Summarize the data and calculate the ROI. If developed properly, each action plan should have annualized monetary values associated with improvements. Also, each individual has indicated the percent of the improvement that is directly related to the program. Finally, each participant has provided a confidence percentage to reflect their uncertainty with the process and the subjective nature of some of the data that may be provided.

Because this process involves some estimates, it may not appear to be very credible. Several adjustments during the analysis make the process very credible and believable. The following adjustments are made (the guiding principles refer to the operating standards listed in Chapter 2):

Step 1: For those participants who do not provide data, it is assumed that they had no improvement to report. This is a very conservative assumption. (Guiding Principle #6)

Step 2: Each value is checked for realism, usability, and feasibility. Extreme values are discarded and omitted from the analysis. (Guiding Principle #8)

Step 3: Because the improvement is annualized, it is assumed the program had no improvement after the first year. Some programs should add value at year two and three. (Guiding Principle #9)

Step 4: The improvement from Step 3 is then adjusted by the confidence level, multiplying it by the confidence percent. The confidence level is actually an error suggested by the participants. (Guiding Principle #7) For example, a participant indicating 80% confidence with the process, is reflecting a 20% error possibility. In a $10,000 estimate with an 80% confidence factor, the participant is suggesting that the value could be in the range of $8000 to $12,000. To be conservative, the lower number is used. Thus, the confidence factor is multiplied by the amount of improvement.

Step 5: The new values are then adjusted by the percent of the improvement related directly to the program using straight multiplication. This isolates the effects of training. (Guiding Principle #5)

The monetary values determined in these five steps are totaled to arrive at a total program benefit. Since these values are already annualized, the total of these benefits becomes the annual benefits for the program. This value is placed in the numerator of the ROI formula to calculate the ROI.

Application

The impact of the action plan process is impressive. In a medium-size manufacturing facility, a training program was developed for first-level supervisors that focused on improving interpersonal skills with employees. Several of the areas tackled were productivity improvement, scrap reduction, absenteeism, turnover, grievances, and safety. These areas were discussed thoroughly and supervisors learned skills to make improvements in each area. Supervisors were required to develop action plans for improvement and report the results in a follow-up six months after the program. In this situation, the improvement measures were predetermined from the needs assessment. The following results were documented from a pilot group:

- ☐ The department unit hour was increased from 65 to 75. This is a basic measure of productivity, where a unit hour of 60 is considered to be average and acceptable work.
- ☐ Scrap was reduced from 11 to 7.4%.
- ☐ Absenteeism was reduced from 7 to 3.25%.
- ☐ The annual turnover rate was drastically reduced from 30 to 5%.
- ☐ Grievances were reduced 80%.
- ☐ Lost time accidents were reduced 95%.

These results were achieved by supervisors practicing what they had learned and reporting results of action plans. Although these results are impressive, three additional steps are needed to develop the ultimate evaluation, the return on investment. First, the amount of the improvement that is actually linked to the program must be determined, working with each measure. In this situation, supervisors estimated the percent of the improvement directly linked to the program. For example, while the absenteeism improvement showed an overall decrease of 3.75%, the supervisors collectively estimated that only 46% of the absenteeism reduction was actually linked to the program. Thus, a 3.75% absenteeism reduction actually becomes 1.725%. This figure can be further adjusted by factoring in a confidence level (provided by supervisors when they supplied the estimate). In this example, supervisors were 84% confident of their allocation of the absenteeism improvement. This adjustment means that 1.725% then becomes 1.45% when adjusted for the 84% confidence level. These two adjustments isolate the effects of the training program on the output measure and are fully described in the next chapter.

The second step to develop the ROI is to convert the data to monetary value. A value for a single absence must be determined and used to calculate the annual benefit of the improvement. There are at least ten ways to place values on data, and they are fully described in Chapter 5. In this example, supervisors had developed an estimated value of one absence, which was used previously in several applications where the cost of absenteeism was needed. Thus, the total number of absences avoided was calculated and multiplied by the value of one absence to obtain the training program's annual impact on absenteeism reduction. This process shows clearly the economic value of the program on that specific output measure. These two steps, isolating the effects of training and converting data to monetary values are performed for each of the six improvement measures, and the total value represents the annual economic benefit of the program.

The third step necessary to move to an ROI is to develop the fully loaded costs of the program. In this step, the costs related to the needs assessment and program development are prorated. In addition, all direct training costs are captured, along with the cost of the participants' salaries and benefits for the time they were attending training. The fully loaded cost for all participants reflects the total investment in this program for this group. This process is fully explained in Chapter 6.

With these three additional steps, the ROI can be calculated using the formulas described in Chapter 2 (net benefits divided by costs). In this example, total annual benefits directly attributed to the program after converting all six improvement items to monetary units are $775,000. The fully loaded costs for the program, where needs assessment, program development, and the cost for the evaluation were included, resulted in a value of $65,000. Thus, the ROI becomes as follows:

$$ROI = \frac{\text{Net Program Benefits}}{\text{Program Costs}} = \frac{\$775,000 - \$65,000}{\$65,000} \times 100 = 1092\%$$

This impressive ROI has credibility because of the conservative nature of the adjustments made to the data. Without these three additional steps, the target audience may be left wondering how much of the results were actually linked to the training program and how much the benefits exceeded the costs.

Advantages/Disadvantages

Although there are many advantages, there are at least two concerns with action plans. The process relies on direct input from the participant usually with no assurance of anonymity. As such, there is a possibility that the information is biased and unreliable. Also, action plans can be time consuming for the participant and, if the participant's supervisor is not involved in the process, there may be a tendency for the participant not to complete the assignment.

As this section has illustrated, the action plan approach has many inherent advantages. Action plans are simple and easy to administer; are easily understood by participants; are used with a wide variety of programs; are appropriate for all types of data; are able to measure reaction, learning, behavior changes, and results; and may be used with or without other evaluation methods. The two disadvantages may be overcome with careful planning and implementation. Because of the tremendous flexibility and versatility of the process, and the conservative adjustments that can be made in analysis, action plans have become an important data collection tool for the ROI analysis.

PERFORMANCE CONTRACTS

The performance contract is essentially a slight variation of the action planning process with a preprogram commitment. Based on the principle of mutual goal setting, a performance contract is a written agreement between a participant and the participant's supervisor. The participant agrees to improve performance in an area of mutual concern related to the content of the HRD program. The agreement is in the form of a project to be completed or a goal to be accomplished soon after the program is completed. The agreement spells out what is to be accomplished, at what time, and with what results.

Performance contracting is administered much the same way as the action planning process. Although the steps can vary according to the specific kind of contract and the organization, a common sequence of events is as follows:

- ☐ With supervisor approval, the employee (participant) decides to attend an HRD program.
- ☐ The participant and manager mutually agree on a topic for improvement with specific measure(s).
- ☐ Specific, measurable goals are set.
- ☐ The participant is involved in the program where the contract is discussed and plans are developed to accomplish the goals.
- ☐ After the program, the participant works on the contract against a specific deadline.
- ☐ The participant reports the results to his or her immediate manager.
- ☐ The supervisor and participant document the results and forward a copy to the HRD department along with appropriate comments.

The individuals mutually select the topic/measure to be improved prior to program inception. The process of selecting the area for improvement is similar to the process used in the action planning process. The topic can cover one or more of the following areas:

☐ *Routine performance*—includes specific improvements in routine performance measures such as production targets, efficiency, and error rates.
☐ *Problem solving*—focuses on specific problems such as an unexpected increase in accidents, a decrease in efficiency, or a loss of morale.
☐ *Innovative or creative applications*—includes initiating changes or improvements in work practices, methods, procedures, techniques, and processes.
☐ *Personal development*—involves learning new information or acquiring new skills to increase individual effectiveness.

The topic selected should be stated in terms of one or more objectives. The objectives should state what is to be accomplished when the contract is complete. These objectives should be:

☐ written
☐ understandable (by all involved)
☐ challenging (requiring an unusual effort to achieve)
☐ achievable (something that can be accomplished)
☐ largely under the control of the participant
☐ measurable and dated

The details required to accomplish the contract objectives are developed following the guidelines under the action plans presented earlier. Also, the methods for analyzing data and reporting progress are essentially the same, as with the action planning process.

SELECTING THE APPROPRIATE METHOD

This chapter has presented a variety of methods to capture postprogram data for an ROI analysis. Collectively, they offer a wide range of opportunities to collect data in a variety of situations. Several issues should be considered when deciding which method is appropriate for a situation.

Type of Data

Perhaps one of the most important issues to consider when selecting the method is the type of data to be collected. Some methods are more appropriate for Level 4, while others are best for Level 3. Still others are best for Levels 2 or 1. Table 3-1 shows the most appropriate type of data for a specific method. Questionnaires and surveys, observations, interviews, and focus groups are suited for all levels. Tests are appropriate for Level 2. Questionnaires and surveys are best for Level 1, although interviews and focus groups can be used, but they are often too costly. Performance monitoring, performance contracting, action planning, and questionnaires can easily capture Level 4 data.

Participants' Time for Data Input

Another important factor in selecting the data collection method is the amount of time that participants must take with data collection. Time requirements should always be minimized, and the method should be positioned so that it is value-added activity (i.e., the participants understand that this activity is something they perceive as valuable so they will not resist). This requirement often means that sampling is used to keep the total participant time to a reasonable amount. Some methods, such as business performance monitoring, require no participant time, while others such as interviews and focus groups, require a significant investment in time.

Table 3-1. Collecting Postprogram Data: The Methods

	Level 1	Level 2	Level 3	Level 4
☐ Questionnaires/Surveys	✓	✓	✓	✓
☐ Tests		✓		
☐ Interviews			✓	
☐ Focus Groups			✓	
☐ Observations		✓	✓	
☐ Action Planning			✓	✓
☐ Performance Contracting			✓	✓
☐ Performance Monitoring				✓

Management's Time for Data Input

The time that a participant's immediate manager must allocate to data collection is another important issue in the method selection. This time requirement should always be minimized. Some methods, such as performance contracting, may require much involvement from the manager prior to, and after, the program. Other methods, such as questionnaires administered directly to participants, may not require any manager time.

Cost of Method

Cost is always a consideration when selecting the method. Some data collection methods are more expensive than others. For example, interviews and observations are very expensive. Surveys, questionnaires, and performance monitoring are usually inexpensive.

Disruption of Normal Work Activities

Another key issue in selecting the appropriate method, and perhaps the one that generates the most concern with managers, is the amount of disruption the data collection will create. Routine work processes should be disrupted as little as possible. Some data collection techniques, such as performance monitoring, require very little time and distraction from normal activities. Questionnaires generally do not disrupt the work environment, and can often be completed in only a few minutes, or even after normal work hours. On the other extreme, some items such as observations and interviews may be too disruptive for the work unit.

Accuracy of Method

The accuracy of the technique is another factor when selecting the method. Some data collection methods are more accurate than others. For example, performance monitoring is usually very accurate; whereas, questionnaires can be distorted and unreliable. If actual on-the-job behavior must be captured, unobtrusive observation is clearly one of the most accurate processes.

Built-In Design Possibility

Because it is important to build in data collection for many of the evaluation plans, the relative ease at which the method can be built into the program is important; it must become an integral part of the program. Some methods, such as action plans, can be easily built into the design of the program. Other methods, such as observation, are more difficult.

For some situations, the program is redesigned to allow for a follow-up session where evaluation is addressed along with additional training. For example, an interactive selling skills program (a consecutive three day program) was redesigned as a two-day workshop to build skills, followed by a one-day session three weeks later. Thus, the follow-up session provided an opportunity for additional training and evaluation. During the first part of the last day, Level 3 evaluation data was collected using a focus group process. Also, specific barriers and problems encountered in applying the skills were discussed. The second half of the day was devoted to additional skill building and refinement along with techniques to overcome the particular barriers to using the skills. Thus, in effect, the redesigned program provided a mechanism for follow-up.

Utility of an Additional Method

Because there are many different methods to collect data, it is tempting to use too many data collection methods. Multiple data collection methods add time and costs to evaluation and may result in very little additional value. Utility refers to the added value of the use of an additional data collection method. When more than one method is used, this question should always be addressed. Does the value obtained from the additional data warrant the extra time and expense of the method? If the answer is no, the additional method should not be implemented.

Cultural Bias for Data Collection Method

The culture or philosophy of the organization can dictate which data collection methods are used. For example, some organizations are accustomed to using questionnaires and prefer to use them in their culture. Other organizations will not use observation because their culture does not support the potential "invasion of privacy" associated with it.

DATA TABULATION ISSUES

Data must be collected using one or more of the methods outlined in this chapter. As the data are collected, several other issues need to be addressed and clarified.

Use the Most Credible Source

This is a principle discussed earlier, but it is worth repeating. The data used in the analysis must be the most credible data available. If data are collected from more than once source, the most credible one is used, if there is clearly a difference. This leads to a guiding principle.

Guiding Principle #3
When collecting and analyzing data, use only the most credible sources.

Missing Data

It is rare for all the participants to provide data in a follow-up evaluation. The philosophy described in this chapter is to use only the available data for the total benefits. This philosophy is based on making every attempt possible to collect data from every participant, if at all possible. In reality, the return rate of questionnaires or the participation rate of other data collection methods will probably be in the 60–80% range. Below 50% should be considered questionable because of the extreme negative impact it will have on the results. This leads to a guiding principle:

Guiding Principle #6
If no improvement data are available for a population or from a specific source, it is assumed that little or no improvement has occurred.

Data Summary

Data should be tabulated and summarized, ready for analysis. Ideally, tabulation should be organized by particular evaluation levels and issues.

Tables can be summarized, analyzed, and then reported eventually in the impact study.

Extreme Data

As data are entered, there should be some review of the data for its reasonableness. Extreme data items and unsupported claims should be omitted. This leads to a guiding principle:

Guiding Principle #8
Extreme data items and unsupported claims should not be used in ROI calculations.

These rules for initially adjusting, summarizing, and tabulating data are critical in preparing for the analysis. They take a very conservative approach, and, consequently, build credibility with the target audience. More use on these principles will be presented later.

FINAL THOUGHTS

This chapter has provided an overview of collection approaches that can be used in the ROI analysis. A variety of options are available, which can usually match any budget or situation. Some methods are gaining more acceptance for ROI calculations. In addition to performance monitoring, follow-up questionnaires and action plans, as described in this chapter, are regularly used to collect data for an ROI analysis. Other methods can be helpful to develop a complete picture of application of the training and subsequent business impact.

CASE STUDY—PART B, LINEAR NETWORK SYSTEMS

Needs Assessment

An improper or inadequate needs assessment may result in a program designed to address skills that are not needed or are already in place. The needs assessment was conducted at Level 4 (business needs), Level 3 (job performance needs), and Level 2 (skill and knowledge needs). Without a multiple level needs assessment, it is difficult to evaluate a program designed to change job behavior (Level 3) and business impact improvement (Level 4). Thus, the needs assessment became a very critical issue for identifying performance deficiencies at all three levels and was an important component in LNS's plan to develop first-level managers.

Business Performance Measures

The needs assessment identified several business performance measures where improvement was needed, all related to inadequate leadership skills. These included the following data items:

☐ productivity, measured by the percentage of shipments met
☐ employee turnover
☐ absenteeism

There was some skepticism among senior management that productivity could be enhanced through leadership training, although most of the first-level managers agreed that they could boost productivity with improved teamwork. Employee turnover was high and, although there were many factors that influenced turnover, most managers felt that turnover was a variable under their control. Finally, absenteeism was extremely high, particularly on second shifts and on Mondays and Fridays.

LNS had developed an adequate measurement system, which monitored, among other variables, productivity, turnover, and absenteeism measures by the production unit. Each first-level manager received absenteeism and turnover data monthly, and productivity measures were available weekly for the production departments. Support departments can significantly influence the measures by providing excellent support and assistance.

Top management approved the leadership program proposal, including the structure and timing.

Evaluation Levels

Because LNS management was interested in the accountability of training, and the consulting firm was eager to show results of training, both parties were anxious to conduct an ROI evaluation for this project. ROI data can be very convincing for marketing a program to other groups. With this approach, business impact data would be collected, converted to monetary values, and compared to the program cost to develop the ROI (Level 5). In addition, Levels 1, 2, and 3 data would be collected to measure reaction, learning, and application. Thus, all five levels of evaluation were pursued.

There was another important reason for evaluating this program at all five levels. Because this program is linked to key organizational measures, a success would show a direct linkage to the company's bottom-line. A significant payoff to the company would clearly show management that leadership training is a high impact process and that it can make a difference by improving important business performance measures.

Objectives

Because Levels 3 and 4 data must be collected, it is essential that specific objectives be measurable and directly related to the Level 3 and 4 data obtained from the needs assessment. Therefore, program objectives were revised to include the following. After attending this program, participants should be able to:

- ☐ Describe and identify applications for two motivational models.
- ☐ Describe and identify applications for two leadership models.
- ☐ Set measurable performance goals each month for each employee.
- ☐ Apply performance feedback skills each day with each employee.
- ☐ Reduce employee turnover from an average annual rate of 29 to 25% in 4 months.
- ☐ Reduce absenteeism from a weekly average of 5 to 3% in 4 months.
- ☐ Increase productivity by 2 percentage points in 4 months.

The specific targets were difficult to develop and required the complete cooperation of the plant manager and the department heads.

Discussion Questions
1. What is your reaction to these measures? Do you think this program could influence each measure?
2. What are the recommended postprogram data collection methods?
3. Complete data collection plan for evaluation (see Figure 3-3).

Data Collection Plan

Program:_____ Responsibility:_____ Date:_____

Level	Objective(s)	Measures/Data	Data Collection Method	Data Sources	Timing	Responsibilities
1	Reaction/ Satisfaction					
2	Learning					
3	Application/ Implementation					
4	Business Results					
5	ROI	Comments: _____				

Figure 3-3 Evaluation plan: data collection.

REFERENCES

Alreck, P.L., and R.B. Settle. *The Survey Research Handbook: Guidelines and Strategies for Conducting a Survey*, 2nd ed. New York, NY: McGraw-Hill, 1995.

Harrell, K.D. "Level III Training Evaluation: Considerations for Today's Organizations," *Performance Improvement*, May/June 2001, p. 24.

Kvale, S. *InterViews: An Introduction to Qualitative Research Interviewing.* Thousand Oaks, CA: Sage Publications, 1996.

Mondschein, M. *Measurit: Achieving Profitable Training.* Leawood, KS: Leathers Publishing, 1999.

Phillips, J.J., and P.P. Phillips. "Performance Management Training," *In Action: Measuring Return on Investment*, vol. 3, Phillips, J.J. (Ed.), Alexandria, VA: American Society for Training and Development, 2001, pp. 15–36.

Phillips, J.J., and P.P. Phillips. "Evaluating the Impact of a Graduate Program in a Federal Agency," *In Action: Measuring ROI in the Public Sector*, Alexandria, VA: American Society for Training and Development, 2002, pp. 149–172.

Robson, C. *Real World Research: A Resource for Social Scientists and Practitioner-Researchers*, 2nd ed. Malden, MA: Blackwell Publishers, 2002.

Shrock, S., and W.C.C. Coscarelli. *Criterion-Referenced Test Development: Technical and Legal Guidelines for Corporate Training and Certification*, 2nd ed. Washington, DC: International Society for Performance Improvement, 2000.

Subramony, D.P., *et al.* "Using Focus Group Interviews," *Performance Improvement*. International Society for Performance Improvement, September 2002.

Westgaard, O. *Tests That Work: Designing and Delivering Fair and Practical Measurement Tools in the Workplace*. San Francisco, CA: Jossey-Bass/Pfeiffer, 1999.

FURTHER READING

Brinkerhoff, R.O., and A.M. Apking. *High-Impact Learning: Strategies for Leveraging Business Results from Training*. Cambridge, MA: Perseus Publishing, 2001.

Combs, W.L., and S.V. Falletta. *The Targeted Evaluation Process: A Performance Consultant's Guide to Asking the Right Questions and Getting the Results You Trust*. ASTD, 2000.

Folkman, J. *Employee Surveys That Make a Difference: Using Customized Feedback Tools to Transform Your Organization*. Provo, UT: Executive Excellence Publishing, 1998.

Gubrium, J.F., and J.A. Holstein (Ed.). *Handbook of Interview Research: Context & Method*. Thousand Oaks, CA: Sage Publications, 2002.

Hayes, B.E. *Measuring Customer Satisfaction: Survey Design, Use, and Statistical Analysis Methods*, 2nd ed. Milwaukee, WI: ASQ Quality Press, 1998.

Knox, A.B. *Evaluation for Continuing Education: A Comprehensive Guide to Success*. San Francisco, CA: Jossey-Bass, 2002.

Kraut, Allen I. (Ed.). *Organizational Surveys: Tools for Assessment and Change*. San Francisco, CA: Jossey-Bass Publishers, 1996.

Morgan, D.L. *The Focus Group Guidebook*. Thousand Oaks, CA: Sage Publications, 1998.

Schwarz, N., and S. Sudman (Ed.). *Answering Questions: Methodology for Determining Cognitive and Communicative Processes in Survey Research*. San Francisco, CA: Jossey-Bass Publishers, 1996.

Spradley, J.P. *Participant Observation*. Australia: Wadsworth/Thomson Learning, 1980.

Yin, R.K. *Case Study Research: Design and Methods*, 2nd ed. Thousand Oaks, CA: Sage Publications, 1994.

CHAPTER 4

Isolating the Effects of Training

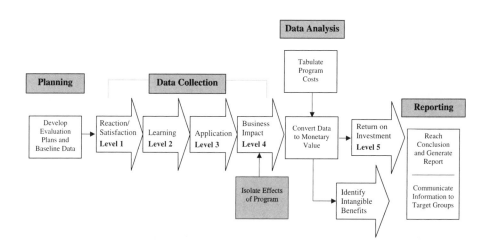

The following situation is repeated often. A significant increase in performance is noted after a major training program was conducted and the two events appear to be linked. A key manager asks, "How much of this improvement was caused by the training program?" When this potentially embarrassing question is asked, it is rarely answered with any degree of accuracy and credibility. While the change in performance may be linked to the training program, other nontraining factors usually have con-

111

tributed to the improvement. As depicted in the ROI model above, this chapter explores the techniques to isolate the effects of training. These strategies are utilized in some of the best organizations because they attempt to measure the return on investment in training and development.

The cause-and-effect relationship between training and performance can be very confusing and difficult to prove, but can be accomplished with an acceptable degree of accuracy. The challenge is to develop one or more specific strategies to isolate the effects of training early in the process, usually as part of an evaluation plan. Upfront attention ensures that appropriate strategies will be used with minimum costs and time commitments.

PRELIMINARY ISSUES

The Need for Isolating the Effects of Training

While isolating the effects of training seems to be a logical, practical, and necessary issue, it is still much debated. Some professionals argue that to isolate the effects of training goes against everything taught in systems thinking and team performance improvement (Brinkerhoff and Dressler, 2002). Others argue that the only way to link training to actual business results is to isolate its effect on those business measures (Russ-Eft and Preskill, 2001). Much of the debate centers around misunderstandings and the challenge of isolating the effects of the process. The first point in the debate is the issue of complementary processes. It is true that training is often implemented as part of a total performance improvement initiative. There are always other influences that must work in harmony with training to improve business results. It is often not an issue of whether training is part of the mix, but how much training is needed, what specific content is needed, and the most appropriate delivery needed to drive training's share of performance improvement.

The issue of isolating the effects of training is not meant to suggest that training should stand alone as a single influencing variable to driving significant business performance. The isolation issue comes into play, however, when there are different owners of the processes that are influencing business results and they must have more information about relative contribution. In many situations, this question has to be addressed: How much of the improvement was caused by training? Without an answer, or a specific method to address the issue, tremendous credibility is lost, particularly with the senior management team.

The other point in the debate is the difficulty of achieving the isolation. The classic approach is to use control group arrangements in which one group receives training and another does not. This is one of the techniques described in this chapter and is the most credible. However, the control group may not be appropriate in the majority of studies. Consequently, other methods must be used. Researchers sometimes use time-series analysis, also discussed in this chapter as trend-line analysis. Beyond that, many researchers either give up and suggest that it cannot be addressed with credibility or they choose to ignore the issue, hoping that it will not be noticed by the sponsor. Neither of these responses is acceptable to the senior management team who is attempting to understand the linkage between training and business success. A credible estimation adjusted for error will often satisfy their requirements. The important point is to *always* address this issue, even if an expert estimation is used with an error adjustment. In this way, the issue of isolating the effects of training becomes an essential step in the analysis. Thus, a guiding principle is established on this issue.

Guiding Principle #5
At least one method must be used to isolate the effects of
the project.

The premise of this chapter is that isolating the effects of training is a required step. Nine different techniques are presented in this chapter to address this issue. At least one of them will *always* be used.

Chain of Impact: The Initial Evidence

Before presenting the techniques, it is helpful to examine the chain of impact implied in the different levels of evaluation. As illustrated in Figure 4-1, the chain of impact must be in place for the program to drive business results.

Measurable business impact achieved from a training program should be derived from the application of skills/knowledge on the job over a specified period of time after a program has been conducted. This on-the-job application of training is referred to as Level 3 in the five

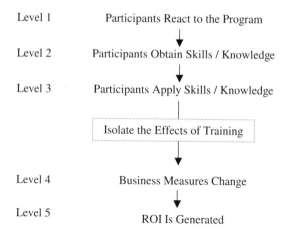

Level 1   Participants React to the Program

Level 2   Participants Obtain Skills / Knowledge

Level 3   Participants Apply Skills / Knowledge

Isolate the Effects of Training

Level 4   Business Measures Change

Level 5   ROI Is Generated

Figure 4-1. The chain of impact.

evaluation levels described in Chapter 2 and reported elsewhere (Kirkpatrick, 1998). Continuing with this logic, successful application of program material on the job should stem from participants learning new skills or acquiring new knowledge in the training program, which is measured as a Level 2 evaluation. Therefore, for a business results improvement (Level 4 evaluation), this chain of impact implies that measurable on-the-job applications are realized (Level 3 evaluation) and new knowledge and skills are learned (Level 2 evaluation). Without the preliminary evidence of the chain of impact, it is difficult to isolate the effects of training. If there is no learning or application of the material on the job, it is virtually impossible to conclude that the training program caused any performance improvements. This chain of impact requirement with the different levels of evaluation is supported in the literature (Alliger and Janak, 1989). From a practical standpoint, this issue requires data collection at four levels for an ROI calculation. If data are collected on business results, it should also be collected for other levels of evaluation to ensure that the training program helped to produce the business results. This issue is so critical that it becomes the first guiding principle for the ROI methodology.

Guiding Principle #1
When a higher-level evaluation is conducted, data must be collected at lower levels.

This approach is consistent with the approach practiced by leading organizations who participated in ASTD's benchmarking project. It was reported that most organizations collecting Level 4 data on business results also collected data at the previous three levels (Bassi and Lewis, 1999). The chain of impact does not prove that there was a direct connection to training; the isolation is necessary to make this connection and pinpoint the amount of improvement caused by training. Many research efforts have attempted to develop correlations between the different levels. This research basically states that if a significant correlation exists, the chain of impact is in place. If a significant correlation does not exist, there were many barriers that caused the process to break down. This is logical when the chain of impact is considered.

Most research in this area adds very little to the understanding of evaluation. Correlations between two levels show the connection (or disconnect) between the two. It doesn't mean that the levels are flawed. Instead, it implies that some factor prevented the learning process from adding value. For example, most of the breakdowns occur between Levels 2 and 3. Much research has shown that as much as 90% of what was learned is not used on the job (Kauffman, 2002).

There are usually a variety of barriers that impede the transfer of the learning to the job. Many barriers are in place and readily inhibit the success of training. It doesn't mean that the next level of evaluation (Level 3) is inappropriate, it just indicates that some factor is preventing the skills and knowledge from transferring to the job. Thus, a correlation analysis between the levels adds very little understanding to what must occur in practice for training to add business value. Also, correlation analysis does not show the cause-and-effect relationship. Even if there's a strong correlation, the critical step of isolating the effect of training must still be undertaken to ensure a causal relationship between the training and the business improvement.

Identifying Other Factors: A First Step

As a first step in isolating training's impact on performance, all of the key factors that may have contributed to the performance improvement should be identified. This step reveals other factors that may have influenced the results, underscoring that the training program is not the sole source of improvement. Consequently, the credit for improvement is shared with several possible variables and sources, an approach that is likely to gain the respect of management.

Several potential sources identify major influencing variables. The sponsors may be able to identify factors that should influence the output measure if they have requested the program. The client will usually be aware of other initiatives or programs that may impact the output. Even if the program is operational, the client may have much insight into the other influences that may have driven the performance improvement.

Program participants are often aware of other influences that may have caused performance improvement. After all, it is the impact of their collective efforts that is being monitored and measured. In many situations, they witness previous movements in the performance measures and can pinpoint the reasons for changes. They are normally the experts in this issue.

Analysts and program developers are another source for identifying variables that have an impact on results. The needs analysis will routinely uncover these influencing variables. Program designers typically analyze these variables while addressing the training transfer issue.

In some situations, participants' supervisors may be able to identify variables that influence the performance improvement. This is particularly useful when training program participants are entry-level or low-skill employees (operatives) who may not be fully aware of the variables that can influence performance.

Finally, middle and top management may be able to identify other influences, based on their experience and knowledge of the situation. Perhaps they have monitored, examined, and analyzed the other influences. The authority positions of these individuals often increase the credibility and acceptance of the data.

Taking time to focus attention on variables that may have influenced performance brings additional accuracy and credibility to the process. It moves beyond the scenario where results are presented with no mention of other influences, a situation that often destroys the credibility of a training impact report. It also provides a foundation for some of the techniques described in this book by identifying the variables that must be isolated to show the effects of training. A word of caution is appropriate here. Halting the process after this step would leave many unknowns about actual training impact and might leave a negative impression with the client or senior management, since it may have identified variables that management did not previously consider. Therefore, it is recommended that the HRD staff go beyond this initial step and use one or more of the techniques that isolate the impact of training, which is the focus of this chapter.

Use of Control Groups

The most accurate approach to isolate the impact of training is the use of control groups in an experimental design process (Wang, 2002). This approach involves the use of an experimental group that attends training and a control group that does not. The composition of both groups should be as similar as possible and, if feasible, the selection of participants for each group should be on a random basis. When this is possible and both groups are subjected to the same environmental influences, and the difference in the performance of the two groups can be attributed to the training program.

As illustrated in Figure 4-2, the control group and experimental group do not necessarily have preprogram measurements. Measurements are taken after the program is implemented. The difference in the performance of the two groups shows the amount of improvement that is directly related to the training program.

Control group arrangements appear in many settings, including both private and public sectors. For example, in an impact study to measure the return on investment for telephonic customer service skills, Verizon Communications used both an experimental group and a control group (Keuler, 2001). The training program was designed to improve Verizon customer feedback and was expected to reduce the overall number of calls that escalated to the supervisory level. The difference between the two groups revealed the extent to which the skills were transferred to the job (Level 3) and also the impact it was having in the workplace (Level 4). Thus, control group differences can be used to isolate the effects on both Level 3 and Level 4 data.

In another example, a turnover reduction program for communication specialists in a government agency used both a control group and an experimental group (Phillips and Phillips, 2002). The experimental group was compiled of individuals in a special program designed to

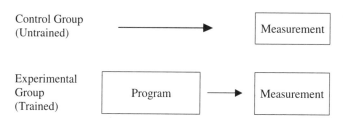

Figure 4-2. Post-test only, control group design.

allow participants to achieve a master's degree in information science on agency time and at agency expense. The control group was carefully selected to match up with the experimental group in terms of job title, tenure with the agency, and the college degree obtained. The control/experimental group differences were very dramatic, showing the impact of the retention solution program.

One caution to keep in mind is that the use of control groups may create an image that the HRD staff is creating a laboratory setting, which can cause a problem for some administrators and executives. To avoid this stigma, some organizations run a program using pilot participants as the experimental group and do not inform the nonparticipating control group. Another example will illustrate this approach. An international specialty manufacturing company developed a program for its customer service representatives who sell directly to the public. The program was designed to improve selling skills and produce higher levels of sales. Previously, sales skills acquisition was informal, on the job, or by trial and error. The HRD manager was convinced that formal training would significantly increase sales. Management was skeptical and wanted proof—a familiar scenario. The program was pilot-tested by teaching sales skills to 16 customer service representatives randomly selected from the 32 most recently hired. The remaining 16 served as a control group and did not receive training. Prior to training, performance was measured using average daily sales (sales divided by number of days) for 30 days (or length of service, if shorter) for each of the two groups. After training, the average daily sales were recorded for another 30 days. A significant difference in the sales of the two groups emerged, and because the groups were almost identical and were subjected to the same environmental influences, it was concluded that the sales differences were a result of training and not other factors. In this setting, the pilot group was the experimental group. The comparison group (control group) was easily selected. The technique was used without the publicity and potential criticism that is typical when using the control group arrangement.

The control group process does have some inherent problems that may make it difficult to apply in practice. The first major problem is that the process is inappropriate for many situations. For some types of training programs, it is not proper to withhold training from one particular group while training is given to another. This is particularly important for critical skills that are needed immediately on the job. For example, in entry-level training, employees need basic skills to perform their job. It would be improper to withhold training from a group of new employees just so they can be compared to a group that receives the training. Although this would reveal the impact of initial training, it would be devastating to those individuals who are struggling to learn necessary skills, trying to cope with the job situation. In the previous example, a control group is feasible. The training that was provided was not necessarily essential to the job and the organization was not completely convinced that it would add value in terms of the actual sales.

This particular barrier keeps many control groups from being implemented. Management is not willing to withhold training in one area to see how it works in another. However, in practice, there are many opportunities for a natural control group agreement to develop in situations where training is implemented throughout an organization. If it will take several months for everyone in the organization to receive the training, there may be enough time for a parallel comparison between the initial group being trained and the last group trained. In these cases, it is critical to ensure that the groups are matched as closely as possible so the first two groups are very similar to the last two groups. These naturally occurring control groups often exist in major training program implementation. The challenge is to address this issue early enough to influence the implementation schedule so that similar groups can be used in the comparison.

The second major problem is the selection of the groups. From a practical perspective it is virtually impossible to have identical control and experimental groups. Dozens of factors can affect employee performance, some of them individual and others contextual. To tackle the issue on a practical basis, it is best to select three to five variables that will have the greatest influence on performance. For example, in an interactive selling skills program in a retail store chain, three groups were trained and their performances were compared to three similar groups, which were the control groups (Phillips and Phillips, 2001). The selection of the particular groups was based on four variables that store executives thought would influence performance most from one store to another: previous sales performance, actual market area, store size, and customer traffic. In this example, there were literally dozens of variables that could affect store performance, ranging from individual differences (e.g., sales experience, education, and tenure) to managerial and leadership differences within the department and store (e.g., leadership style and managerial control), as well as in-store policies on merchandising and marketing. Perhaps the most differences occur externally with the market area and surrounding competition. The challenge was to take a realistic approach and to address a reasonable number of measures. In this example, the regional store executives selected the four measures that probably account for at least 80% of the differences. Thus, using the 80–20 rule, the challenge of selecting groups is manageable. When the output can be influenced by as many as 40–50 measures, it is almost impossible to consider all the measures with a store sample size of 420. Thus, the practical use of the control group must take into consideration the constraints in a work setting and focus on the most critical influences, besides training, that will make a difference in the output measure.

A third problem with the control group arrangement is contamination, which can develop when participants in the training program instruct others in the control group. Sometimes the reverse situation occurs when members of the control group model the behavior from the trained group. In either case, the experiment becomes contaminated because the influence of training filters to the control group. This can be minimized by ensuring that control groups and experimental groups are at different locations, have different shifts, or are on different floors in the same building. When this is not possible, it is sometimes helpful to explain to both groups that one group will receive training now and another will receive training at a later date. Also, it may be helpful to appeal to the sense of responsibility of those being trained and ask them not to share the information with others.

Closely related to the previous problem is the issue of time. The longer a control group and experimental group comparison operates, the likelihood of other influences to affect the results increases. More variables will enter into the situation, contaminating the results. On the other end of the scale, there must be enough time so that a clear pattern can emerge between the two groups. Thus, the timing for control group comparisons must strike a delicate balance of waiting long enough for their performance differences to show, but not too long so that the results become seriously contaminated.

A fifth problem occurs when the different groups function under different environmental influences. Because they may be in different locations, the groups may have different environmental influences. Sometimes the selection of the groups can help prevent this problem from occurring. Also, using more groups than necessary and discarding those with some environmental differences is another tactic.

A sixth problem with using control groups is that it may appear to be too research-oriented for most business organizations. For example, management may not want to take the time to experiment before proceeding with a program or they may not want to withhold training from a group just to measure the impact of an experimental program. Because of this concern, some HRD practitioners do not entertain the idea of using control groups. When the process is used, however, some organizations conduct it with pilot participants as the experimental group and nonparticipants as the control group. Under this arrangement, the control group is not informed of their control group status.

Because this is an effective approach for isolating the impact of training, it should be considered as a strategy when a major ROI impact study is planned. In these situations it is important for the program impact to be isolated to a high level of accuracy; the primary advantage of the control group process is accuracy. About one third of the more than 100 published studies on the ROI methodology use the control group process.

TREND LINE ANALYSIS

Another useful technique for approximating the impact of training is trend line analysis. With this approach, a trend line is drawn, using previous performance as a base, and extending the trend into the future. When training is conducted, actual performance is compared to projected value, the trend line. Any improvement of performance over what the trend line predicted can then be reasonably attributed to training, if two conditions are met:

1. The trend that has developed prior to the program is expected to continue if the program had not been implemented to alter it (i.e., If the training program had not been implemented, would this trend continue on the same path established before the training?). The process owner(s) should be able to provide input to reach this conclusion. If the answer is "no," the trend line analysis will not be used. If the answer is "yes," the second condition is considered.

2. No other new variables or influences entered the process after the training was conducted. The key word is "new," realizing that the trend has been established because of the influences already in place, and no additional influences enter the process beyond the training and development program. If the answer is "yes," another method would have to be used. If the answer is "no," the trend line analysis develops a reasonable estimate of the impact of training.

Figure 4-3 shows an example of this trend line analysis taken from a shipping department in a warehouse operation. The percent reflects the

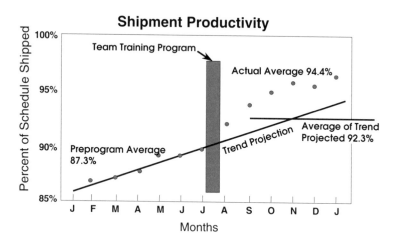

Figure 4-3. Trend line of productivity.

level of actual shipments compared to scheduled shipments. Data is presented before and after a team-training program, which was conducted in July. As shown in the figure, there was an upward trend on the data prior to conducting the training. Although the program apparently had a dramatic effect on shipment productivity, the trend line shows that improvement would have continued anyway, based on the trend that had been previously established. It is tempting to measure the improvement by comparing the average six-months shipments prior to the program (87.3%) to the average of six months after the program (94.4%) yielding a 6.9% difference. However, a more accurate comparison is the six-month average after the program compared to the trend line (92.3%). In this example, the difference is 2.1%. In this case, the two conditions outlined above were met (yes on the first; no on the second). Thus, using this more modest measure increases the accuracy and credibility of the process to isolate the impact of the program.

Preprogram data must be available before this technique can be used and the data should have some reasonable degree of stability. If the variance of the data is high, the stability of the trend line becomes an issue. If this is an extremely critical issue and the stability cannot be assessed from a direct plot of the data, more detailed statistical analyses can be used to determine if the data is stable enough to make the projection (Salkind, 2000).

The trend line, projected directly from the historical data using a straight edge, may be acceptable. If additional accuracy is needed, the trend line can be projected with a simple routine, available in many calculators and software packages, such as Microsoft Excel™.

The use of the trend line analysis becomes more dramatic and convincing when a measure, moving in an undesirable direction, is completely turned around with the training program. For example, Figure 4-4 shows a trend line of the sexual harassment complaints in a large hospital chain (Phillips and Hill, 2001). As the figure presents, the complaints were increasing in a direction undesired by the organization. The workshop and other subsequent activities connected with the program turned the situation around so that the actual results are in the other direction. The trend line process shows when a dramatic improvement has occurred. The trend line projected value shows a number that is significantly higher than the actual results and the preprogram and postprogram differences.

A primary disadvantage of this trend line approach is that it is not always accurate. The use of this approach assumes that the events that influenced the performance variable prior to the program are still in place after the program, except for the implementation of the training program (i.e., the trends that were established prior to training will continue in the same relative direction). Also, it assumes that no new influences entered the situation at the time training was conducted. This is seldom the case.

The primary advantage of this approach is that it is simple and inexpensive. If historical data are available, a trend line can quickly be drawn

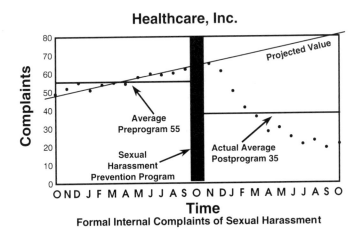

Figure 4-4. Sexual harassment complaints.

and differences estimated. While not exact, it does provide a very quick assessment of training's potential impact. About 15% of the more than 100 published studies on the ROI methodology use the trend line analysis technique. When other variables enter the situation, additional analysis is needed.

FORECASTING METHODS

A more analytical approach to trend line analysis is the use of forecasting methods that predict a change in performance variables. This approach represents a mathematical interpretation of the trend line analysis discussed above when other variables entered the situation at the time of training. The basic premise is that the actual performance of a measure, related to training, is compared to the forecasted value of that measure. The forecasted value is based on the other influences. A linear model, in the form of $y = ax + b$, is appropriate when only one other variable influences the output performance and that relationship is characterized by a straight line. Instead of drawing the straight line, a linear equation is developed, which calculates a value of the anticipated performance improvement.

An example will help explain the application of this process. A large retail store chain with a strong sales culture implemented a sales training program for sales associates. The three-day program was designed to enhance sales skills and prospecting techniques. The application of the skills should increase the sales volume for each associate. An important measure of the program's success is the sales per employee six months after the program compared to the same measure prior to the program. The average daily sales per employee prior to training, using a one-month average, were $1100 (rounded to the nearest $100). Six months after the program, the average daily sales per employee were $1500 (the sixth month). Both of these sales numbers are average values for a specific group of participants. Two related questions must be answered: Is the difference in these two values attributable to the training program? Did other factors influence the actual sales level?

After reviewing potential influencing factors with several store executives, only one factor, the level of advertising, appeared to have changed significantly during the period under consideration. When reviewing the previous sales per employee data and the level of advertising, a direct relationship appeared to exist. As expected, when advertising expenditures were increased, the sales per employee increased proportionately.

The advertising staff had developed a mathematical relationship between advertising and sales. Using the historical values, a simple linear model yielded the following relationship: $y = 140 + 40x$, where y is the daily sales per employee and x is the level of advertising expenditures per week (divided by 1000). This equation was developed by the marketing department using the method of least squares to derive a mathematical relationship between two columns of data (i.e., advertising and sales). This is a routine option on some calculators and is included in many software packages. Figure 4-5 shows the linear relationship between advertising and sales.

The level of weekly advertising expenditures in the month preceding training was $24,000 and the level of expenditures in the sixth month after training was $30,000. Assuming that the other factors possibly influencing sales were insignificant, store executives determined the impact of the advertising by plugging in the new advertising expenditure amount, 30, for x and calculating the daily sales, which yields $1340. Thus, the new sales level caused by the increase in advertising is $1340, as shown in Figure 4-5. Since the new actual value is $1500, then $160 (i.e., 1500 –1340) must be attributed to the training program. The effect of both the training and advertising is shown in the figure.

A major disadvantage with this approach occurs when several variables enter the process. The complexity multiplies and the use of sophisticated statistical packages for multiple variable analyses is necessary.

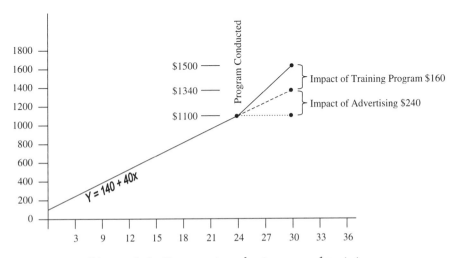

Figure 4-5. Forecasting the impact of training.

Even then, a good fit of the data to the model may not be possible. Unfortunately, some organizations have not developed mathematical relationships for output variables as a function of one or more inputs. Without them, the forecasting method is difficult to use.

The primary advantage of this process is that it can accurately predict business performance measures without training, if appropriate data and models are available. The presentation of specific methods is beyond the scope of this book and is contained in other works (Armstrong, 2001). Approximately 5% of published studies on the ROI methodology utilizes the forecasting technique.

PARTICIPANT ESTIMATE OF TRAINING'S IMPACT

An easily implemented method to isolate the impact of training is to obtain information directly from program participants. The effectiveness of this approach rests on the assumption that participants are capable of determining or estimating how much of a performance improvement is related to the training program. Because their actions have produced the improvement, participants may have very accurate input on the issue. They should know how much of the change was caused by applying what they have learned in the program. Although an estimate, this value will typically have credibility with management because participants are at the center of the change or improvement.

When using this technique, several assumptions are made.

1. A training (or performance improvement) has been conducted with a variety of different activities, exercises, and learning opportunities all focused on improving performance.
2. One or more business measures have been identified prior to training and have been monitored following the process. Data monitoring has revealed an improvement in the business measure.
3. There is a need to link the training to the specific amount of performance improvement and develop the monetary impact of the improvement. This information forms the basis for calculating the actual ROI.

With these assumptions, the participants can pinpoint the actual results linked to the training program and provide data necessary to develop the ROI. This can be accomplished using a focus group or with a questionnaire.

Focus Group Approach

The focus group works extremely well for this challenge if the group size is relatively small—in the 8–12 range. If much larger, the groups should be divided into multiple groups. Focus groups provide the opportunity for members to share information equally, avoiding domination by any one individual. The process taps the input, creativity, and reactions of the entire group.

The meeting should take about one hour (slightly more if there are multiple factors affecting the results or there are multiple business measures). The facilitator should be neutral to the process (i.e., the same individual conducting the training should not conduct this focus group). Focus group facilitation and input must be objective.

The task is to link the business results of the training to business performance. The group is presented with the improvement and they provide input on isolating the effects of training.

The following steps are recommended to arrive at the most credible value for training impact.

1. **Explain the task.** The task of the focus group meeting is outlined. Participants should understand that there has been improvement in performance. While many factors could have contributed to the performance, the task of this group is to determine how much of the improvement is related to the training.

2. **Discuss the rules.** Each participant should be encouraged to provide input, limiting his or her comments to two minutes (or less) for any specific issue. Comments are confidential and will not be linked to a specific individual.

3. **Explain the importance of the process.** The participant's role in the process is critical. Because it is their performance that has improved, the participants are in the best position to indicate what has caused this improvement; they are the experts in this determination. Without quality input, the contribution of this training (or any other processes) may never be known.

4. **Select the first measure and show the improvement.** Using actual data, show the level of performance prior to and following training; in essence, the change in business results is reported.

5. **Identify the different factors that have contributed to the performance.** Using input from experts—others who are knowledgeable about the improvements—identify the factors that have influenced the improvement (e.g., the volume of work has

changed, a new system has been implemented, or technology has been enhanced). If these are known, they are listed as the factors that may have contributed to the performance improvement.

6. **The group is asked to identify other factors that have contributed to the performance.** In some situations, only the participants know other influencing factors and those factors should surface at this time.

7. **Discuss the linkage.** Taking each factor one at a time, the participants individually describe the linkage between that factor and the business results. For example, for the training influence, the participants would describe how the training has driven the actual improvement by providing examples, anecdotes, and other supporting evidence. Participants may require some prompting to provide comments. If they cannot provide dialogue of this issue, there's a good chance that the factor had no influence.

8. **The process is repeated for each factor.** Each factor is explored until all the participants have discussed the linkage between all the factors, and the business performance improvement. After this linkage has been discussed, the participants should have a clear understanding of the cause and effect relationship between the various factors and the business improvement.

9. **Allocate the improvement.** Participants are asked to allocate the percent of improvement to each of the factors discussed. Participants are provided a pie chart, which represents a total amount of improvement for the measure in question, and are asked to carve up the pie, allocating the percentages to different improvements with a total of 100%. Some participants may feel uncertain with this process, but should be encouraged to complete this step using their best estimate. Uncertainty will be addressed later in the meeting.

10. **Provide a confidence estimate.** The participants are then asked to review the allocation percentages and, for each one, estimate their level of confidence in the allocation estimate. Using a scale of 0–100%, where 0% represents no confidence and 100% is certainty, participants express their level of certainty with their estimates in the previous step. A participant may be more comfortable with some factors than others so the confidence estimate may vary. This confidence estimate serves as a vehicle to adjust results.

11. **Participants are asked to multiply the two percentages.** For example, if an individual has allocated 35% of the improvement

to training and is 80% confident, he or she would multiply 35% × 80%, which is 28%. In essence, the participant is suggesting that at least 28% of the teams' business improvement is linked to the training program. The confidence estimate serves as a conservative discount factor, adjusting for the error of the estimate. The pie charts with the calculations are collected without names and the calculations are verified. Another option is to collect pie charts and make the calculations for the participants.

12. **Report results.** If possible, the average of the adjusted values for the group is developed and communicated to the group. Also, the summary of all of the information should be communicated to the participants as soon as possible.

Participants who do not provide information are excluded from the analysis. Table 4-1 illustrates this approach with an example of one participant's estimations.

The participant allocates 50% of the improvement to training. The confidence percentage is a reflection of the error in the estimate. A 70% confidence level equates to a potential error range of ±30% (100% − 70% = 30%). The 50% allocation to training could be 30% more (50% + 15% = 65%) or 30% less (50% = 15% = 35%) or somewhere in between. Thus, the participant's allocation is in the range of 35 to 65%. In essence, the confidence estimate frames this error range. To be conservative, the lower side of the range is used (35%). This leads to another guiding principle:

Table 4-1. Example of a Participant's Estimation

Factor Which Influenced Improvement	Percent of Improvement Caused By	Confidence Expressed as a Percent
1. Training Program	50%	70%
2. Change in Procedures	10%	80%
3. Adjustment in Standards	10%	50%
4. Revision to Incentive Plan	20%	90%
5. Increased Management Attention	10%	50%
6. Other _____	___%	___%
Total	100%	

Guiding Principle #7
Estimates of improvement should be adjusted for the potential error of the estimate.

This approach is equivalent to multiplying the factor estimate by the confidence percentage to develop a usable training factor value of 35% (50% × 70%). This adjusted percentage is then multiplied by the actual amount of the improvement (postprogram minus preprogram value) to isolate the portion attributed to training. The adjusted improvement is now ready for conversion to monetary values and, ultimately, used in developing the return on investment.

This approach provides a credible way to isolate the effects of training when other methods will not work. It is often regarded as the low cost solution to the problem because it takes only a few focus groups and a small amount of time to arrive at this conclusion. In most of these settings, the actual conversion to monetary value is not conducted by the group, but developed in another way. For most data, the monetary value may already exist as a standard, acceptable value. The issue of converting data to monetary value is detailed in the next chapter. However, if participants must provide input on the value of the data, it can be approached in the same focus group meeting as another phase of the process, where the participants provide input into the actual monetary value of the unit. To reach an accepted value, the steps are very similar to the steps for isolation.

Questionnaire Approach

Sometimes focus groups are not available or considered unacceptable for use of the data collection. The participants may not be available for a group meeting or the focus groups become too expensive. In these situations, it may be helpful to collect similar information via a questionnaire. With this approach, participants must address the same issues as those addressed in the focus group, but now on a series of impact questions imbedded into a follow-up questionnaire.

The questionnaire may focus solely on isolating the effects of training, as detailed in the previous example, or it may focus on the monetary value derived from the program, with the isolation issue being only a part of the data collected. This is a more versatile approach for using questionnaires when it is not certain exactly how participants will provide business impact data. In some programs, the precise measures that will be influenced by the program may not be known. This is sometimes the case in programs involving leadership, team building, communications, negotiations, problem solving, innovation, and other types of training and performance improvement initiatives. In these situations, it is helpful to obtain information from participants on a series of impact questions, showing how they have used what they have learned and the subsequent impact in the work unit. It is important for participants to know about these questions before they receive the questionnaire. The surprise element can be disastrous in data collection. More on this issue later. The recommended series of questions are:

Impact Questions

1. How have you and your job changed as a result of attending this program (skills and knowledge application)?
2. What impact do these changes bring to your work or work unit?
3. How is this impact measured (specific measure)?
4. How much did this measure change after you participated in the program (monthly, weekly, or daily amount)?
5. What is the unit value of the measure?
6. What is the basis for this unit value? Please indicate the assumptions made and the specific calculations you performed to arrive at the value.
7. What is the annual value of this change or improvement in the work unit (for the first year)?
8. Recognizing that many other factors influence output results in addition to training; please identify the other factors that could have contributed to this performance.
9. What percent of this improvement can be attributed directly to the application of skills and knowledge gained in the program? (0–100%)
10. What confidence do you have in the above estimate and data, expressed as a percent? (0% = no confidence; 100% = certainty)
11. What other individuals or groups could estimate this percentage or determine the amount?

Perhaps an illustration of this process can reveal its effectiveness and acceptability. In a large global organization, the impact of a leadership program for new managers was being assessed. Because the decision to calculate the impact of training was made after the program had been conducted, the control group arrangement was not feasible as a method to isolate the effects of training. Also, before the program was implemented, no specified business impact data (Level 4) were identified that was directly linked to the program. Participants may drive one or more of a dozen business performance measures. Consequently, it was not appropriate to use trend line analysis. Participants' estimates proved to be the most useful way to assess the impact of training on the business performance. In a detailed follow-up questionnaire, participants were asked a variety of questions regarding the applications of what was learned from the program. As part of the program, the individuals were asked to develop action plans and implement them, although there was no specific follow-up plan needed. The series of impact questions listed above provided an estimation of the impact.

Although this series of questions is challenging, when set up properly and presented to participants in an appropriate way, they can be very effective for collecting impact data. Table 4-2 shows a sample of the calculations from these questions for this particular program. In this snapshot of the data, the input from seven participants is presented. The total value for the program would be the total of the input from all who provided data.

Although this is an estimate, the approach has considerable accuracy and credibility. Four adjustments are effectively utilized with this approach to reflect a conservative approach:

1. The individuals who do not respond to the questionnaire or provide usable data on the questionnaire are assumed to have no improvements. This is probably an over-statement of results since some individuals will have improvements, but not report them on the questionnaire. This is Guiding Principle #6, discussed in Chapter 3.
2. Extreme data and incomplete, unrealistic, and unsupported claims are omitted from the analysis, although they may be included in the intangible benefits. This is Guiding Principle #8, discussed in Chapter 3.
3. Since only annualized values are used, it is assumed that there are no benefits from the program after the first year of implementation. In reality, leadership training should be expected to add value for several years after training has been conducted. This is Guiding Principle #9, discussed in Chapter 5.

Table 4-2. Sample of Input from Participants in a Leadership Program for New Managers

Participant Number	Annual Improvement Value	Basis for Value	Confidence	Isolation Factor	Adjusted Value
11	$36,000	Improvement in efficiency of group. $3,000 month × 12 (Group Estimate)	85%	50%	$15,300
42	90,000	Turnover Reduction. Two turnover statistics per year. Base salary × 1.5 = 45,000	90%	40%	32,400
74	24,000	Improvement in customer response time. (8 hours to 6 hours) Estimated value: $2,000/month	60%	55%	7,920
55	$2,000	5% improvement in my effectiveness ($40,500 × 5%)	75%	50%	750
96	$10,000	Absenteeism Reduction (50 absences per year × $200)	85%	75%	6,375
117	$8,090	Team project completed 10 days ahead of schedule. Annual salaries $210,500 = $809 per day × 10 days	90%	45%	3,279
118	159,000	Under budget for the year by this amount.	100%	30%	47,700

4. The confidence level, expressed as a percent, is multiplied by the improvement value to reduce the amount of the improvement by the potential error. This is Guiding Principle #4, discussed earlier.

When presented to senior management, the results of this impact study were perceived to be an understatement of the program's success. The data and the process were considered to be credible and accurate.

Collecting an adequate amount of quality data from the series of impact questions is the critical challenge with this process. Participants must be primed to provide data and this can be accomplished in several ways.

1. Participants should know in advance that they are expected to provide this type of data along with an explanation of why this is needed and how it will be used.
2. Ideally, participants should see a copy of this questionnaire and discuss it while they're involved in the training program. If possible, a verbal commitment to provide the data should be obtained at that time.
3. Participants could be reminded of the requirement prior to the time to collect data. The reminder should come from others involved in the process—even the immediate manager.
4. Participants could be provided with examples of how the questionnaire can be completed, using most-likely scenarios and typical data.
5. The immediate manager could coach participants through the process.
6. The immediate manager could review and approve the data.

These steps help keep the data collection process, with its chain of impact questions, from being a surprise. It will also accomplish three critical tasks.

1. **The response rate will increase.** Because participants commit to provide data during the session, a greater percentage will respond.
2. **The quantity of data will improve.** Participants will understand the chain of impact and understand how data will be used. They will complete more questions.
3. **The quality of the data is enhanced.** With up-front expectations, there is greater understanding of the type of data needed and

improved confidence in the data provided. Perhaps subconsciously, participants begin to think through consequences of training and specific impact measures. The result: improved quality of input.

Participant estimation is a critical technique to isolate the effect of training, however, the process has some disadvantages. It is an estimate and, consequently, does not have the accuracy desired by some HRD managers. Also, the input data may be unreliable since some participants are incapable of providing these types of estimates. They might not be aware of exactly which factors contributed to the results or they may be reluctant to provide data. If the questions come as a surprise, the data will be scarce.

Several advantages make this strategy attractive. It is a simple process, easily understood by most participants and by others who review evaluation data. It is inexpensive, takes very little time and analysis, and thus results in an efficient addition to the evaluation process. Estimates originate from a credible source—the individuals who actually produced the improvement.

The advantages seem to offset the disadvantages. Isolating the effects of training will never be precise and this estimate may be accurate enough for most clients and management groups. The process is appropriate when the participants are managers, supervisors, team leaders, sales associates, engineers, and other professional and technical employees.

This technique is the fallback isolation strategy for many types of programs. If nothing else works, this method is used. A fallback approach is needed if the effect of the training is always isolated. The reluctance to use the process often rests with trainers, training managers, learning specialists, and performance improvement specialists. They are reluctant to use a technique that is not an airtight case. Estimates are typically avoided. However, the primary audience for the data (the sponsor or senior manager) will readily accept this approach. Living in an ambiguous world, they understand that estimates have to be made and may be the only way to approach this issue. They understand the challenge and appreciate the conservative approach, often commenting that the actual value is probably greater than the value presented. When organizations begin to use this routinely, it sometimes becomes the method of choice for isolation. Because of this, approximately 50% of the more than 100 published studies on the ROI methodology use this as a technique to isolate the effects of training.

SUPERVISOR ESTIMATE OF TRAINING'S IMPACT

In lieu of (or in addition to) participant estimates, the participants' supervisor may be asked to provide the extent of training's role in producing a performance improvement. In some settings, participants' supervisors may be more familiar with the other factors influencing performance. Consequently, they may be better equipped to provide estimates of impact. The recommended questions to ask supervisors, after describing the improvement caused by the participants, are:

1. In addition to training, what other factors could have contributed to this success?
2. What percent of the improvement in performance measures of the participant resulted from the training program? (0–100%)
3. What is the basis for this estimate?
4. What is your confidence in this estimate, expressed as a percentage? (0% = no confidence; 100% = complete confidence)
5. What other individuals or groups would know about this improvement and could estimate this percentage?

These questions are similar to those in the participant's questionnaire. Supervisor estimates should be analyzed in the same manner as participant estimates. To be more conservative, estimates may be adjusted by the confidence percentage. If feasible, it is recommended that inputs be obtained from both participants and supervisors. When participants' estimates have been collected, the decision of which estimate to use becomes an issue. If there is some compelling reason to think that one estimate is more credible than another, it should be used. The most conservative approach is to use the lowest value and include an appropriate explanation. Another potential option is to recognize that each source has its own unique perspective and that an average of the two is appropriate, placing an equal weight on each input.

An example illustrates how manager input can closely parallel participants' input. Table 4-3 shows the comparison of participant input to manager input for a training program for technicians involved with ISDN lines in a telecommunications company. Both the participants and the managers were asked to allocate the various factors that contributed to the overall improvement. In this case, both participants and managers gave almost the same allocation, bringing increased credibility to the participants' estimate. In this situation, the managers were familiar and involved with the various factors that contribute to improved perform-

Table 4-3. Estimate of Training's Impact

Factor	Participants	Managers
ISDN knowledge, skills, or experience graduates had *before* they attended the training	13%	14%
ISDN knowledge, skills, or experience graduates gained *from* the training	37%	36%
ISDN knowledge, skills, or experience graduates acquired on their own *after* the training	16%	12%
ISDN reference material or job aids unrelated to the training, e.g., bulletins, methods, and procedure documentation	7%	9%
Coaching or feedback from peers	18%	18%
Coaching or feedback from graduates' managers	2%	5%
Observation of others	7%	6%

ance. They understood the factors enough to provide credible input. This may not always be the case; managers removed from a particular job by distance or function are unable to make this type of allocation.

This approach has the same disadvantages as participant estimates. It is subjective and, consequently, may be viewed with skepticism by senior management. Also, supervisors may be reluctant to participate, or be incapable of providing accurate impact estimates. In some cases they may not know about other factors that contributed to the improvement.

The advantages of this approach are similar to the advantages of participant estimation. It is simple and inexpensive and enjoys an acceptable degree of credibility because it comes directly from the supervisors of those individuals who received the training. When combined with participant estimation, the credibility is enhanced considerably. Also, when factored by the level of confidence, its value further increases.

MANAGEMENT ESTIMATE OF TRAINING'S IMPACT

In some cases, upper management may estimate the percent of improvement that should be attributed to the training program. For example, in Litton Guidance and Control Systems, the senior management team adjusted the results from a self-directed team process (Graham, Bishop, and Birdsong, 1994). After considering additional factors, such as technology, procedures, and process change (which could have contributed to the improvement), management applied a subjective factor (in this case 60%) to represent the portion of the results that should be attributed to the training program. The 60% factor was developed in a meeting with top managers and therefore had the benefit of group ownership. While this process is very subjective, the input is received from the individuals who often provide or approve funding for the program. Sometimes their level of comfort with the process is the most important consideration.

This method is not necessarily recommended because of its subjective nature. Senior managers may not understand all the factors or have no indication of the relative difference of the factors that could have affected the business measure driven by training. Consequently, the use of this method should be avoided or used only when it is necessary to secure buy-in from the senior management team.

In some situations, the training impact will be large, providing a very high ROI. Top managers may feel more comfortable making an adjustment in the actual data. In essence, they are applying their discount factor for an unknown factor, although attempts have been made to identify each factor. While there's no scientific basis for this technique, it provides some assurance that the data are appropriately discounted.

CUSTOMER INPUT OF TRAINING'S IMPACT

One helpful approach in some narrowly focused situations is to solicit input on the impact of training directly from customers. In these situations, customers are asked why they chose a particular product or service or to explain how individuals applying skills and abilities have influenced their reaction to the product or service learned in a training program. This strategy focuses directly on what the training program is often designed to improve. For example, after a teller training program was conducted following a bank merger, market research data showed that the percentage of customers who were dissatisfied with teller knowledge was reduced by 5% when compared to market survey data before training (Rust, Zahorik, and Keiningham, 1994). Since only the training increased teller knowledge, the 5% reduction of dissatisfied customers was directly attributable to the training program.

In another example, a large real estate company provided a comprehensive training program for agents, focusing on presentation skills. As customers listed their homes with an agent, they received a survey, exploring the reasons for deciding to list their home with the company.

Among the reasons listed were the presentation skills of the agent. Responses on this question and related questions provided evidence of the percentage of new listings attributed to the training program.

This approach can be used only in situations where customer input can be obtained. Even then, customers may not be able to provide accurate data. However, because customer input is critical, the approach is useful in those situations where it can be utilized.

Expert Estimation of Training's Impact

External or internal experts can sometimes estimate the portion of results that can be attributed to training. When using this strategy, experts must be carefully selected based on their knowledge of the process, program, and situation. For example, an expert in quality might be able to provide estimates of how much change in a quality measure can be attributed to training and how much can be attributed to other factors in the implementation of a TQM program.

This approach would most likely be used in a scenario involving the success of a program developed by an external supplier. In a detailed evaluation of previous studies, a certain amount of the results have been attributed to training. This figure from the supplier is used to extrapolate it to the current situation. This approach should be pursued cautiously because the situation may be very different. However, if it is a program application with many similarities in the situation, this value may be a rough estimate—a very rough estimate. Because of these concerns, this approach should be used with explanations. Also, it is important to check the actual studies that have been conducted to ensure that a credible, objective process was used in data collection and analysis.

This technique has an advantage in that its credibility often reflects the reputation of the expert or independent consultant. It is a quick source of input from a reputable expert or independent consultant. Sometimes top management will place more confidence in external experts than in their own internal staff.

Calculating the Impact of Other Factors

Although not appropriate in all cases, there are some situations where it may be feasible to calculate the impact of factors (other than training) that influenced the improvement and then conclude that training is credited with the remaining portion. In this approach, training takes credit for improvement that cannot be attributed to other factors.

An example will help explain the approach. In a consumer-lending program for a large bank, a significant increase in consumer loan volume was generated after a training program was conducted for consumer loan officers (Phillips, 1994). Part of the increase in volume was attributed to training while the remainder was due to the influence of other factors operating during the same time period. Two other factors were identified by the evaluator: A loan officer's production improved with time, and falling interest rates stimulated an increase in consumer volume.

In regard to the first factor, as loan officers make loans their confidence improves. They use consumer lending policy manuals and gain knowledge and expertise through trial and error. The amount of this factor was estimated by using input from several internal experts in the marketing department.

For the second factor, industry sources were used to estimate the relationship between increased consumer loan volume and falling interest rates. These two estimates together accounted for a certain percent of increased consumer loan volume. The remaining improvement was attributed to the training program.

This method is appropriate when the other factors are easily identified and the appropriate mechanisms are in place to calculate their impact on the improvement. In some cases it is just as difficult to estimate the impact of other factors as it is for the impact of the training program, leaving this approach less advantageous. This process can be very credible if the method used to isolate the impact of other factors is credible.

USING THE TECHNIQUES

With several techniques available to isolate the impact of training, selecting the most appropriate techniques for the specific program can be difficult. Some techniques are simple and inexpensive, while others are more time consuming and costly. When attempting to make the selection decision, several factors should be considered:

- ☐ feasibility of the technique
- ☐ accuracy provided with the technique, when compared to the accuracy needed

☐ credibility of the technique with the target audience
☐ specific cost to implement the technique
☐ the amount of disruption in normal work activities as the technique is implemented
☐ participant, staff, and management time needed with the particular technique

Multiple techniques or sources for data input should be considered since two sources are usually better than one. When multiple sources are utilized, a conservative method is recommended to combine the inputs. A conservative approach builds acceptance. The target audience should always be provided with explanations of the process and the various subjective factors involved. Multiple sources allow an organization to experiment with different techniques and build confidence with a particular technique. For example, if management is concerned about the accuracy of participants' estimates, a combination of a control group arrangement and participants' estimates could be attempted to check the accuracy of the estimation process.

It is not unusual for the ROI in training and development to be extremely large. Even when a portion of the improvement is allocated to other factors, the numbers are still impressive in many situations. The audience should understand that, although every effort was made to isolate the impact, it is still a figure that is not precise and may contain error. It represents the best estimate of the impact given the constraints, conditions, and resources available. Chances are it is more accurate than other types of analyses regularly utilized in other functions within the organization.

FINAL THOUGHTS

This chapter presented a variety of techniques that isolate the effects of training. The techniques represent the most effective approaches to tackle this issue and are utilized by some of the most progressive organizations. Too often results are reported and linked to training without any attempt to isolate the portion of results that can be attributed to the training. It is impossible to link training to business impact if this issue is ignored. If the training and development function is to continue to improve its professional image as well as meet its responsibility for obtaining results, this issue must be addressed early in the process.

CASE STUDY—PART C,
LINEAR NETWORK SYSTEMS

Data Collection Plan

The consultant and the HRD Manager decided that the action planning process would be used in the follow-up evaluation. First level managers should know how to develop action plans and their managers should be able to provide assistance and support with the process. The action plan would show how the newly acquired skills are applied to improve measures such as productivity, turnover, and absenteeism. A portion of the program allowed for a discussion of action plans, and the program facilitator was required to approve the action plan verifying that it meets basic requirements. A model action plan would be provided to help ensure that supervisors understand the process.

After discussions with management, it was felt that within four months supervisors should be able to apply leadership skills to achieve measurable results. Although a six-month time frame was recommended, senior management indicated that they might want to proceed with the program in other plants before six months and therefore preferred a three-month period. Four months was a compromise.

Because all of the action plans involve different time frames, each participant was asked to provide a progress report in four months, or in some cases, the completed project. This would provide a snapshot of the performance improvement within that time frame.

Although the action plan, by design, collected Levels 3 and 4 data, a follow-up questionnaire was planned to gain more evidence of on-the-job behavior change (Level 3). Responsibilities for data collection at Levels 1 and 2 usually rest with the facilitator and that was the case here. The Area Training Coordinator was assigned the responsibility for collecting the questionnaire data (Level 3) and monitoring performance (Level 4). The data collection plan is presented as Figure 4-6.

Isolating the Effects of Training

One of the most important challenges facing program evaluators is determining the specific technique that isolates the effects of the training program, recognizing that other factors may influence outcome measures at the same time the program is being conducted. This is one of the most important issues (usually raised by management) when they want to know exactly how much of the results are related specifically to the program.

DATA COLLECTION PLAN

Program: Leadership Development Program   **Responsibility:** _____   **Date:** _____

Level	objective(s)	Measures/Data	Data Collection Method	Data Sources	Timing	Responsibilities
1	**REACTION/SATISFACTION** • Positive reaction • Identify planned actions	• Average rating of at least 4.2 on 5.0 scale on quality, usefulness, and achievement of program objectives. • 100% submit planned actions	• Standard feedback questionnaire	• Participants	• End of program	• Facilitator
2	**LEARNING/SKILLS** • Knowledge on motivational models • Knowledge on leadership models/skills • Skills on motivating employees • Knowledge/skills on providing counseling/feedback • Knowledge on measuring employee performance • Problem solving skills	• Demonstrated ability to provide employee feedback/motivating/ problem solving/ leadership skills • Scale of 1-5 on assessment of knowledge	• Skill practice • Facilitator assessment • Participant assessment	• Participants • Facilitator • Participants	• During program	• Facilitator
3	**APPLICATION and IMPLEMENTATION** • Extent and frequency of skill use • Complete all steps of action plan	• Scale of 1-5 on assessment of application • The number of steps completed on action plan	• Follow-up questionnaire • Action plan	• Participants • Participants	• 4 months after program • 4 months after program	• Area Training Coordinator
4	**BUSINESS IMPACT** • Identify at least 2 measures that need improvement	• Varies	• Action plan	• Participants	• 4 months after program	• Area Training Coordinator
5	ROI • 25%	**Comments**				

Figure 4-6. Data collection plan.

<table>
<tr><td colspan="2" align="center">Discussion Questions</td></tr>
</table>

Discussion Questions
1. What method(s) should be used to isolate the effects of training?
2. Should more than one technique be used to isolate the effects of training? Please explain.

REFERENCES

Alliger, G.M., and E.A. Janak. "Kirkpatrick's Levels of Training Criteria: Thirty Years Later." *Personnel Psychology*, vol. 42, 1989, pp. 331–342.

Armstrong, J.S. (Ed.). *Principles of Forecasting: A Handbook for Researchers and Practitioners.* Boston, MA: Kluwer Academic Publishers, 2001.

Bassi, L.J., and E.M. Lewis. *Linking Training and Performance: Benchmarking Results.* Alexandria, VA: American Society for Training and Development, 1999.

Brinkerhoff, R.O., and D. Dressler. "Using Evaluation to Build Organizational Performance and Learning Capability: A Strategy and a Method." *Performance Improvement,* July 2002.

Graham, M., K. Bishop, and R. Birdsong. "Self-Directed Work Teams," *In Action: Measuring Return on Investment,* vol. 1, Phillips, J.J. (Ed.). Alexandria, VA: American Society for Training and Development, 1994, pp. 105–122.

Kaufman, R. "Resolving the (Often-Deserved) Attacks on Training." *Performances Impermanency,* July 2002, vol 41, no 6.

Keuler, D.J. "Measuring ROI for Telephonic Customer Service Skills," *In Action: Measuring Return on Investment,* vol. 3, Phillips, P.P. (Ed.). Alexandria, VA: American Society for Training and Development, 2001, pp. 131–158.

Kirkpatrick, D. *Evaluating Training Programs: The Four* Levels, 2nd ed. San Francisco, CA: Berrett-Koehler Publishers, 1998.

Phillips, J.J. "Measuring ROI in an Established Program," *HR Scorecard.* Boston, MA: Butterworth–Heinemann, 1994, pp. 187–197.

Phillips, J.J., and D. Hill. "Sexual Harassment Prevention," *In Action: Measuring Return on Investment,* vol. 2, Phillips, J.J. (Ed.). Alexandria, VA: American Society for Training and Development, 2001, pp. 17–35.

Phillips, P.P., and J.J. Phillips. "Measuring Return on Investment on Interactive Selling Skills," *In Action: Measuring Return on Investment,* vol. 3, Phillips, P.P. (Ed.). Alexandria, VA: American Society for Training and Development, 2001, pp. 149–172.

Phillips, P.P., and J.J. Phillips. "Evaluating the Impact of a Graduate Program in a Federal Agency," *In Action: Measuring ROI in the Public Sector*, Phillips, P.P. (Ed.). Alexandria, VA: American Society for Training and Development, 2002, pp. 149–172

Riley, T., H. Davani, P. Chason, and K. Findley. "Practices and Pitfalls: A Practitioner's Journey Into Level 3 Evaluation." *Performance Improvement*, May/June 2002.

Russ-Eft, D., and H. Preskill. *Evaluation in Organizations: A Systematic Approach to Enhancing Learning, Performance, and Change.* Cambridge, MA: Perseus Publishing, 2001.

Rust, R.T., A.J. Zahorik, and T.L. Keiningham. *Return on Quality: Measuring the Financial Impact of Your Company's Quest for Quality.* Chicago, IL: Probus Publishers, 1994.

Salkind, N.J. *Statistics for People Who (Think They) Hate Statistics.* Thousand Oaks, CA: Sage Publications, Inc., 2000.

Wang, G. "Control Group Methods for HPT Program Evaluation and Measurement." *Performance Improvement Quarterly,* 15(2), 2002, pp. 32–46.

Wang, G., Z. Dou, and N. Lee. "A Systems Approach to Measuring Return on Investment (ROI) for HRD Interventions." *Human Resource Development Quarterly,* 13(2), 2002, pp. 203–224.

FURTHER READING

Chelimsky, E., and W.R. Shadish, (Ed.). *Evaluation for the 21st Century: A Handbook.* Thousand Oaks, CA: Sage Publications, 1997.

Creswell, J.W. *Research Design: Qualitative & Quantitative Approaches.* Thousand Oaks, CA: Sage Publications, 1994.

Miller, D.C., and N.J. Salkind. *Handbook of Research Design & Social Measurement,* 6th ed. Thousand Oaks, CA: Sage Publications, 2002.

Rossi, P.H., H.E. Freeman, and M.W. Lipsey. *Evaluation: A Systematic Approach,* 6th ed. Thousand Oaks, CA: Sage Publications, 1999.

Mark, M.M., G.T. Henry, and G. Julnes. *Evaluation: An Integrated Framework for Understanding, Guiding, and Improving Policies and Programs.* San Francisco, CA: Jossey-Bass, 2000.

Phillips, J.J. *The Consultant's Scorecard: Tracking Results and Bottom-Line Impact of Consulting Projects.* New York, NY: McGraw-Hill, 2000.

CHAPTER 5

Converting Data to Monetary Benefits

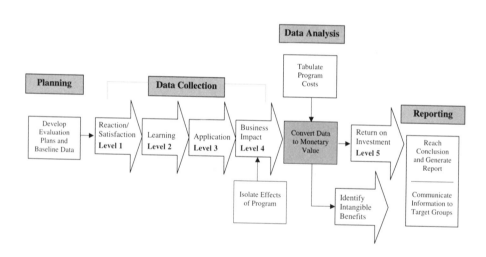

Traditionally most impact evaluation studies stop with a tabulation of business results, which is a Level 4 evaluation. In those situations, the program is considered successful if it produced improvements such as productivity increases, quality enhancements, absenteeism reductions, or customer satisfaction improvements. While these results are important, it is more insightful to convert the data to monetary value and show the total impact of the improvement. The monetary value is also needed to compare the cost of the program to develop the ROI. This evaluation is the ultimate level of the five-level evaluation framework presented in Chapter 1. This chapter shows how leading organizations are moving beyond just tabulating business results and are adding another step of converting data to monetary value. Chapter 3 outlined the methods used to collect data. Chapter 4 described a variety of techniques to isolate the effects of training. This chapter outlines techniques that convert the data to monetary value.

PRELIMINARY ISSUES

Sorting Out Hard and Soft Data

After collecting performance data, many organizations find it helpful to divide data into hard and soft categories. Hard data are the traditional measures of organizational performance, as they are objective, easy to measure, and easy to convert to monetary values. Hard data are often very common measures, achieve high credibility with management, and are available in every type of organization. They are destined to be converted to monetary value and included in the ROI formula.

Hard data represent the output, quality, cost, and time of work-related processes. Table 5-1 shows a sampling of typical hard data under these four categories. Almost every department or unit will have hard data performance measures. For example, a government office approving applications for work visas in a foreign country will have these four measures among its overall performance measurement: the number of applications processed (Output), cost per application processed (Cost), the number of errors made processing applications (Quality), and the time it takes to process and approve an application (Time). Ideally, training programs for employees in this unit should be linked to one or more hard data measures.

Because many training programs are designed to develop soft skills, soft data are needed in evaluation. Soft data are usually subjective, sometimes difficult to measure, almost always difficult to convert to monetary values, and are behaviorally oriented. When compared to hard data, soft data are usually less credible as a performance measure. Soft data measures may or may not be converted to monetary values.

Soft data items can be grouped into several categories; Table 5-2 shows one such grouping. Measures such as employee turnover, absenteeism, and grievances appear as soft data items, not because they are difficult to measure, but because it is difficult to accurately convert them to monetary values.

Table 5-1. Examples of Hard Data

OUTPUT	TIME
Units Produced	Equipment Downtime
Items Assembled	Overtime
Items Sold	On Time Shipments
Forms Processed	Time to Project Completion
Loans Approved	Processing Time
Inventory Turnover	Cycle Time
Patients Visited	Meeting Schedules
Applications Processed	Repair Time
Productivity	Efficiency
Work Backlog	Work Stoppages
Shipments	Order Response Time
New Accounts Opened	Late Reporting
	Lost Time Days

COSTS	QUALITY
Budget Variances	Scrap
Unit Costs	Rejects
Cost By Account	Error Rates
Variable Costs	Rework
Fixed Costs	Shortages
Overhead Costs	Deviation from Standard
Operating Costs	Product Failures
Number of Cost Reductions	Inventory Adjustments
Accident Costs	Percent of Tasks Completed Properly
Sales Expense	Number of Accidents

General Steps to Convert Data

Before describing the specific techniques to convert either hard or soft data to monetary values, the general steps used to convert data in each strategy are briefly summarized. These steps should be followed for each data conversion.

Focus on a unit of measure. First, identify a unit of improvement. For output data, the unit of measure is the item produced, service provided, or sale consummated. Time measures are varied and include items such as the time to complete a project, cycle time, or customer response time. The unit is usually expressed as minutes, hours, or days. Quality is a common measure, and the unit may be one error, reject, defect, or

Table 5-2. Examples of Soft Data

WORK HABITS	CUSTOMER SERVICE
Absenteeism	Churn Rate
Tardiness	Number of Satisfied Customers
Visits to the Dispensary	Customer Satisfaction Index
First Aid Treatments	Customer Loyalty
Violations of Safety Rules	Customer Complaints
Excessive Breaks	

WORK CLIMATE	DEVELOPMENT/ADVANCEMENT
Number of Grievances	Number of Promotions
Number of Discrimination	Number of Pay Increases
Charges	Number of Training Programs Attended
Employee Complaints	Requests for Transfer
Job Satisfaction	Performance Appraisal Ratings
Employee Turnover	Increases in Job Effectiveness
Litigation	

JOB ATTITUDES	INITIATIVE
Job Satisfaction	Implementation of New Ideas
Organizational Commitment	Successful Completion of Projects
Perceptions of Job Responsibilities	Number of Suggestions Implemented
Employee Loyalty	Number of Goals
Increased Confidence	

rework item. Soft data measures are varied, and the unit of improvement may include items such as a grievance, an absence, an employee turnover statistic, or a change of one point in the customer satisfaction index.

Determine a value of each unit. Place a value (V) on the unit identified in the first step. For measures of production, quality, cost, and time, the process is relatively easy. Most organizations have records or reports reflecting the value of items such as one unit of production or the cost of a defect. Soft data are more difficult to convert to a value, as the cost of one absence, one grievance, or a change of one point in the employee attitude survey is often difficult to pinpoint. The techniques in this chapter provide an array of possibilities to make this conversion. When more than one value is available, either the most credible or the lowest value is used.

Calculate the change in performance data. The change in output data is developed after the effects of training have been isolated from other influences. The change (ΔP) is the performance improvement, measured as hard or soft data, that is directly attributable to the training program. The value may represent the performance improvement for an individual, a team, a group or several groups of participants.

Determine an annual amount for the change. Annualize the ΔP value to develop a total change in the performance data for one year. Using a year has become a standard approach with many organizations that wish to capture the total benefits of a training program. Although the benefits may not be realized at the same level for an entire year, some programs will continue to produce benefits beyond one year. In some cases, the stream of benefits may involve several years. However, using one year of benefits is considered a conservative approach for short term solutions (most training on performance improvement initiatives are short term solutions). For long term solutions, a longer, but conservative period is used. The time frame is establishing before the study begins. This leads to a guiding principle:

Guiding Principle #9
Only the first year of benefits (annual) should be used in the ROI analysis of short-term projects/initiatives.

Calculate the total value of the improvement. Develop the total value of improvement by multiplying the annual performance change (ΔP) by the unit value (V) for the complete group in question. For example, if one group of participants for a program is being evaluated, the total value will include total improvement for all participants in the group. This value for annual program benefits is then compared to the cost of the program, usually through the return on investment formula presented in Chapter 1.

TECHNIQUES FOR CONVERTING DATA TO MONETARY VALUES

An example taken from a team building program at a manufacturing plant describes the five-step process of converting data to monetary values. This program was developed and implemented after a needs assessment revealed that a lack of teamwork was causing an excessive number of grievances. Thus, the actual number of grievances resolved at Step 2 in the grievance process was selected as an output measure. Table 5-3 shows the steps taken to assign a monetary value to the data arrived at a total program impact of $546,000.

Ten techniques are available to convert data to monetary values. Some techniques are appropriate for a specific type of data or data category, while other techniques can be used with virtually any type of data. The HRD staff's challenge is to select the particular technique that best matches the type of data and situation. Each technique is presented next, beginning with the most credible approach.

Table 5-3. An Example to Illustrate the Steps to Convert Data to Monetary Values

Setting: Team-Building Program in a Manufacturing Plant

Step 1   Focus on a Unit of Improvement.
One grievance reaching Step 2 in the 4-step grievance resolution process.

Step 2   Determine a Value of Each Unit.
Using internal experts, the labor relations staff, the cost of an average grievance was estimated to be $6500 when considering time and direct costs. (V = $6500)

Step 3   Calculate the Change in Performance Data.
Six months after the program was completed, total grievances per month reaching Step 2 declined by ten. Seven of the ten grievance reductions were related to the program as determined by supervisors (Isolating the Effects of Training).

Step 4   Determine an Annual Amount for the Change.
Using the six-month value, 7 per month yields an annual improvement of 84 ($\Delta P = 84$) for the first year

Step 5   Calculate the Annual Value of the Improvement
Annual Value = ΔP times V
$\qquad$ = 84 times $6500
$\qquad$ = $546,000

CONVERTING OUTPUT DATA TO CONTRIBUTION

When a training program has produced a change in output, the value of the increased output can usually be determined from the organization's accounting or operating records. For organizations operating on a profit basis, this value is usually the marginal profit contribution of an additional unit of production or unit of service provided. For example, a production team in a major appliance manufacturer is able to boost production of small refrigerators with a series of comprehensive training programs. The unit of improvement, therefore, is the profit margin of one refrigerator. In organizations that are performance rather than profit driven, this value is usually reflected in the savings accumulated when an additional unit of output is realized for the same input requirements. For example, in a visa section of a government office, an additional visa application is processed at no additional cost. Thus, an increase in output translates into a cost savings equal to the unit cost of processing a visa.

The formulas and calculations used to measure this contribution depend on the organization and its records. Most organizations have this type of data readily available for performance monitoring and goal setting. Managers often use marginal cost statements and sensitivity analyses to pinpoint the value associated with changes in output (Boulton, Libert, and Samek, 2000). If the data are not available, the HRD staff must initiate or coordinate the development of appropriate values.

In one case involving a commercial bank, a sales seminar for consumer loan officers was conducted that resulted in additional consumer loan volume (output). To measure the return on investment in the training program, it was necessary to calculate the value (profit contribution) of one additional consumer loan. This was a relatively easy item to calculate from the bank's records (Phillips, 2000). As shown in Table 5-4, several components went into this calculation.

The first step was to determine the yield, which was available from bank records. Next, the average spread between the cost of funds and the yield received on the loan was calculated. For example, the bank could obtain funds from depositors at 5.5% on average, including the cost of operating the branches. The direct costs of making the loan, such as salaries of employees directly involved in consumer lending and advertising costs for consumer loans, had to be subtracted from this difference. Historically, these direct costs amounted to 0.82% of the loan value. To cover overhead costs for other corporate functions, an additional 1.61%

Table 5-4. Loan Profitability Analysis

Profit Component	Unit Value
Average loan size	$15,500
Average loan yield	9.75%
Average cost of funds (including branch costs)	5.50%
Direct costs for consumer lending	0.82%
Corporate overhead	1.61%
Net Profit per Loan	1.82%

was subtracted from the value. The remaining 1.82% of the average loan value represented the bank's profit margin on a loan.

The good news about this strategy is that standard values are available for many of the measures. The challenge is to quickly find the appropriate and credible value. As the previous example illustrates, the value was already developed for other purposes. This value was then used in the evaluation of the training program. Table 5-5 provides additional detail on the common measures of output data, showing how they are typically developed and some of the comments concerning them. As the table illustrates, standard values are almost always available in the organization. However, if no value has been developed for a particular measure, one of the techniques listed in the chapter can be used to develop the value.

CALCULATING THE COST OF QUALITY

Quality is a critical issue, and its cost is an important measure in most manufacturing and service firms. Since many training programs are designed to improve quality, the HRD staff must place a value on the improvement in certain quality measures. For some quality measures, the task is easy. For example, if quality is measured with a defect rate, the value of the improvement is the cost to repair or replace the product. The most obvious cost of poor quality is the scrap or waste generated by mistakes. Defective products, spoiled raw materials, and discarded paperwork are all the results of poor quality. This scrap and waste translates directly into a monetary value. For example, in a production environment, the cost of a defective product is the total cost incurred to the point the mistake is identified minus the salvage value.

Table 5-5. Typical Output Measures

Output Measures	Example	Technique	Comments
Production unit	One unit assembled	Standard value	Available in almost every manufacturing unit
Service unit	Packages delivered on time	Standard value	Developed for most service providers when it is a typical service delivery unit
Sales	Monetary increase in revenue	Standard value (profit margin)	The profit from one additional dollar of sales is a standard item
Market share	10% increase in market share in one year	Standard value	Margin of increased sales
Productivity measure	10% change in productivity index	Standard value	This measure is very specific to the type of production or productivity measured. It may include per unit of time

Employee mistakes and errors can cause expensive rework. The most costly rework occurs when a product is delivered to a customer and must be returned for correction. The cost of rework includes both labor and direct costs. In some organizations, the cost of rework can be as much as 35% of operating costs (Campanella, 1999). In one example of a program involving customer service training for dispatchers in an oil company, a measure of rework is the number of pullouts. A pullout occurs when a delivery truck cannot fill an order for fuel at a service station. The truck returns to the terminal for an adjustment to the order. Tabulating the cost of a sample of actual pullouts develops the average cost of the pullout. The cost elements include driver time involved, the cost of the truck, the cost of terminal use, and an estimate of administrative costs.

In another example, involving couriers with DHL Worldwide Express (Spain), a program was implemented to train new couriers. Several measures were involved in the payoff of the program. One of those was a quality measure known as repackaging error. This occurs when a parcel is damaged due to mishandling and has to be repackaged before it can be delivered to the customer. The time and repackaging costs are small; nevertheless, when spread over several parcels, couriers, and the country, the value can be significant. The company had already developed a cost for this error and the standard value was used in the ROI study involving courier training.

Perhaps the costliest element of poor quality is customer and client dissatisfaction. In some cases, serious mistakes can result in lost business. Customer dissatisfaction is difficult to quantify, and attempts to arrive at a monetary value may be impossible using direct methods. Usually the judgment and expertise of sales, marketing, or quality managers may be the best sources by which to try to measure the impact of dissatisfaction. A growing number of quality experts are now measuring customer and client dissatisfaction with market surveys (Johnson and Gustafsson, 2000). However, other strategies discussed in this chapter may be more appropriate to measure the cost of customer dissatisfaction.

The good news about quality measures is that there has been much effort to develop the value for improving the particular measure. This is due in part to total quality management, continuous process improvement, and Six Sigma. All of these processes have focused on individual quality measures and the cost of quality. Consequently, specific standard values have been developed. If standard values are not available for any of the quality measures, one of the techniques in this chapter can be used to develop the value.

CONVERTING EMPLOYEE TIME

Reduction in employee time is a common objective for training and performance improvement programs. In a team environment, a program could enable the team to perform tasks in a shorter time frame, or with fewer people. On an individual basis, time management workshops are designed to help professional, sales, supervisory, and managerial employees save time in performing daily tasks. The value of the time saved is an important measure of the program's success, and this conversion is a relatively easy process.

The most obvious time savings are from labor reduction costs in performing work. The monetary savings is found by multiplying the hours saved times the labor cost per hour. For example, after attending a time management training program, participants estimated that each saves an average of 74 minutes per day, worth $31.25 per day or $7500 per year (Stamp, 1992). This time savings was based on the average salary plus benefits for the typical participant.

The average wage with a percent added for employee benefits will suffice for most calculations. However, employee time may be worth more. For example, additional costs in maintaining an employee (office space, furniture, telephone, utilities, computers, secretarial support, and other overhead expenses) could be included in the average labor cost. Thus, the average wage rate may quickly escalate to a large number. However, the conservative approach is to use the salary plus employee benefits.

In addition to the labor cost per hour, other benefits can result from a time savings. These include improved service, avoidance of penalties for late projects, and the creation of additional opportunities for profit. These values can be estimated using other methods discussed in this chapter.

A word of caution is in order when the time savings are developed. Time savings is only realized when the amount of time saved translates into a additional contribution. If a training program results in a savings in manager time, a monetary value is realized only if the manager used the additional time in a productive way. If a team-based program generates a new process that eliminates several hours of work each day, the actual savings will be realized only if there is a cost savings from a reduction in employees, a reduction in overtime pay, or increased productivity. Therefore, an important preliminary step in developing time savings is to determine if a "true" savings will be realized (Harbour, 1996).

USING HISTORICAL COSTS

Sometimes historical records contain the value of a measure and reflect the cost (or value) of a unit of improvement. This strategy involves identifying the appropriate records and tabulating the actual cost components for the item in question. For example, a large construction firm implemented a training program to improve safety performance. The program improved several safety-related performance measures, ranging from OSHA fines to total worker compensation costs. Examining the company's records using one year of data, the HRD staff calculated the average cost for each safety measure.

In another example, a large city had implemented an absenteeism reduction program for its city bus drivers. The HR vice president was interested in showing the return on investment for the program (Phillips and Stone, 2002). To show the impact of the absenteeism reduction, the cost of one absence was needed. As part of the study, the external consulting firm developed a detailed cost of an absence, considering the full costs of a driver pool maintained to cover an unexpected absence. All of the costs were calculated in a fully loaded profile to present the cost of an absence. As this impact study revealed, the time to develop historical costs is sometimes expensive, leaving the researchers often looking for an easier way. Consequently, using historical cost data may not be the technique of choice because of the time and effort involved. In those situations, one or more of the techniques listed in the remainder of the chapter should be used.

Using Internal and External Experts' Input

When faced with converting soft data items for which historical records are not available, it might be feasible to consider input from experts on the processes. With this approach, internal experts provide the cost (or value) of one unit of improvement. Those individuals who have knowledge of the situation and the respect of the management group are often the best prospects for expert input. These experts must understand the processes and be willing to provide estimates as well as the assumptions used in arriving at the estimate. When requesting input from experts, it is best to explain the full scope of what is needed, providing as many specifics as possible. Most experts have their own methodology to develop this value.

An example will help clarify this approach. In one manufacturing plant, a team building program was designed to reduce the number of grievances filed at Step 2 (see Table 5-3). This is the step in which the grievance is recorded in writing and becomes a measurable soft data item. Except for the actual cost of settlements and direct external costs, the company had no records of the total costs of grievances (i.e., there were no data for the time required to resolve a grievance). Therefore, an estimate was needed from an expert. The manager of labor relations, who had credibility with senior management and thorough knowledge of the grievance process, provided an estimate of the cost. He based his estimate on the average settlement when a grievance was lost, the direct costs related to the grievances (arbitration, legal fees, printing, research), the estimated amount of supervisory, staff, and employee time associated with the grievance, and a factor for reduced morale and other "soft" consequences. This internal estimate, although not a precise figure, was appropriate for this analysis and had adequate credibility with management.

When internal experts are not available, external experts are sought. External experts must be selected based on their experience with the unit of measure. Fortunately, many experts are available who work directly with important measures such as creativity, innovation, employee attitudes, customer satisfaction, employee turnover, absenteeism, and grievances. They are often willing to provide estimates of the cost (or value) of these items. Because the credibility of the value is directly related to his or her reputation, the credibility and reputation of the expert are critical.

Sometimes one or more techniques may be used in a complementary way to develop the costs. Consider, for example, the process for developing the cost of a sexual harassment complaint (Phillips and Hill, 2001). In this case study, the cost of a formal complaint filed with the vice president of Human Resources was developed. For this analysis, the assumption was made that if no complaints were filed, there would be no costs of sexual harassment communication, investigation, and defense. Consequently, two approaches were used to arrive at the cost of a complaint. First, the direct cost was captured for an entire year of all activities and processes connected with sexual harassment. This figure was taken directly from the cost statements. Second, the other cost values were estimated (e.g., time of the staff and management involved in these activities), using input from internal experts, the EEOC, and affirmative action staff. Figure 5-1 shows how these two values were combined to

Figure 5-1. Calculating the cost of a sexual harassment complaint.

yield a total value of $852,000 for 35 complaints, which yielded an approximate value of $24,000 for a complaint.

USING VALUES FROM EXTERNAL DATABASES

For some soft data items, it may be appropriate to use estimates of the cost (or value) of one unit based on the research of others. This technique taps external databases that contain studies and research projects focusing on the cost of data items. Fortunately, many databases are available that report cost studies of a variety of data items related to training programs. Data are available on the cost of turnover, absenteeism, grievances, accidents, and even customer satisfaction. The difficulty lies in finding a database with studies or research efforts for a situation similar to the program under evaluation. Ideally, the data would come from a similar setting in the same industry, but that is not always possible. Sometimes data on all industries or organizations would be sufficient, perhaps with an adjustment to fit the industry under consideration.

An example illustrates the use of this process. A new program was designed to reduce turnover of branch employees in a regional banking group (Phillips and Phillips, 2002). To complete the evaluation and calculate the ROI, the cost of turnover was needed. To develop the turnover value internally, several costs would have to be identified, including the cost of recruiting, employment processing, orientation, training new employees, lost productivity while a new employee is trained, quality problems, scheduling difficulties, and customer satisfaction problems. Additional costs include regional manager time to work with the turnover issues and, in some cases, exit costs of litigation, severance, and unemployment. Obviously, these costs are significant. Most HRD managers do not have the time to calculate the cost of turnover, particularly when it is needed for a one-time event such as evaluating a training program. In this example, turnover cost studies in the same industry placed the value at about 1.1 to 1.25 times the average annual salaries of the employees. Most turnover cost studies report the cost of turnover as a multiple of annual base salaries. In this example, management decided to be conservation and adjusted the value downward to .9 of the average base salary of the employees.

USING ESTIMATES FROM PARTICIPANTS

In some situations, program participants estimate the value of a soft data improvement. This technique is appropriate when participants are capable of providing estimates of the cost (or value) of the unit of measure improved by applying the skills learned in the program. When using this approach, participants should be provided with clear instructions, along with examples of the type of information needed. The advantage of this approach is that the individuals closest to the improvement are often capable of providing the most reliable estimates of its value.

An example illustrates this process. A group of supervisors attended an interpersonal skills training program, "Improving Work Habits," which was designed to lower the absenteeism rate of the employees in their work units. Successful application of the training program should result in a reduction in absenteeism. To calculate the ROI for the program, it was necessary to determine the average value of one absence in the company. As is the case with most organizations, historical records for the cost of absenteeism were not available. Experts were not available, and external studies were sparse for this particular industry. Consequently, supervisors (program participants) were asked to estimate the cost of an absence.

In a group-interview format, each participant was asked to recall the last time an employee in his or her work group was unexpectedly absent, and describe what was necessary to compensate for the absence. Because the impact of an absence will vary considerably from one employee to another within the same work unit, the group listened to all explanations. After reflecting on what must be done when an employee is absent, each supervisor was asked to provide an estimate of the average cost of an absence in the company. Although some supervisors are reluctant to provide estimates, with prodding and encouragement they will usually provide a value. The values are averaged for the group, and the result is the cost of an absence to be used in evaluating the program. Although this is an estimate, it is probably more accurate than data from external studies, calculations using internal records, or estimates from experts. And because it comes from supervisors who deal with the issue daily, it will usually have credibility with senior management.

USING ESTIMATES FROM SUPERVISORS AND MANAGERS

In some situations, participants may be incapable of placing a value on the improvement. Their work may be so far removed from the output of the process that they cannot reliably provide estimates. In these cases, the team leaders, supervisors, or managers of participants may be capable of providing estimates. Consequently, they may be asked to provide a value for a unit of improvement linked to the program. For example, a training program for customer service representatives was designed to reduce customer complaints. Applying the skills and knowledge learned from the program resulted in a reduction in complaints, but the value of a single customer complaint was needed to determine the value of improvement. Although customer service representatives had knowledge of some issues surrounding customer complaints, they were not well versed in the full impact, so their supervisors were asked to provide a value.

In other situations, supervisors are asked to review and approve participants' estimates. After the program is completed, participants estimated the value of their improvements that were directly related to their participation in the program. Their immediate managers are then asked to review the estimates and the process used by the participants to arrive at the estimates. Supervisors could confirm, adjust, or discard the values provided by the participants.

In some situations senior management provides estimates of the value of data. With this approach, senior managers interested in the process or program are asked to place a value on the improvement based on their perception of its worth. This approach is used in situations in which it is very difficult to calculate the value or other sources of estimation are unavailable or unreliable. An example will illustrate this strategy. A hospital chain was attempting to improve customer satisfaction with a training program for all employees. The program was designed to improve customer service, and thus improve the external customer satisfaction index. To determine the value of the program, a value for a unit of improvement (one point on the index) was needed. Because senior management was very interested in improving the index, they were asked to provide input on the value of one unit. In a regular executive staff meeting, each senior manager and hospital administrator was asked to describe what it means for a hospital when the index increases. After some discussion, each individual was asked to provide an estimate of the monetary value gained when the index moves one point. Although initially reluctant to provide the information, with some encouragement, monetary values were provided, totaled, and averaged. The result was an estimate of the worth of one unit of improvement, which was used as a basis of calculating the benefit of the program. Although this process is subjective, it does have the benefit of ownership from senior executives, the same executives who approved the program budget.

LINKING WITH OTHER MEASURES

When standard values, records, experts, and external studies are unavailable, a feasible approach might be developing a relationship between the measure in question and some other measure that may be easily converted to a monetary value. This approach involves identifying, if possible, existing relationships showing a strong correlation between one measure and another with a standard value.

For example, the classical relationship depicted in Figure 5-2 shows a correlation between job satisfaction and employee turnover. In a consulting project designed to improve job satisfaction, a value is needed for changes in the job satisfaction index. A predetermined relationship showing the correlation between improvements in job satisfaction and reductions in turnover can link the changes directly to turnover. Using standard data or external studies, the cost of turnover can easily be developed as described earlier. Thus, a change in job satisfaction is converted to a monetary value, or at least an approximate value. It is not always exact because of the potential for error and other factors, but the estimate is sufficient for converting the data to monetary values.

In some situations, a chain of relationships may be established to show the connection between two or more variables. In this approach, a measure that may be difficult to convert to a monetary value is linked to other measures that, in turn, are linked to measures on which a value can be placed. Ultimately these measures are traced to a monetary value

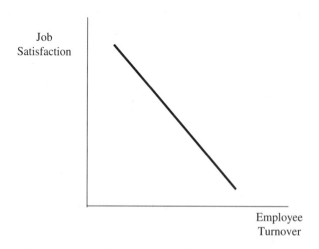

Figure 5-2. Relationship between employee satisfaction and turnover.

that is often based on profits. Figure 5-3 shows the model used by Sears, one of the world's largest retail store chains (Ulrich, 1998). The model connects job attitudes (collected directly from the employees) with customer service, which is directly related to revenue growth. The rectangles in the chart represent survey information, while the ovals represent hard data. The shaded measurements are collected and distributed in the form of Sears total performance indicators.

As the model in Figure 5-3 shows, a 5-point improvement in employee attitudes will drive a 1.3-point improvement in customer satisfaction. This, in turn, drives a 0.5% increase in revenue growth. Thus, if employee attitudes at a local store improved by 5 points, and previous revenue growth was 5%, the new revenue growth would be 5.5%. These links between measures, often called the *service-profit chain*, create a promising way to place monetary values on hard-to-quantify measures.

USING HRD STAFF ESTIMATES

The final technique for converting data to monetary values is to use HRD staff estimates. Using all the available information and experience, the staff members most familiar with the situation provide estimates of the

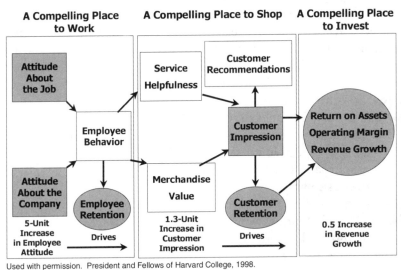

Used with permission. President and Fellows of Harvard College, 1998.

Figure 5-3. Linkage of job satisfaction and revenue.

value. For example, an international oil company created a dispatcher training program designed to reduce dispatcher absenteeism, along with other performance measure problems. The HRD staff estimated the cost of an absence to be $200 (Payne, 1994). This value was then used in calculating the savings for the reduction of absenteeism following training for the dispatchers. Although the staff may be capable of providing accurate estimates, this approach may be perceived as being biased, since the HRD staff wanted it to be large (a motive). It should be used only when other approaches are not available.

SELECTING THE APPROPRIATE MEASURES

With so many techniques available, the challenge is to select one or more techniques appropriate to the situation. The following guidelines can help determine the proper selection.

Use the technique appropriate for the type of data. Some techniques are designed specifically for hard data, while others are more appropriate for soft data. Consequently, the actual type of data will often dictate the technique. Hard data, while always preferred, are not always available. Soft data are often required, and thus must be addressed with the techniques appropriate for soft data.

Move from most accurate to least accurate techniques. The ten techniques are presented in order of accuracy and credibility, beginning with the most credible. Standard, accepted values are most credible; HRD staff estimates are least credible. Working down the list, each technique should be considered for its feasibility in the situation. The technique with the most accuracy and credibility is recommended.

Consider availability and convenience when selecting the technique. Sometimes the availability of a particular source of data will drive the selection. In other situations, the convenience of a technique may be an important factor in its selection.

When estimates are sought, use the source who has the broadest and most credible perspective on the issue. To improve the accuracy of an estimate, the broadest perspective on the issue is needed. The individual providing an estimate must be knowledgeable of all the processes and the issues surrounding the value of the data item.

Use multiple techniques when feasible. Sometimes it is helpful to have more than one techniques for obtaining a value for the data. When multiple sources are available, more than one source should be used to serve as a comparison or to provide another perspective. When multiple sources are used, the data must be integrated using a convenient decision rule such as the lowest value, a preferred approach because of the conservative nature of the lowest value.

This leads to a guiding principle:

Guiding Principle #4
When analyzing data, choose the most conservative
among alternatives.

By most conservative, it is the approach that yields the lowest ROI. Thus, if the benefits are in consideration (numerator), it is the lowest value that yields that lowest ROI.

Minimize the amount of time required to select and implement the appropriate technique. As with other processes, it is important to keep the time invested as low as possible, so that the total time and effort for the ROI does not become excessive. Some strategies can be implemented with less time than others. This block in the ROI model can quickly absorb more time than the remainder of all the steps. Too much time at this step can dampen an otherwise enthusiastic attitude about the process.

ACCURACY AND CREDIBILITY OF DATA

The Credibility Problem

The techniques presented in this chapter assume that each data item collected and linked with training can be converted to a monetary value. Although estimates can be developed using one or more of these techniques, the process of converting data to monetary values may lose credibility with the target audience, who may doubt its use in analysis. Very subjective data, such as a change in employee morale or a reduction in the number of employee conflicts, are difficult to convert to monetary values. The key question for this determination is this: "Could these results be presented to senior management with confidence?" If the process does not meet this credibility test, the data should not be converted to monetary values and instead listed as an intangible benefit. Other data, particularly hard data items, could be used in the ROI calculation, leaving the very subjective data as intangible improvements.

When converting data to monetary value, it is important to be consistent in the approach. Specific rules for making conversions will ensure this consistency and, ultimately, enhance the reliability of the study. When it is questionable if a data item should be converted, a four-part test is suggested starting with the question "Is there a standard value?" If the answer is yes, it is used; if not, the next part of the test is considered. The next question "Is there a method available to convert data to monetary value?" If this answer is no, the item is listed as an intangible. If it can be converted using one of the methods in this chapter the next step is considered. The next question is, "Can the conversion be accomplished with minimum resources?" If the answer is no, the item should be considered an intangible; if yes, the final step is considered. The last question is, "Can the conversion process be described to an executive audience and obtain their buy-in in two minutes?" If yes, the value can be placed in the ROI calculation; if no, it is listed as an intangible. These guidelines are very critical in converting data consistently. The four-part test is also described in Table 8-4 in Chapter 8, *Identifying Intangible Measures*. The important point is to be consistent and methodical when converting data.

The accuracy of data and the credibility of the conversion process are important concerns. HRD professionals sometimes avoid converting data because of these issues. They are more comfortable in reporting that a training program resulted in reducing absenteeism from 6 to 4% without attempting to place a value on the improvement. They assume that each person receiving the information will place a value on the absenteeism reduction. Unfortunately, the target audience may know little about the cost of absenteeism and will usually underestimate the actual value of the improvement. Consequently, there should be some attempt to include this conversion in the ROI analysis.

How the Credibility of Data Is Influenced

When ROI data is presented to selected target audiences, its credibility will be an issue. The degree to which the target audience will believe the data will be influenced by the following factors.

Reputation of the source of data. The actual source of the data represents the first credibility issue. How credible is the individual or groups providing the data? Do they understand the issues? Are they knowledgeable of all the processes? The target audience will often place more credibility on data obtained from those who are closest to the source of the actual improvement or change.

Reputation of the source of the study. The target audience scrutinizes the reputation of the individual, group, or organization presenting the data. Do they have a history of providing accurate reports? Are they unbiased with their analyses? Are they fair in their presentation? Answers to these and other questions will form an impression about the reputation.

Audience bias. The audience may have a bias—either positive or negative—to a particular study or the data presented from the study. Some executives have a positive feeling about a particular program and will need less data to convince them of its value. Other executives may have a negative bias toward the program and will need more data to make this comparison. The potential bias of the audience should be understood so that the data can be presented to counter any attitude.

Motives of the evaluators. The audience will look for motives of the person(s) conducting the study. Do the individuals presenting the data have an axe to grind? Do they have a personal interest in creating a favorable or unfavorable result? Are the stakes high if the study is unfavorable? These and other issues will cause the target audience to examine the motives of those who have conducted the study.

Methodology of the study. The audience will want to know specifically how the research was conducted. How were the calculations made? What steps were followed? What processes were used? A lack of information on the methodology will cause the audience to become wary and suspicious of the results. They will substitute their own perception of the methodology.

Assumptions made in the analysis. The audience will try to understand the assumptions made in the analysis. What are the assumptions in the study? Are they standard? How do they compare with other assumptions in other studies? When assumptions are omitted, the audience will substitute their own, often unfavorable assumptions. In ROI studies, conservative guiding principles influence calculations and conclusions.

Realism of the outcome data. Impressive ROI values could cause problems. When outcomes appear to be unrealistic, it may be difficult for the target audience to believe them. Huge claims often fall on deaf ears, causing reports to be thrown away before they are reviewed.

Types of data. The target audience will usually have a preference for hard data. They are seeking business performance data tied to output, quality, costs, and time. These measures are usually easily understood and closely related to organizational performance. Conversely, soft data are sometimes viewed suspiciously from the outset, as many senior executives are concerned about its soft nature and limitations of the data on the analysis.

Scope of analysis. The smaller the scope, the more credible the data. Is the scope of the analysis narrow? Does it involve just one group or all of the employees in the organization? Limiting the study to a small group, or series of groups, of employees makes the process more accurate and believable.

Collectively, these factors will influence the credibility of an ROI impact study and provide a framework from which to develop the ROI report. Thus, when considering each of the issues, the following key points are suggested for developing an ROI impact study and presenting it to the management group:

- ☐ Use the most credible and reliable source for estimates.
- ☐ Present the material in an unbiased, objective way.
- ☐ Be prepared for the potential bias of the audience.
- ☐ Fully explain the methodology used throughout the process, preferably on a step-by-step basis.
- ☐ Define the assumptions made in the analysis, and compare them to assumptions made in other similar studies.
- ☐ Consider factoring or adjusting output values when they appear to be unrealistic.
- ☐ Use hard data whenever possible and combine with soft data if available.
- ☐ Keep the scope of the analysis very narrow. Conduct the impact with one or more groups of participants in the program, instead of all participants or all employees.

Making Adjustments

Two potential adjustments should be considered before finalizing the monetary value. In some organizations where soft data are used and values are derived with imprecise methods, senior management is sometimes offered the opportunity to review and approve the data. Because of the subjective nature of this process, management may factor (reduce) the data so that the final results are more credible.

The other adjustment concerns the time value of money. Since an investment in a program is made at one time period and the return is realized in a later time period, a few organizations adjust the program benefits to reflect the time value of money, using discounted cash flow techniques. The actual monetary benefits of the program are adjusted for this time period. The amount of this adjustment, however, is usually small compared with the typical benefits realized from training and performance improvement programs.

FINAL THOUGHTS

In conclusion, organizations are attempting to be more aggressive when defining the monetary benefits of training and development. Progressive HRD managers are no longer satisfied with reporting business performance results from training. Instead, they are taking additional steps to convert business results data to monetary values and compare them with the program's cost to develop the ultimate level of evaluation, the return on investment. This chapter presented ten specific techniques to convert business results to monetary values, offering an array of possibilities to fit any situation and program.

CASE STUDY—PART D, LINEAR NETWORK SYSTEMS

Isolating the Effects of Training

In discussions with management and participants in the training program, two factors were identified which could have an influence on each of the business performance measures, in addition to the training program. First, the implementation of the total quality management program placed emphasis on improving all three measures in this case. Quality was defined in a broad sense, including being at work (absenteeism), remaining with the company (turnover), and ensuring that customer shipments were on time (productivity).

The second factor was the various team-building activities that were initiated as LNS attempted to move to a team-based structure. First level managers were encouraged to use employee input, conduct meetings with employees, and to take action to improve productivity. If successful, team building should increase productivity and reduce turnover and absenteeism.

Because it was important to determine the precise impact of the training program, it was necessary to isolate the effects of training from the other two factors. One of the most effective approaches is the use of a control group arrangement in which one group receives training and another similarly situated group does not receive training. LNS explored the control group arrangement in this setting. Initially it appeared to be an excellent opportunity to use this plant location as a pilot group and select another similar plant as a control group. However, no other plant had the same product line, same type of processes, same workforce characteristics, and same environmental conditions, all important variables to reflect performance. Thus, the control group arrangement was not considered a feasible approach.

The approach utilized to isolate the effects of training was participants' estimates. Participants would be asked to indicate how much of their improvement was linked directly to their training. Participants provided the information in a portion of the action plan. Each participant is presented with a six-month average of the data prior to training to compare with posttraining data. After training, managers regularly receive reports for each of the items as part of their operating data.

Converting Data to Monetary Values

The next task in setting up the ROI process is to select the technique to convert data to monetary values. The challenge facing the evaluation team is to determine the most credible and accurate techniques for placing values on each of the Business Impact (Level 4) data items.

Discussion Questions

1. What is the most appropriate technique to assign a value to productivity?
2. What is the most logical way to convert employee turnover to a monetary value?
3. What is the most appropriate method to place a monetary value on an absence?
4. For other potential improvement measures, what range of potential techniques can be used to convert data to monetary values?

REFERENCES

Boulton, R.E.S., B.D. Libert, and S.M. Samek. *Cracking the Value Code: How Successful Businesses Are Creating Wealth in the New Economy.* New York, NY: HarperBusiness, 2000.

Campanella, Jack (Ed.). *Principles of Quality Costs,* 3rd ed. Milwaukee, WI: American Society for Quality, 1999.

Harbour, J.L. *Cycle Time Reduction: Designing and Streamlining Work for High Performance.* New York, NY: Quality Resources, 1996.

Johnson, M.D., and A. Gustafsson. *Improving Customer Satisfaction, Loyalty, and Profit: An Integrated Measurement and Management System.* San Francisco, CA: Jossey-Bass, 2000.

Payne, R. "Improving Customer Service Skills," *In Action: Measuring Return on Investment,* vol. 1. J.J. Phillips (Ed.). Alexandria, VA: American Society for Training and Development, 1994, pp. 169–186.

Phillips, J.J. *The Consultant's Scorecard: Tracking Results and Bottom-Line Impact of Consulting Projects.* New York, NY: McGraw-Hill, 2000.

Phillips, J.J., and D. Hill. "Sexual Harassment Prevention," *The Human Resources Scorecard: Measuring the Return on Investment.* Boston, MA: Butterworth–Heinemann, 2001, pp. 354–372.

Phillips, J.J., and R.D. Stone. "Absenteeism Reduction Program," *In Action: Measuring ROI in the Public Sector.* Alexandria, VA: American Society for Training and Development, 2002, pp. 221–234.

Phillips, P.P. "Executive Leadership Development," *The Human Resources Scorecard: Measuring the Return on Investment.* Boston, MA: Butterworth–Heinemann, 2001, pp. 449–476.

Phillips, P.P., and J.J. Phillips. "A Strategic Approach to Retention Improvement," *In Action: Retaining Your Best Employees,* P.P. Phillips (Ed.). Alexandria, VA: American Society for Training and Development, 2002.

Stamp, D. *The Workplace of the 21st Century.* Bellevue, WA: Priority Management Systems, 1992.

Ulrich, D. (Ed.). *Delivering Results.* Boston, MA: Harvard Business School, 1998.

Further Reading

Barsky, J. *Finding the Profit in Customer Satisfaction: Translating Best Practices into Bottom-Line Results.* New York, NY: Contemporary Books, 1999.

Daffy, C. *Once a Customer Always a Customer: How to Deliver Customer Service that Creates Customers for Life.* Dublin, Ireland: Oak Tree Press, 1999.

Donovan, J., R. Tully, and B. Wortman. *The Value Enterprise: Strategies for Building a Value-Based Organization.* Toronto, Canada: McGraw-Hill Ryerson, 1998.

Greenberg, P. CRM at the Speed of Light: Capturing and Keeping Customers in Internet Real Time. Berkeley, CA: Osborne/McGraw-Hill, 2001.

Harry, M., and R. Schroeder. Six Sigma: The Breakthrough Management Strategy Revolutionizing the World's Top Corporations. New York, NY: Currency, 2000.

Heskett, J.L., E. Sasser, Jr., and L.A. Schlesinger. (1997). The Service Profit Chain. New York, NY: The Free Press.

Jones, S. (Ed.). Doing Internet Research. Thousand Oaks, CA: Sage Publications, 1999.

MacGregor Serven, L.B. Value Planning: The New Approach to Building Value Every Day. New York, NY: John Wiley & Sons, Inc., 1998.

McCarthy, D.G. The Loyalty Link: How Loyal Employees Create Loyal Customers. New York, NY: John Wiley & Sons, Inc., 1997.

Niven, P.R. Balanced Scorecard Step-by-Step: Maximizing Performance and Maintaining Results. New York, NY: John Wiley & Sons, Inc., 2002.

Pande, P.S., R.P. Neuman, and R.R. Cavanagh. The Six Sigma Way: How GE, Motorola, and Other Top Companies Are Honing Their Performance. New York, NY: McGraw-Hill, 2000.

Phillips, J.J. The Consultant's Scorecard: Tracking Results and Bottom-Line Impact of Consulting Projects. New York, NY: McGraw-Hill, 2000.

Phillips, P.P. The Human Resources Scorecard: Measuring the Return on Investment. Boston. MA: Butterworth–Heinemann, 2001.

Vavra, T.G. Customer Satisfaction Measurement Simplified: A Step-by-Step Guide for ISO 9001:2000 Certification. Milwaukee, WI: ASQ Quality Press, 2000.

CHAPTER 6

Tabulating Program Costs

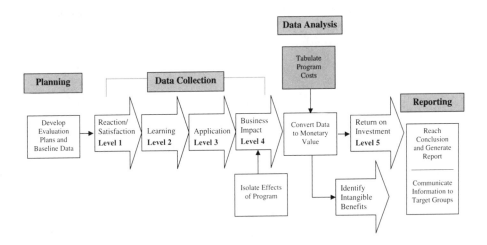

The cost of providing training and performance improvement is increasing—creating more pressure for HRD managers to know how and why money is spent. The total cost of training is required, which means that the cost profile goes beyond the direct costs and includes all indirect costs. Fully loaded cost information is used to manage resources, develop standards, measure efficiencies, and examine alternative delivery processes.

Tabulating program costs is an essential step in developing the ROI calculation, and these costs are used as the denominator in the ROI formula. It is just as important to focus on costs as it is on benefits. In practice, however, costs are often more easily captured than benefits. This chapter explores the costs accumulation and tabulation steps, outlining the specific costs that should be captured, and presents economical ways in which costs can be developed.

COST STRATEGIES

Importance of Costs

Many influences have caused the increased attention now given to monitoring training costs accurately and thoroughly. Every organization should know approximately how much money it spends on training and development. Many organizations calculate this expenditure and make comparisons with that of other organizations, although comparisons are difficult to make because of the different bases for cost calculations. Some organizations calculate training and development (T&D) costs as a percentage of payroll costs and set targets for increased investment. In the United States, the average is about 2%, whereas in Europe it is 3.0%, in Asia 3.8%, and in Latin America it is 3.8% (Marquardt, King, and Koon, 2001).

An effective system of cost monitoring enables an organization to calculate the magnitude of total training expenditures. Collecting this information also helps top management answer two important questions:

1. How much do we spend on training compared with other organizations?
2. How much should we spend on training?

The training and development staff should know the relative cost effectiveness of programs and their components. Monitoring costs by program allows the staff to evaluate the relative contribution of a program and to determine how those costs are changing. If a program's cost rises, it might be appropriate to reevaluate the program's impact and overall success. It may be useful to compare specific components of costs with those of other programs or organizations. For example, the cost per participant for one program could be compared with the cost per participant for a similar program. Huge differences may signal a problem. Also, costs associated with design, development, or delivery could be compared with those of other programs within the organization and used to develop cost standards.

Accurate costs are necessary to predict future costs. Historical costs for a program provide the basis for predicting future costs of a similar program or budgeting for a program. Sophisticated cost models make it possible to estimate or predict costs with reasonable accuracy.

When a return on investment or cost benefit analysis is needed for a specific program, costs must be developed. One of the most significant reasons for collecting costs is to obtain data for use in a benefits-versus-costs comparison. In this comparison, cost data are equally important as the program's economic benefits.

To improve the efficiency of the training and development function, controlling costs is necessary. Competitive pressures place increased attention on efficiencies. Most training and development departments have monthly budgets with cost projections listed by various accounts and, in some cases, by program. Cost monitoring is an excellent tool for identifying problem areas and taking corrective action. In the practical and classical management sense, the accumulation of cost data is a necessity.

Capturing costs is challenging because the figures must be accurate, reliable, and realistic. Although most organizations develop costs with much more ease than developing the economic value of benefits, the true cost of training is often an elusive figure even in some of the best organizations. While the total HRD direct budget is usually a number that is easily developed, it is more difficult to determine the specific costs of a program, including the indirect costs related to it. To develop a realistic ROI, costs must be accurate and credible. Otherwise, the painstaking difficulty and attention to the benefits will be wasted because of inadequate or inaccurate costs.

Pressure to Disclose All Costs

Today there is increased pressure to report all training costs, or what is referred to as fully-loaded costs. This takes the cost profile beyond the direct cost of training and includes the time that participants are involved in training, including their benefits and other overhead. For years, management has realized that there are many indirect costs of training. Now they are asking for an accounting of these costs. Perhaps this point is best illustrated in a situation that recently developed in state government. The management controls of a large state agency were being audited by a state auditor. A portion of the audit focused on training costs. The following comments are taken from the auditor's report.

Costs tracked at the program level focus on direct or "hard" costs and largely ignore the cost of time spent participating in or supporting training. The costs of participant time to prepare for and attend training are not tracked. For one series of programs, including such costs raised the total training cost dramatically. The agency stated that the total two-year cost for the specific program was about $600,000. This figure generally includes only direct costs and, as such, is substantially below the costs of the time spent by staff in preparing for and attending the program. When accounting for prework and attendance, the figure comes to a total of $1.39 million. If the statewide average of 45.5% for fringe benefits is considered, the total indirect cost of staff time to prepare for and attend the program becomes $2 million. Finally, if the agency's direct costs of $600,000 are added to the $2 million total indirect cost just noted, the total becomes over $2.6 million. Among other factors that would drive actual total costs higher still are:

☐ cost of travel, meals, and lodging for training participants;
☐ allocated salaries and fringes of staff providing administrative and logistic support; and
☐ opportunity costs of productivity lost by staff in doing prework and attending training.

Failure to consider all indirect or "soft" costs may expose the agency to noncompliance with the Fair Labor Standards Act (FLSA), particularly as training spreads through rank-and-file staff. Since FLSA requires that such staff be directly compensated for overtime, it is no longer appropriate for the agency to ask employees to complete training prework on their own time. Continuing to handle such overtime work this way may also encourage false overtime reporting, skew overtime data, and/or increase the amount of uncompensated overtime.

Numerous barriers exist to hamper agency efforts in determining "How much does training cost?"

☐ Cost systems tend to hide administrative, support, internal, and other indirect or "soft" costs.
☐ Costs generally are monitored at the division level rather than at the level of individual programs or activities.
☐ Cost information required by activity-based cost systems is not being generated.

As this case vividly demonstrates, the cost of training is much more than direct expenditure, and the training and development departments are expected to report fully loaded costs in their reports.

Fully Loaded Costs

The conservative approach to calculating the ROI has a direct connection to cost accumulation. A guiding principle focuses directly on this issue.

Guiding Principle #10
Project/program costs should be fully loaded for ROI analysis.

With this approach, all costs that can be identified and linked to a particular program are included. The philosophy is simple: When in doubt in the denominator, put it in (i.e., if it is questionable whether a cost should be included, it is recommended that it be included, even if the cost guidelines for the organization do not require it). This parallels a rule for the numerator, which states, "when in doubt, leave it out" (i.e., if it is questionable whether a benefit should be included in the numerator, it should be omitted from the analysis). When an ROI is calculated and reported to target audiences the process should withstand even the closest scrutiny in terms of its accuracy and credibility. The only way to meet this test is to ensure that all costs are included. Of course, from a realistic viewpoint, if the controller or chief financial officer insists on not using certain costs, then it is best to leave them out.

The Danger of Costs without Benefits

It is dangerous to communicate the costs of training without presenting benefits. Unfortunately, many organizations have fallen into this trap for years. Costs are presented to management in all types of ingenious ways such as cost of the program, cost per employee, and cost per development hour. While these may be helpful for efficiency comparisons, it may be troublesome to present them without benefits. When most executives review training costs, a logical question comes to mind: What benefit was received from the program? This is a typical management reaction, particularly when costs are perceived to be high. Because of this, some organizations have developed a policy of not communicating training cost data for a specific program unless the benefits can be captured and presented along with the costs. Even if the benefit data are subjective and intangible, they are included with the cost data. This helps to keep a balance with the two issues.

Policies and Guidelines

For some organizations, it may be helpful to detail the philosophy and policy on costs in guidelines for the HRD staff or others who monitor and report costs. Cost guidelines detail specifically what costs are included with training and how cost data are captured, analyzed, and reported. Cost guidelines can range from a one-page document to a fifty-page manual in a large, complex organization. The simpler approach is better. When fully developed, they should be reviewed by the finance and accounting staff. The final document serves as the guiding force in collecting, monitoring, and reporting costs. When an ROI is calculated and reported, costs are included in a summary form and the cost guidelines are referenced in a footnote or attached as an appendix.

Cost Tracking Issues

Sources of Costs

It can be helpful to first consider the sources of training and performance improvement cost. There are three major categories of sources, as illustrated in Table 6-1. The HRD staff expenses usually represent the

Table 6-1. Sources of Costs

Source of Costs	Cost Reporting Issues
1. HRD Staff expenses	A. Costs are usually accurate. B. Variable expenses may be underestimated.
2. Participant expenses (direct and indirect)	A. Direct expenses are usually not fully loaded. B. Indirect expenses are rarely included in costs.
3. External expenses (equipment and services)	A. Sometimes understated. B. May lack accountability.

greatest segment of costs and are sometimes transferred directly to the client or program sponsor. The second major cost category consists of participant expenses, both direct and indirect. These costs are not identified in many training and performance improvement projects, but, nevertheless, reflect a significant amount. The third cost source is the payments made to external organizations. These include payments directly to hotels and conference centers, equipment suppliers, and services prescribed in the project. As Table 6-1 shows, some of these cost categories are understated. The finance and accounting records should be able to track and reflect the costs from these three different sources. The process presented in this chapter has the capability of tracking these costs, as well.

Training Process Steps and Cost

Another important way to consider training and performance improvement costs is in the characteristics of how the project unfolds. Figure 6-1 shows the typical training and development cycle, beginning with the initial analysis and assessment, and progressing to the evaluation and reporting of the results. These functional process steps represent the typical flow of work. As a performance problem is addressed, a solution is developed or acquired and implemented in the organization. Implementation is often grouped with delivery. The entire process is routinely reported to the client or sponsor and evaluation is undertaken to show the project's success. There is also a group of costs to support the process—administrative support and overhead costs. To fully understand costs, the project should be analyzed in these different categories, as described later in this chapter.

Prorated versus Direct Costs

Usually all costs related to a program are captured and expensed to that program. However, three categories are usually prorated over several sessions of the same program. Needs assessment, design and development, and acquisition are all significant costs that should be prorated over the shelf life of the program. Using a conservative approach, the shelf life of the program should be very short. Some organizations will consider one year of operation for the program, others may consider two or three years. If there is some dispute about the specific time period to be used in the proration formula, the shorter period should be used. If possible, the finance and accounting staff should be consulted.

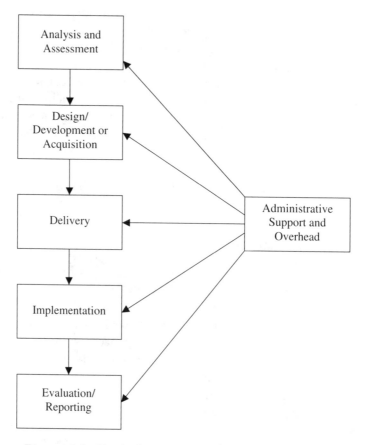

Figure 6-1. Typical training and development cycle.

A brief example will illustrate proration for development costs. In a large technology company, an e-learning program was developed at a cost of $98,000. Developers anticipated that the program would have a three-year life cycle before it would have to be updated. The revision costs at the end of the three years were estimated to be about one-half of the original development costs, or $49,000. It was estimated that 400 participants would take the program in a three-year period with an ROI calculation planned for 20 participants. Since the program will have one-half of its residual value at the end of three years, one-half of the cost should be written off for this three-year period. Thus, the $49,000, representing half of the development costs, would be spread over the 400 participants as a prorated development cost or $122.50 per participant.

Thus, an ROI for 20 participants would have a development cost of $2450 included in the cost profile.

Employee Benefits Factor

When presenting salaries for participants and HRD staff associated with programs, the benefits factor should be included. This number is usually well known in the organization and is used in other cost applications. It represents the cost of all employee benefits expressed as a percent of base salaries. In some organizations this value is as high as 50–60%. In others, it may be as low as 25–30%. The average in the United States is approximately 38% (*Nation's Business*, 2002).

MAJOR COST CATEGORIES

The most important task is to define which specific costs are included in a tabulation of the program costs. This task involves decisions that will be made by the HRD staff and usually approved by management. If appropriate, the finance and accounting staff may need to approve the list. Table 6-2 shows the recommended cost categories for a fully loaded,

Table 6-2. Training Program Cost Categories

Cost Item	Prorated	Expensed
Needs Assessment and Analysis	✓	
Design and Development	✓	
Acquisition	✓	
Delivery/Implementation		✓
☐ Salaries/Benefits—Facilitators		✓
☐ Salaries/Benefits—Coordination		✓
☐ Program Materials and Fees		✓
☐ Travel/Lodging/Meals		✓
☐ Facilities		✓
☐ Participants Salaries/Benefits		✓
Contact Time		✓
Travel Time		✓
Preparation Time		✓
Evaluation	✓	
Overhead/Training and Development	✓	

conservative approach to estimating costs. Each category is described below.

Needs Assessment and Analysis

One of the most often overlooked items is the cost of conducting a needs assessment. In some programs this cost is zero because the program is conducted without a needs assessment. However, as more organizations focus increased attention on needs assessment, this item will become a more significant cost in the future. All costs associated with the needs assessment should be captured to the fullest extent possible. These costs include the time of staff members conducting the assessment, direct fees and expenses for external consultants who conduct the needs assessment, and internal services and supplies used in the analysis. The total costs are usually prorated over the life of the program. Depending on the type and nature of the program, the shelf life should be kept to a very reasonable number in the one- to two-year time frame. The exception would be very expensive programs that are not expected to change significantly for several years.

Design and Development Costs

One of the most significant items is the cost of designing and developing the program. These costs include internal staff time in both design and development and the purchase of supplies, videos, CD-ROMs, and other material directly related to the program. It would also include the use of consultants. As with needs assessment costs, design and development costs are usually prorated, perhaps using the same time frame. One to two years is recommended unless the program is not expected to change for many years and the costs are significant.

When pilot programs are implemented, a prorating dilemma may surface. For expensive pilot programs, the complete design and development costs could be very significant. In this situation, prorating may not be an issue because the pilot program is completely at risk. If all of those costs are included in the ROI analysis, it may be difficult, if not impossible, for a project to produce a positive ROI. The following rules can help work through this dilemma.

1. If the pilot project is completely at risk, all the costs should be placed in the ROI evaluation decision (i.e., if the pilot project does not have a positive ROI with all the costs included, it will not be

implemented). In this scenario, it is best to keep the design and development costs to a minimum. Perhaps the program could be implemented without all of the "bells and whistles." The videos, CD-ROMs, and other expensive development tools may be delayed until the use of skills and content are proven. This approach is often unreasonable.

2. If program implementation is not at risk, the cost of the development should be prorated over the anticipated life cycle. This is the approach taken in most situations. It is plausible to have a significant investment in the design and development of a pilot program when it is initiated, with the understanding that if it is not adding value, it can be adjusted, changed, or modified to add value. In these cases, a prorated development cost would be appropriate.

Regardless of the approach taken, these should be discussed before the evaluation begins. A dispute over prorating should not occur at the time the results are being tabulated. This discussion should also involve the sponsor of the program and a representative from finance and accounting.

Acquisition Costs

In lieu of development costs, many organizations purchase programs to use directly or in a modified format. The acquisition costs for these programs include the purchase price for the facilitator materials, train-the-trainer sessions, licensing agreements, and other costs associated with the right to deliver the program. These acquisition costs should be prorated using the same rationale above; one to two years should be sufficient. If modification of the program is needed or some additional development is required, these costs should be included as development costs. In practice, many programs have both acquisition costs and development costs.

Delivery Costs

Usually the largest segment of training costs would be those associated with delivery. Five major categories are included.

☐ **Salaries of facilitators and coordinators.** The salaries of facilitators or program coordinators should be included. If a coordinator is involved in more than one program, the time should be allocated to the specific program under review. If external facilitators are used, all charges should be included for the session. The important issue is to capture all of the direct time of internal employees or external consultants who work directly with the program. The benefits factor should be included each time direct labor costs are involved. This factor is a widely accepted value, usually generated by the finance and accounting staff, and in the 30–50% range.

☐ **Program materials and fees.** Specific program materials such as notebooks, textbooks, CD-ROMs, case studies, exercises, and participant workbooks should be included in the delivery costs, along with license fees, user fees, and royalty payments. Pens, paper, certificates, calculators, and personal copies of software are also included in this category.

☐ **Travel, lodging, and meals.** Direct travel for participants, facilitators, or coordinators are included. Lodging and meals are included for participants during travel, as well as meals during the stay for the program. Refreshments should also be included.

☐ **Facilities.** The direct cost of the facilities should be included. For external programs, this is the direct charge from the conference center, hotel, or motel. If the program is conducted in-house, the conference room represents a cost for the organization, then the cost should be estimated and included even if it is not the practice to include facilities' cost in other reports. The cost of internal facilities can easily be estimated by obtaining a room rental rate of the same size room at a local hotel. Sometimes this figure is available on a square foot basis from the finance and accounting staff (e.g., the value per square foot per day). In other situations, the cost of commercial real estate, on a square foot basis, could be determined locally from commercial real estate agents or the newspaper. The important point is to quickly come to a credible estimate for the value of the cost of the room.

This is an important issue that is often overlooked. With encouragement from the finance and accounting staff, some HRD staff members do not charge an amount for the use of internal facilities. The argument is that the room is there, regardless of its use for training. However, the complete cost of training should include the item, because the room would probably not exist unless there was routine training taking place. In the total cost picture, this is a very minor charge. It might have more value from the gesture than influencing the ROI calculation.

☐ **Participants' salaries and benefits.** The salaries plus employee benefits of participants, for the time away from work, represent an expense that should be included. Participant time away from work may include three components: contact time (at the keyboard for clearance), travel time, and preparation time. For situations where the program has been conducted, these costs can be estimated using average or midpoint values for salaries in typical job classifications. When a program is targeted for an ROI calculation, participants can provide their salaries directly and in a confidential manner. It should be noted that this account should be used instead of cost opportunity or replacement costs.

For major training and development programs, there may be a separate category for implementation. If the program involves meetings, follow-ups, manager reinforcement, and a variety of other activities beyond the specific training program, an additional category for implementation may be appropriate. In some extreme examples, on-site coordinators are available to provide assistance and support for the program as it is implemented throughout the region, branch, or division. The total expense of these coordinators is implementation expenses that should be included. The specific cost categories for implementation are often mirrored in the delivery categories. However, in most situations, the implementation is considered part of the delivery and is placed in that category. The remainder of this book presents them as a combined category.

Evaluation

Usually the total evaluation cost is included in the program costs to compute the fully loaded cost. ROI costs include the cost of developing the evaluation technique, designing instruments, collecting data, data analysis, and report preparation and distribution. Cost categories include time, materials, purchased instruments, or surveys. A case can be made to prorate the evaluation costs over several programs instead of charging the total amount as an expense. For example, if 25 sessions of a program are conducted in a three-year period and one group is selected for an ROI calculation, then the ROI costs could logically be prorated over the 25 sessions, since the results of the ROI analysis should reflect the success of the other programs and will perhaps result in changes that will influence the other programs as well.

Overhead

A final charge is the cost of overhead, the additional costs in the training function not directly related to a particular program. The overhead category represents any training department cost not considered in the above calculations. Typical items include the cost of clerical support, the departmental office expenses, salaries of training managers, and other fixed costs. Some organizations obtain an estimate for allocation by dividing the total overhead by the number of program participant training days or hours for the year. This becomes a standard value to use in calculations.

An example illustrates the simplicity of this approach. An organization with 50 training and development programs tabulates all of the expenditures in the budget not allocated directly to a particular program ($548,061 in this example). This part of the budget is then viewed as total overhead, unallocated to specific training and development programs. The allocation of days may be appropriate in others. Next, this number is divided by the total number of participant days or hours (e.g., 5-day program is offered 10 times a year, 50 days should be put in the total days category, or 400 hours for an 8-hour day). In this example, the total days were approximately 7400. The total unallocated overhead of $548,061 is divided by 7400 days to arrive at $74. Thus, an overhead amount of $74 is charged for overhead for each day of training. A three-day leadership program would be charged $222 for overhead. The amount is usually small and will have very little impact on the ROI calculation. The hours approach may be helpful if there is a significant amount of e-learning and participants are involved in programs an hour at a time. The gesture of including the number as part of a fully loaded cost profile builds credibility with the sponsor and senior executives.

Cost Reporting

An example, using an actual case study, shows how the total costs are presented. Table 6-3 shows the cost for a major executive leadership program (Phillips, 2001). This was a very extensive leadership program involving four one-week off-site training sessions with personal coaches and learning coaches assigned to the participants. Working in teams, participants tackled a project that was important to top executives. Each team reported the results to management. The project teams could hire consultants, as well. These costs are listed as project costs. The costs for the first group, involving 22 participants, is detailed in the table.

Table 6-3. Cost Tabulation Example

PROGRAM COSTS

Analysis/Design/Development	
External Consultants	$525,330
Training Department	28,785
Management Committee	26,542
Delivery	
Conference Facilities (Hotel)	142,554
Consultants/External	812,110
Training Department Salaries and Benefits (for direct work with the program)	15,283
Training Department Travel Expenses	37,500
Management Committee (time)	75,470
Project Costs ($25,000 × 4)	100,000
Participant Salaries and Benefits (class sessions) (Average daily salary × benefits factor × number of program days)	84,564
Participant Salaries and Benefits (project work)	117,353
Travel and Lodging for Participants	100,938
Cost of Materials (handouts, purchased materials)	6,872
Research and Evaluation	
Research	110,750
Evaluation	125,875
Total Costs	**$2,309,926**

The issue of prorating costs was an important consideration. In this case, it was reasonably certain that a second group would be conducted. The analysis, design, and development expenses of $580,657 could, therefore, be prorated over two sessions. Consequently, in the actual ROI calculation, half of this number was used to arrive at the total value ($290,328). This left a total program cost of $2,019,598 to include in the analysis ($2,309,926 −$290,328). On a participant basis, this was $91,800, or $22,950 for each week of formal sessions. Although this program was very expensive, it was still close to a rough benchmark of weekly costs of several senior executive leadership programs, involving the same time commitments.

Cost Accumulation and Estimation

There are two basic ways to accumulate costs. One is by a description of the expenditure such as labor, materials, supplies, travel, etc. These are expense account classifications. The other is by categories in the HRD process or function such as program development, delivery, and evaluation. An effective system monitors costs by account categories according to the description of those accounts but also includes a method for accumulating costs by the HRD process/functional category. Many systems stop short of this second step. While the first grouping sufficiently gives the total program cost, it does not allow for a useful comparison with other programs or indicate areas where costs might be excessive by relative comparisons.

Cost Classification Matrix

Costs are accumulated under both of the above classifications. The two classifications are obviously related and the relationship depends on the organization. For instance, the specific costs that comprise the analysis part of a program may vary substantially with the organization.

An important part of the classification process is to define the kinds of costs in the account classification system that normally apply to the major process/functional categories. Table 6-4 is a matrix that represents the categories for accumulating all HRD-related costs in the organization. Those costs, which normally are a part of a process/functional category, are checked in the matrix. Each member of the HRD staff should know how to charge expenses properly. For example, consider equipment that is rented to use in the development and delivery of a program. Should all or part of the cost be charged to development? Or should it be charged to delivery? More than likely, the cost will be allocated in proportion to the extent in which the item was used for each category.

Cost Accumulation

With expense account classifications clearly defined and the process/functional categories determined, it is easy to track costs on individual programs. This is accomplished by using special account numbers and project numbers. An example illustrates the use of these numbers.

Table 6-4. Cost Classification Matrix

Expense	Process / Functional Categories			
Account Classification	Analysis	Development	Delivery	Evaluation
00 Salaries and Benefits—HRD Staff	X	X	X	X
01 Salaries and Benefits—Other Staff		X	X	
02 Salaries and Benefits—Participants			X	X
03 Meals, Travel, and Incidental Expenses—HRD Staff	X	X	X	X
04 Meals, Travel, and Accommodations—Participants			X	
05 Office Supplies and Expenses	X	X		X
06 Program Materials and Supplies		X	X	
07 Printing and Copying	X	X	X	X
08 Outside Services	X	X	X	X
09 Equipment Expense Allocation	X	X	X	X
10 Equipment—Rental		X	X	
11 Equipment—Maintenance			X	
12 Registration Fees	X			
13 Facilities Expense Allocation			X	
14 Facilities Rental			X	
15 General Overhead Allocation	X	X	X	X
16 Other Miscellaneous Expenses	X	X	X	X

A project number is a three-digit number representing a specific HRD program. For example:

New Professional Associates' Orientation	112
New Team Leader Training	215
Statistical Quality Control	418
Valuing Diversity	791

Numbers are assigned to the process/functional breakdowns. Using the example presented earlier, the following numbers are assigned:

Analysis	1
Development	2
Delivery	3
Evaluation	4

Using the two-digit numbers assigned to account classifications in Table 6-4, an accounting system is complete. For example, if workbooks are reproduced for the Valuing Diversity workshop, the appropriate charge number for that reproduction is 07-3-791. The first two digits denote the account classification, the next digit the process/functional category (delivery), and the last three digits the project number viewing diversity. This system enables rapid accumulation and monitoring of HRD costs. Total costs can be presented by:

☐ HRD program (Valuing Diversity workshop),
☐ process/functional categories (delivery), and
☐ expense account classification (printing and reproduction).

Cost Estimation

The previous sections covered procedures for classifying and monitoring costs related to HRD programs. It is important to monitor and compare ongoing costs with the budget or with projected costs. However, a significant reason for tracking costs is to predict the cost of future programs. Usually this goal is accomplished through a formal cost estimation method unique to the organization.

Some organizations use cost estimating worksheets to arrive at the total cost for a proposed program. Figure 6-2 shows an example of a cost estimating worksheet, which calculates analysis, development, delivery, and evaluation costs. The worksheets contain a few formulas that make it easier to estimate the cost. In addition to these worksheets,

Analysis Costs	Total
Salaries & Employee Benefits—HRD Staff	
(No. of People x Average Salary x Employee Benefits	
Factor x No. of Hours on Project)	_____
Meals, Travel, and Incidental Expenses	_____
Office Supplies and Expenses	_____
Printing and Reproduction	_____
Outside Services	_____
Equipment Expenses	_____
Registration Fees	_____
General Overhead Allocation	_____
Other Miscellaneous Expenses	_____
Total Analysis Cost	_____

Development Costs	Total
Salaries & Employee Benefits	
(No. of People x Avg. Salary x Employee Benefits	
Factor x No. of Hours on Project)	_____
Meals, Travel, and Incidental Expenses	_____
Office Supplies and Expenses	_____
Program Materials and Supplies	_____
CD ROM _____	
Videotape _____	
Audiotapes _____	
Slides _____	
Manuals and Materials _____	
Other _____	
Printing and Reproduction	_____
Outside Services	_____
Equipment Expense	_____
General Overhead Allocation	_____
Other Miscellaneous Expense	_____
Total Development Costs	_____

Delivery Costs	Total
Participant Costs (A)*	_____
Salaries & Employee Benefits (No. of	
Participants x Avg. Salary x Employee	
Benefits Factor x Hrs. or Days of	
Training Time)	_____
Meals, Travel, & Accommodations (No. of	
Participants x Avg. Daily Expenses x	
Days of Training)	_____
Program Materials and Supplies	_____

Figure 6-2. Cost estimating worksheet.

Participant Replacement Costs (if
    applicable) (B)*
Lost Production (Explain Basis) (C)*
Facilitator Costs
    Salaries & Benefits
    Meals, Travel, & Incidental Expense
    Outside Services
Facility Costs
Facilities Rental
Facilities Expense Allocation
Equipment Expense
General Overhead Allocation
Other Miscellaneous Expense
Total Delivery Costs

Evaluation Costs   **Total**
Salaries & Employee Benefits—HRD Staff
  (No. of People x Avg. Salary x Employee Benefits
  Factor x No. of Hours on Project)
Meals, Travel, and Incidental Expense
Participant Costs
Office Supplies and Expense
Printing and Reproduction
Outside Services
Equipment Expense
General Overhead Allocation
Other Miscellaneous Expenses
   Total Evaluation Costs
   TOTAL PROGRAM COSTS

*Use A, B, or
C—Not a
combination

Figure 6-2. Continued.

current charge rates for services, supplies, and salaries are available. These data become outdated quickly and are usually prepared periodically as a supplement.

The most appropriate basis for predicting costs is to analyze the previous costs by tracking the actual costs incurred in all phases of a program, from analysis to evaluation. This way, it is possible to see how much is spent on programs and how much is being spent in the different categories. Until adequate cost data are available, it is necessary to use the detailed analysis in the worksheets for cost estimation.

FINAL THOUGHTS

Costs are important for a variety of uses and applications. They help the HRD staff manage the resources carefully, consistently, and efficiently. They also allow for comparisons between different elements and cost categories. Cost categorization can take several different forms; the most common are presented in this chapter. Costs should be fully loaded in the ROI calculation. From a practical standpoint, including certain cost items may be optional, based on the organization's guidelines and philosophy. However, because of the scrutiny involved in ROI calculations, it is recommended that all costs be included, even if it goes beyond the requirements of the company policy.

CASE STUDY—PART E, LINEAR NETWORK SYSTEMS

Converting Data to Monetary Values

As part of the next step in the ROI process, LNS's data are converted to monetary values. The value of improved productivity was a standard value developed by engineering and production control. Each 1% of improvement in productivity would save the plant $21,000, annually.

The company had no detailed historical records on turnover costs, although the company expected these costs to be significant when considering the cost of employment, recruiting, training, and lost productivity. The consultant provided information from external studies, which showed that turnover can cost one times the annual pay of the employees (100% of annual direct compensated). Annual wages of nonsupervisory employees averaged $31,000. Management thought that a figure of one times the annual pays would be too high for the cost of turnover since the training period was relatively short, recruiting costs were normally quite low, and exit costs were not very significant. After discussing this with senior management, the compromise figure of $24,800 was reached for the cost of turnover (80% of annual direct compensated). This appeared to be a very conservative estimate. Sixteen first level managers were trained in this program, and they supervised a total of 385 employees.

The consultant located some previous studies about the cost of absenteeism in a similar manufacturing sector, which showed a range of $89–$210 per absence with an average of $180. Brief estimates taken in the training session, with input from the 16 managers, yielded an average cost of $98. This was considered the most credible valve because it was developed using the process described in the last chapter, using estimates from participants. LNS employees worked an average of 228 days per year.

Costs

Because the consulting firm provided standard material for the new program, development costs were insignificant. The consultant also decided to include all direct costs of participant materials as well as the participants' salaries. Although the first level managers were not replaced while they were in training, the salaries and benefits of managers were included for the time during the training sessions. The average salary of the first level managers was $47,500. The employee benefits factor was 39% of salaries. A total of 3 days were consumed in the program. The total charge for the program from the consulting firm was $51,000, including customization time, facilitation, and needs assessment. The charge for course materials was $185 per participant; miscellaneous refreshments and food was $195 per participant; the use of the conference room was estimated to be $200 per session, although LNS does not routinely capture and report this as a part of training. The consultant estimated the additional cost of the evaluation to be $10,000.

Discussion Questions
1. What major cost categories should always be included in the analysis?
2. What is the total cost for the program?
3. Should any other costs be included? Please explain.

REFERENCES

"Annual Employee Benefits Report," In *Nation's Business*, January 2002.

Cascio, W.F. *Costing Human Resources: The Financial Impact of Behavior in Organizations*, Australia: South-Western College Publishing, 2000.

Kaplan, R.S., and R. Cooper. *Cost & Effect: Using Integrated Cost Systems to Drive Profitability and Performance*. Boston, MA: Harvard Business School Press, 1998.

Marquardt, M.J., S.B. King, and E. Koon. *International Comparisons: An Annual Accounting of Worldwide Patterns in Employer-Provided Training*. Alexandria, VA: The American Society for Training and Development, 2001.

Phillips, P.P. "Executive Leadership Development," In *The Human Resources Scorecard: Measuring the Return on Investment*, J.J. Phillips, R.D. Stone, and P.P. Phillips. Boston, MA: Butterworth–Heinemann, 2001, pp. 449–476.

Young, S.D., and S.F. O'Byrne. *EVA® and Value-Based Management: A Practical Guide to Implementation*. New York, NY: McGraw-Hill, 2001.

FURTHER READING

Eccles, R.G., R.H. Herz, E.M. Keegan, and D.M.H. Phillips. *The Value-Reporting™ Revolution: Moving Beyond the Earnings Game*. New York, NY: John Wiley & Sons, Inc., 2001.

Epstein, M.J., and B. Birchard. *Counting What Counts: Turning Corporate Accountability to Competitive Advantage*. Reading, MA: Perseus, 1991.

Friedlob, G.T., and F.J. Plewa, Jr. *Understanding Return on Investment*. New York, NY: Wiley, 1991.

Marcum, D., S. Smith, and M. Khalsa. *BusinessThink: Rules for Getting it Right—Now, and No Matter What!* New York, NY: John Wiley & Sons, Inc., 2002.

Rasmussen, N., P.S. Goldy, and P.O. Solli. *Financial Business Intelligence: Trends, Technology, Software Selection, and Implementation*. New York, NY: John Wiley & Sons, Inc., 2002.

CHAPTER 7

Calculating the Return

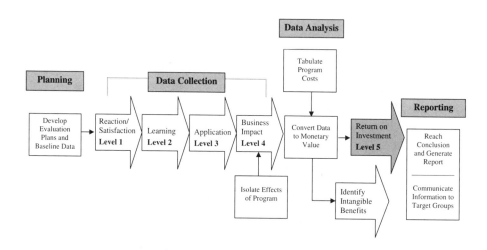

The monetary values for program benefits, developed in Chapter 5, are combined with program cost data, developed in Chapter 6, to calculate the return on investment. This chapter explores several approaches for developing the return on investment, describing the various techniques, processes, and issues involved. Before presenting the formulas for calculating the ROI, a few basic issues are described. An adequate understanding of these issues is necessary to complete this major step in the ROI process. The uses and abuses of ROI are fully explored.

BASIC ISSUES

Definitions

The term *return on investment* is often misused, sometimes intentionally. In these situations, a broad definition for ROI includes any benefit from the program, a vague concept in which even subjective data linked to a program are included in the concept of the return. In this book, the return on investment is more precise and is meant to represent an actual value developed by comparing program costs to benefits. The two most common measures are the benefits/costs ratio and the ROI formula. Both are presented along with other approaches that calculate the return.

For many years, training and development practitioners and researchers have sought to calculate the actual return on the investment for training. If employee training is considered an investment, not an expense, then it is appropriate to place the training and development investment in the same funding mechanism as other investments, such as the investment in equipment and facilities. Although these other investments are quite different, management often views them in the same way. Thus, it is critical to the success of the training and development field to develop specific values that reflect the return on the investment.

Annualized Values

All of the formulas presented in this chapter use annualized values so that the first year impact of the program investment is developed. Using annual values is becoming a generally accepted practice for developing the ROI in many organizations. This approach is a conservative way to develop the ROI, since many short-term training programs have added value in the second or third year. For long-term training programs, annualized values are inappropriate and longer time frames need to be used. For example, in an ROI analysis of a program to send employees to the United States to obtain MBA degrees, a Singapore-based company used a seven-year time frame. The program itself required two years and a five-year impact, with postprogram data used to develop the ROI. However, for most programs lasting one day to one month, first year values are appropriate.

When selecting the approach to measure ROI, it is important to communicate to the target audience the formula used and the assumptions made to arrive at the decision to use it. This action can avoid misunderstandings and confusion surrounding how the ROI value was developed. Although several approaches are described in this chapter, two stand out as the preferred methods: the benefits/costs ratio and the basic ROI formula. These two approaches are described next along with the interpretation of ROI and a brief coverage of the other approaches.

Benefits/Costs Ratio

One of the earliest methods for evaluating training investments is the benefits/costs ratio (BCR). This method compares the benefits of the program to the costs in a ratio. In formula form, the ratio is:

$$BCR = \frac{\text{Program Benefits}}{\text{Program Costs}}$$

In simple terms, the BCR compares the annual economic benefits of the program to the cost of the program. A BCR of one means that the benefits equal the costs. A BCR of two, usually written as 2:1, indicates that for each dollar spent on the program, two dollars were returned as benefits.

The following example will illustrate the use of the benefits/costs ratio. A large metropolitan bus system introduced a new program to reduce unscheduled absences (Phillips and Stone, 2002). The increase in absences left the system facing many delays, thus a large pool of drivers to fill in for the absent drivers was created. The pool had become substantial, representing a significant expenditure. The program involved a change in policy, and a change in the selection process, coupled with meetings and communication. Significant improvements were generated. The benefits of the program were captured in a one-year follow-up and compared to the total cost of the program. The first year payoff for the program was $662,000, based on the two major issues, a no-fault policy and changes in the screening process. The total fully loaded implementation costs was $67,400. Thus, the cost benefit ratio is:

$$BCR = \frac{\$662,000}{\$67,400} = 9.82$$

Therefore, for every dollar invested in this program, almost $10 in benefits were returned.

The principal advantage of using this approach is that it avoids traditional financial measures so that there is no confusion when comparing training investments with other investments in the company. Investments in plants, equipment, or subsidiaries, for example, are not usually evaluated with the benefits/costs method. Some training and development executives prefer not to use the same method to compare the return on training investments with the return on other investments. Consequently, the ROI for training stands alone as a unique type of evaluation.

Unfortunately, there are no standards for what constitutes an acceptable benefits/costs ratio. A standard should be established within an organization, perhaps even for a specific type of program. However, a 1:1 ratio is unacceptable for most programs, and in some organizations, a 1.25:1 ratio is required, where 1.25 times the cost of the program is the benefit.

ROI Formula

Perhaps the most appropriate formula for evaluating training investments is net program benefits divided by cost. The ratio is usually expressed as a percent when the fractional values are multiplied by 100. In formula form, the ROI becomes:

$$\text{ROI (\%)} = \frac{\text{Net Program Benefits}}{\text{Program Costs}} \times 100$$

Net benefits are program benefits minus program costs. The ROI value is related to the BCR by a factor of one. For example, a BCR of 2.45 is the same as an ROI value of 145%. This formula is essentially the same as ROI in other types of investments. For example, when a firm builds a new plant, the ROI is found by dividing annual earnings by the investment. The annual earnings is comparable to net benefits (annual benefits minus the cost). The investment is comparable to program costs, which represent the investment in the program.

An ROI on a training investment of 50% means that the costs are recovered and an additional 50% of the costs are reported as "earnings." A training investment of 150% indicates that the costs have been recovered and an additional 1.5 multiplied by the costs is captured as "earnings." An example illustrates the ROI calculation. Hewlett-Packard took a unique approach to enhancing telephone-based sales

(Seagraves, 2001). Using an innovative, multistep sales skills intervention, tremendous improvement was driven in sales skills. The actual sales improvement, when translated into increased profit, yielded impressive results. The monetary benefit was $3,296,977, the total fully loaded cost was $1,116,291, and when the net benefits were calculated, a value of $2,180,616 was yielded.

$$\text{ROI\%} = \frac{\$2,180,686}{\$1,116,291} \times 100 = 195\%$$

Thus, after the cost of the program had been recovered, Hewlett-Packard received almost $2 for each dollar invested, after the costs were recovered.

Using the ROI formula essentially places training investments on a level playing field with other investments using the same formula and similar concepts. The ROI calculation is easily understood by key management and financial executives who regularly use ROI with other investments.

ROI INTERPRETATION

Choosing the Right Formula

What quantitative measure best represents top management goals? Many managers are preoccupied with the measures of sales, profits (net income), and profit percentages (the ratio of profits to dollar sales). However, the ultimate test of profitability is not the absolute amount of profit or the relationship of profit to sales. The critical test is the relationship of profit to invested capital. The most popular way of expressing this relationship is by means of a rate of return on investment (Anthony and Reece, 1983).

Profits can be generated through increased sales or cost savings. In practice, there are more opportunities for cost savings than profit. Cost savings can be generated when there is improvement in productivity, quality, efficiency, cycle time, or actual cost reduction. When reviewing almost 500 studies with the author's involvement, the vast majority of the studies were based on cost savings. Approximately 85% of the studies had a pay-off based on output, quality, efficiency, time, or cost reduction. The other studies had a pay-off based on sales increases, where the earnings are derived from the profit margin. This issue is important for nonprofits and public sector organizations where the profit opportunity is often unavailable. Most training and performance improvement initiatives will be connected directly to the cost savings portion; thus, ROIs can still be developed in those settings.

In the finance and accounting literature, return on investment is defined as net income (earnings) divided by investment. In the context of training and performance improvement, net income is equivalent to net monetary benefits (program benefits minus program costs). Investment is equivalent to program costs. The term investment is used in three different senses in financial analysis, thus giving three different ROI ratios: return on assets (ROA), return on owners' equity (ROE), and return on capital employed (ROCE).

Financial executives have used the ROI approach for centuries. Still, this technique did not become widespread in industry for judging operating performance until the early twentieth century. Conceptually, ROI has innate appeal because it blends all the major ingredients of profitability in one number; the ROI statistic by itself can be compared with opportunities elsewhere (both inside or outside). Practically, however, ROI is an imperfect measurement that should be used in conjunction with other performance measurements (Horngren, 1982).

It is important for the formula defined above to be utilized in the organization. Deviations from, or misuse of, the formula can create confusion not only among users, but also among the finance and accounting staff. The Chief Financial Office (CFO) and the Finance and Accounting staff should become partners in the implementation of the ROI methodology. Without their support, involvement, and commitment, it is difficult for ROI to be used on a wide-scale basis. Because of this relationship, it is important that the same financial terms be used as those experienced and expected by the CFO.

Table 7-1 shows some misuse of financial terms that appear in the literature. Terms such as return on intelligence (or information) abbreviated as ROI do nothing but confuse the CFO, who is thinking that ROI is the actual return on investment described above. Sometimes return on expectations (ROE), return on anticipation (ROA), or return on client expectations (ROCE) are used, confusing the CFO, who is thinking return on equity, return on assets, and return on capital employed, respectively. Use of these terms in the calculation of a payback of a training and performance improvement program will do nothing but confuse and perhaps lose the support of the finance and accounting staff. Other terms such as return on people, return on resources, return on training, and return on web are often used with almost no consistent financial calculations. The bottom line: don't confuse the CFO. Consider this

Table 7-1. Misuse of Financial Terms

Term	Misuse	CFO Definition
ROI	Return of Information or Return of Intelligence	Return on Investment
ROE	Return on Expectation	Return on Equity
ROA	Return on Anticipation	Return on Assets
ROCE	Return on Client Expectation	Return on Capital Employed
ROP	Return on People	??
ROR	Return on Resources	??
ROT	Return on Training	??
ROW	Return on Web	??

individual to be an ally and use the same terminology, processes, and concepts when applying financial returns for programs.

ROI Objectives: The Ultimate Challenge

When reviewing the specific ROI calculation and formula, it is helpful to position the ROI calculation in the context of all the data. The ROI calculation is only one measure generated with the ROI methodology. Six types of data are developed, five of which are the five levels of evaluation. The data in each level of evaluation is driven by a specific objective, as was described earlier. In terms of ROI, specific objectives are often set, creating the expectations of an acceptable ROI calculation.

Table 7-2 shows the payoff of a sexual harassment prevention program as the results at the different levels are clearly linked to the specific objectives of the program (Phillips and Hill, 2001). As objectives are established, data are collected to indicate the extent to which that particular objective was met. This is the ideal framework that clearly shows the powerful connection between objectives and measurement and evaluation data. The table also shows the chain of impact as reaction leads to learning, which leads to application, which leads to business impact and to ROI. The intangible data shown in the business impact category are items that are purposely not converted to monetary value. Intangible measures could have been anticipated in the project before it was implemented. Others may not be have been anticipated, but were described as a benefit from those involved in the program. In this particular example, there was an expectation of 25% for ROI (ROI

Table 7-2. The Chain of Impact Drives ROI

	Level	Objective	Results
1	Reaction/ Satisfaction	☐ Obtain a positive reaction on the program	☐ Overall rating of 4.11 out of a possible 5
		☐ At least 75% of participants provide an action plan	☐ 93% provided list of action items
2	Learning	☐ Improve knowledge of policy on sexual harassment/knowledge of inappropriate and illegal behavior	☐ Posttest scores average 84; pretest scores average 51 (improvement 65%)
		☐ Skills to investigate and discuss sexual harassment	☐ Participants demonstrated they could use skills successfully
3	Application/ Implementation	☐ Conduct meeting with employees	☐ 96% completed meeting record
		☐ Administer policy to ensure that workplace is free from sexual harassment	☐ Survey showed 4.1 out of 5 scale with behavior change
		☐ Complete action items	☐ 68% report all action items were completed
			☐ 92% reported some action items were completed
4	Business Impact	☐ Reduce the number of formal internal sexual harassment complaints	☐ Complaints reduced from 55 to 35
		☐ Reduce turnover related to sexual harassment activity	☐ Turnover reduced from 24.2 to 19.9%
		☐ Reduce absenteeism related to sexual harassment	☐ Reduced absenteeism
5	ROI	☐ Obtain at least a 25% ROI	☐ ROI = 1052%

objective). This organization uses 25% as a standard for all of their ROI projects and the actual result of 1052% clearly exceeds the expectation by a huge amount.

ROI Targets

Specific expectations for ROI should be developed before an evaluation study is undertaken. While there are no generally accepted standards, four strategies have been used to establish a minimum expected requirement, or hurdle rate, for ROI in a training or performance improvement program. The first approach is to set the ROI using the same values used to invest in capital expenditures, such as equipment, facilities, and new companies. For North America, Western Europe, most of the Asian Pacific area, including Australia and New Zealand, the cost of capital has been reasonable and this internal hurdle rate for ROI is usually in the 15–20% range. Thus, using this strategy, organizations would set the expected ROI the same as the value expected from other investments.

A second strategy is to use an ROI minimum that represents a higher standard than the value required for other investments. This target value is above the percentage required for other types of investments. The rationale: The ROI process for training and performance improvement is still relatively new and often involves subjective input, including estimations. Because of that, a higher standard is required or suggested. For most areas in North America, Western Europe, and the Asia Pacific area, this value is usually set at 25%.

A third strategy is to set the ROI value at a break-even point. A 0% ROI represents a break-even point. This is equivalent to a cost benefit ratio of 1. The rationale for this approach is an eagerness to recapture the cost of training and development only. This is the ROI objective for many public sector organizations. If the funds expended for programs can be captured, there is still value and benefit from the program through the intangible measures, which are not converted to monetary values and the behavior change that is evident in the application and implementation data. Thus, some organizations will use a break-even point, under the philosophy that they are not attempting to make a profit from training and development.

Finally, a fourth, and sometimes recommended, strategy is to let the client or program sponsor set the minimum acceptable ROI value. In this scenario, the individual who initiates, approves, sponsors or supports the program, establishes the acceptable ROI. Almost every program has a major sponsor and that person may be willing to offer the acceptable value. This links the expectations or financial return directly to the expectations of the individual sponsoring the program.

ROI Can Be Very Large

As the examples in this book have demonstrated, the actual ROI value can be quite large—far exceeding what might be expected from other types of investments in plant, equipment, and companies. It is not unusual for programs involved in leadership, team building, management development, supervisor training, and sales training to generate ROIs in the 100–700% range. This does not mean that all ROI studies are positive—many are negative. However, the impact of the training and development can be quite impressive. It is helpful to remember what constitutes the ROI value. Consider, for example, the investment in one week of training for a team leader. If the leader's behavior changes as he or she works directly with the team, a chain of impact can produce a measurable change in performance from the team. This measure now represents the team's measure. That behavior change, translated into a measurement improvement for the entire year, can be quite significant. When the monetary value of the team's improvement is considered for an entire year and compared to the relatively small amount of investment in one team leader, it is easy to see why this number can be quite large.

More specifically, as Figure 7-1 shows, there are some very important factors that contribute to high ROI values. The impact can be quite large when a specific need has been identified and a performance gap exists; a new requirement is introduced and the solution is implemented at the right time for the right people at a reasonable cost; the solution is applied and supported in the work setting; and there's a linkage to one or more business measures. When these conditions are met, high ROI values can be recognized.

It is important to understand that a very high ROI value can be developed that does not necessarily relate directly to the health of the rest of the organization. For example, a high impact ROI can be generated in an organization that is losing money (or in bankruptcy) because the impact is restricted to those individuals involved in the training and performance improvement program and the monetary value of their improvement is connected to that program. At the same time, there can be some disastrous programs generating a very negative ROI in a company that is very profitable. This is a micro-level activity that

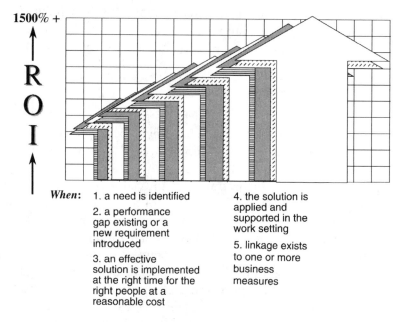

1500% +

R
O
I

When:　1. a need is identified

2. a performance gap existing or a new requirement introduced

3. an effective solution is implemented at the right time for the right people at a reasonable cost

4. the solution is applied and supported in the work setting

5. linkage exists to one or more business measures

Figure 7-1. Rationale for high ROI values.

evaluates the success of a particular program within a particular time frame.

What Happens When the ROI Is Negative?

Perhaps one of the greatest fears of using ROI is the possibility of having a negative ROI. This is a fear that concerns not only the program sponsor or owner, but also those who are involved in the design, development, and delivery of the program. Few individuals want to be involved in a process that exposes a failure. They are concerned that the failure may reflect unfavorably on them. On the positive side, a negative ROI study provides the best opportunity for learning. The ROI methodology reveals problems and barriers. As data are collected through the chain of impact, the reasons for failure become clear. Data on barriers and enablers, captured at Level 3 (Application), usually reveal why the program did not work. While a negative ROI study is the ultimate learning situation, no one wants to invite the opportunity to his or her back door. The preference would be to learn from others. Sometimes the damage created by a negative ROI is the sense of expectations that are not managed properly up front and the fear of the consequences of the negative ROI. The following steps can help minimize or avoid this dilemma:

1. Raise the question about the feasibility of the impact study: Is it appropriate to use the ROI methodology for this particular program? Sometimes, a program, by its very nature, may appear to be a failure, at least in terms of ROI.
2. Make sure there is a clear understanding of the consequences of a negative ROI. This issue should be addressed early and often. The ROI methodology is a process improvement tool and not a performance evaluation tool. The individuals involved should not necessarily be penalized or have their performance evaluated unfavorably because of the negative ROI.
3. Look for warning signs early in the process—they are usually everywhere. Level 1 data can often send strong signals that an evaluation may result in a negative ROI. Maybe the participants react negatively, see no relevance in the program to their jobs, perceive the content to be inappropriate, consider the information outdated, offer no intent to use the material, or refuse to recommend the program to anyone else.
4. Manage expectations. It is best to lower expectations around ROI. Anticipating a high ROI and communicating that to the client or other stakeholders may create a false expectation that will not materialize. Keep the expectations low and the delivery performance high.
5. Using the negative data, reposition the story. Instead of communicating that great results have been achieved with this very effective program, the story now becomes, "We have some great information that reveals how to change the program to obtain improved results." This is more than a play on words—it underscores the importance of learning what went wrong and what can be done in the future.
6. Use the information to drive change. Sometimes the negative ROI can be transformed into a positive ROI with some minor alterations of the program. Implementation issues may need to be addressed in terms of support and use of knowledge and skills in the workplace. In other situations, a complete redesign of the

program may be necessary. In a few isolated cases, discontinuing the program may be the only option. Whatever the option, use the data to drive action so that the overall value of conducting the study has been realized.

These strategies can help minimize the unfavorable, and sometimes disastrous, perceptions of a negative ROI.

ROI Is Not for Every Program

The ROI methodology should not be applied to every program. It takes time and resources to create a valid and credible ROI study. Although this issue is addressed in Chapter 11, *Implementation Issues*, it is appropriate now to underscore the types of programs where this technique is best suited. ROI is appropriate for those programs that:

☐ have a long life cycle. At some point in the life of the program, this level of accountability should be applied to the program.

☐ are very important to the organization in meeting its operating goals. These programs are designed to add value. ROI may be helpful to show that value.

☐ are closely linked to the organization's strategic initiatives. Anything this important needs a high level of accountability.

☐ are very expensive to implement. An expensive program, expending large amounts of company resources, should be subjected to this level of accountability.

☐ are highly visible and sometimes controversial. These programs often require this level of accountability to satisfy the critics.

☐ have a large target audience. If a program is designed for all employees, it may be a candidate for ROI.

☐ command the interest of a top executive group. If top executives are interested in knowing the impact, the ROI methodology should be applied.

These are only guidelines and should be considered in the context of the organization. Other criteria may also be appropriate. These criteria can be used in a scheme to sort out those programs most appropriate for this level of accountability.

It is also helpful to consider the programs where the ROI methodology is not appropriate. ROI is seldom appropriate for programs that:

☐ are very short in duration, such as two-hour briefings. It's difficult to change behavior in such a short time frame.

☐ are legislated or required by regulation. It would be difficult to change anything as a result of this evaluation.

☐ are required by senior management. It may be that these programs will continue regardless of the findings.

☐ serve as operator and technical training. It may be more appropriate to measure only at Levels 1, 2, and 3 to ensure that participants know how to do the job and are doing it properly.

This is not meant to imply that the ROI methodology cannot be implemented for these types of programs. However, when considering the limited resources for measurement and evaluation, careful use of these resources and time will result in evaluating more strategic types of programs. It is also helpful to think about the programs that are appropriate for the first one or two ROI studies. Initially, the use of this process will be met with some anxiety and tentativeness. The programs initially undertaken should not only meet the requirements above, but should also meet other requirements. These programs should:

1. Be as simple as possible. Reserve the complex programs for later.
2. Be a known commodity. This helps ensure that the first study is not negative.
3. Be void of hidden agendas and political sensitivity. The first study should not necessarily be wrapped up in the organization politics.

Deciding the level at which to allocate resources to this process, which programs to pursue for ROI, and the number of programs to pursue in any given time frame are important issues detailed in Chapter 11.

CASE APPLICATION

Background Information

Retail Merchandise Company (RMC), a large national store chain located in most major markets in the United States, attempted to boost sales by conducting an interactive selling skills program for sales associates (Phillips and Phillips, 2001). The program, developed and delivered by an outside vendor, was a response to a clearly defined need to increase the level of interaction between the sales associate and the customer. The program consisted of two days of skills training, followed by three weeks of on-the-job application of the skills. The third day of the program was used for follow-up and additional training. Three groups representing the electronics departments of three stores were initially trained for a pilot implementation. A total of 48 participated.

ROI Analysis

Postprogram data collection was accomplished using three methods. First, the average weekly sales of each associate was monitored (business performance monitoring of output data). Second, a follow-up questionnaire was distributed three months after the training was completed to determine Level 3 success (actual application of the skills on the job). Third, Level 3 data was solicited in a follow-up session, which was conducted on the third day. In this session, participants disclosed their success (or lack of success) with the application of new skills. They also discussed techniques to overcome the barriers to program implementation.

The method used to isolate the effects of training was a control group arrangement. Three store locations were identified (control group) and compared with the three groups in the pilot training (experimental group). The variables of previous store performance, store size, store location, and customer traffic levels were used to match the two groups so that they could be as similar as possible. The method to convert data to monetary values is a direct profit contribution of the increased output. The actual profit obtained from one additional dollar of sales (profit margin) was readily available and used in the calculation.

BCR and ROI Calculations

Although the program was evaluated at all five levels, the emphasis of this study was on Levels 4 and 5 calculation. Levels 1, 2, and 3 data either met or exceeded expectations. Table 7-3 shows the Level 4 data, which is the average weekly sales of both groups after the training. For convenience and at the request of management, a three-month follow up period was used. Management wanted to make the decision to implement the program at other locations if it appeared to be successful in this first three months of operation. Three months may be premature to determine the total impact of the program, but often becomes a convenient time period for evaluation. Data for the first three weeks after training are shown in Table 7-4 along with the last three weeks of the

Table 7-3. Level 4 Data: Average Weekly Sales

Weeks After Training	Postraining Data Trained Groups	Control Groups
1	$9,723	$9,698
2	9,978	9,720
3	10,424	9,812
13	13,690	11,572
14	11,491	9,683
15	11,044	10,092
Average for Weeks 13, 14, 15	$12,075	$10,449

Table 7-4. Annualized Program Benefits

46 participants were still in job after 3 months	
Average Weekly Sales Trained Groups	$12,075
Average Weekly Sales Untrained Groups	10,449
Increase	1,626
Profit Contribution (2% of sales)	32.50
Total Weekly Improvement (32.50 × 46)	1,495
Total Annual Benefits ($1495 × 48 Weeks)	$71,760

evaluation period (weeks 13, 14, and 15). The data show what appears to be a significant difference in the two values.

Two steps are required to move from the Level 4 data to Level 5. First, Level 4 data must be converted to monetary values. Second, the cost of the program must be tabulated. Table 7-4 shows the annualized program benefits. The total benefit was $71,760. Since only 46 participants were still in their current job after three months, to be conservative, the other two participants' potential improvements were removed from the calculation. The profit contribution at the store level, obtained directly from the accounting department, was 2% of sales. For every dollar of additional sales attributed to the program, only two cents would be considered to be the added value. At the corporate level, the number was even smaller, about 1.2%. First year values are used to reflect the total impact of the program. Ideally, if new skills are acquired, as indicated in the

Level 3 evaluation, there should be some value for the use of those skills in year two, or perhaps, even year three. However, for short-term training programs, only first year values are used, requiring the investment to have an acceptable return in a one-year time period.

Guiding Principle #9
Only the first year of benefits (annual) should be used in the ROI analysis of short-term solutions.

Table 7-5 shows the cost summary for this program. Costs are fully loaded, including data for all 48 participants. Since a training supplier conducts the program, there are no direct development costs. The facilitation fee actually covers the prorated development costs as well as the delivery costs. The participants' salaries plus a 35% factor for employee benefits were included in the costs. Facilities costs were included, although the company does not normally capture the costs when internal facilities are used, as was the case with this program. The estimated cost for the coordination and evaluation was also included. The total cost was $32,984. Thus, the benefits/costs ratio becomes:

$$BCR = \frac{\$71,760}{\$32,984} \approx 2.2:1$$

and the return on investment becomes:

$$ROI\ (\%) = \frac{\$71,760 - \$32,984}{\$32,984} \times 100 = 118\%$$

Table 7-5. Cost Summary

48 participants in 3 courses

Facilitation Fees: 3 courses @ $3750	$11,250
Program Materials: 48 @ $35/participant	1,680
Meals/Refreshments: 3 days @ $28/participant	4,032
Facilities: 9 days @ $120	1,080
Participant Salaries Plus Benefits (35% of salaries)	12,442
Coordination/Evaluation	2,500
Total Costs	**$32,984**

The acceptable ROI, defined by the client, was 25%. Thus, the program has an excellent return on investment in its initial trial run after three months of on-the-job applications of the skills.

The decision to implement the program throughout the other store locations becomes much easier. Six types of data are collected to show the full range of success, including the actual ROI. This represents an excellent use of the ROI methodology, where the payoff is developed on the new pilot program. Historically, the decision to go from pilot to full implementation is often based on the reaction data alone. Sometimes, learning, and in limited cases, application data are used. Using the approach described above, those types of data are collected, but more important, business impact, ROI, and intangibles add to the rich database from which to make this critical decision. It is a much less risky process when a full implementation is recommended from the pilot program.

OTHER ROI MEASURES

In addition to the traditional ROI formula previously described, several other measures are occasionally used under the general term of return on investment. These measures are designed primarily for evaluating other types of financial measures, but sometimes work their way into training evaluations.

Payback Period

The payback period is a common method for evaluating capital expenditures. With this approach, the annual cash proceeds (savings) produced by an investment are equated to the original cash outlay required by the investment to arrive at some multiple of cash proceeds equal to the original investment. Measurement is usually in terms of years and months. For example, if the cost savings generated from an HRD program are constant each year, the payback period is determined by dividing the total original cash investment (development costs, outside program purchases, etc.) by the amount of the expected annual or actual savings. The savings represent the net savings after the program expenses are subtracted. To illustrate this calculation, assume that an initial program cost is $100,000 with a three-year useful life. The annual net savings from the program is expected to be $40,000. Thus, the payback period becomes:

$$\text{Payback period} = \frac{\text{Total Investment}}{\text{Annual Savings}} = \frac{\$100,000}{\$40,000} = 2.5 \text{ years}$$

The program will "pay back" the original investment in 2.5 years.

The payback period is simple to use, but has the limitation of ignoring the time value of money. It has not enjoyed widespread use in evaluating training investments.

Discounted Cash Flow

Discounted cash flow is a method of evaluating investment opportunities in which certain values are assigned to the timing of the proceeds from the investment. The assumption, based on interest rates, is that money earned today is more valuable than money earned a year from now.

There are several ways of using the discounted cash flow concept to evaluate capital expenditures. The most popular is probably the net present value of an investment. This approach compares the savings, year by year, with the outflow of cash required by the investment. The expected savings received each year is discounted by selected interest rates. The outflow of cash is also discounted by the same interest rate. If the present value of the savings should exceed the present value of the outlays after discounting at a common interest rate, the investment is usually acceptable in the eyes of management. The discounted cash flow method has the advantage of ranking investments, but it becomes difficult to calculate.

Internal Rate of Return

The internal rate of return (IRR) method determines the interest rate required to make the present value of the cash flow equal to zero. It represents the maximum rate of interest that could be paid if all project funds were borrowed and the organization had to break even on the projects. The IRR considers the time value of money and is unaffected by the scale of the project. It can be used to rank alternatives or to make accept/reject decisions when a minimum rate of return is specified. A major weakness of the IRR method is that it assumes all returns are reinvested at the same internal rate of return. This can make an investment alternative with a high rate of return look even better than it really is, and a project with a low rate of return look even worse. In practice, the IRR is rarely used to evaluate training investments.

Utility Analysis

Another interesting approach for developing the training payoff is utility analysis. Utility analysis measures the economic contribution of a program according to how effective the program was in identifying and modifying behavior, hence the future service contribution of employees. Utility is a function of the duration of a training program's effect on employees' performance, the number of employees trained, the validity of the training program, the value of the job for which training was provided, and the total program cost (Schmidt, Hunter, and Pearlman, 1982). The following formula is offered for assessing the dollar value of a training program:

$$\Delta U = T \times N \times dt \times Sdy - N \times C$$

where:

ΔU = Monetary value of the training program
T = Duration in number of years of a training program's effect on performance
N = Number of employees trained
dt = True difference in job performance between the average trained and the average untrained employees in units of standard deviation
Sdy = Standard deviation of job performance of the untrained group in dollars
C = Cost of training per employee

Of all the factors in this formula, the true difference in job performance and the value of the target job are the most difficult to develop. The validity is determined by noting the performance differences between trained and untrained employees. The simplest method for obtaining this information is to have supervisors rate the performance of each group. Supervisors and experts estimate the value of the target job, Sdy.

Utility analysis has both advantages and disadvantages. As far as disadvantages, it has two primary flaws. First, it is basically a Level 3 ROI analysis, following the concept of the different levels of evaluation presented earlier. Essentially, the process converts behavior change into monetary value (Level 3), ignoring the consequences of the behavior change, which is the business impact (Level 4). Thus, it stops short of following the chain of impact all the way to the consequences of the new behavior in the organization. Simply having new behavior in place does not mean it is being used productively, or adding value to the organization.

The second disadvantage is that utility analysis is based on estimations. Because of the subjective nature of estimations, and the reluctance to use them, the process has not achieved widespread acceptance by training and development professionals as a practical tool for evaluating return on investments. In a recent survey of 100 published case studies on ROI, only 5% use the utility analysis technique (Phillips, 2001).

The advantage of utility analysis is that researchers have developed a proliferation of models. One of the principle proponents of the process identifies six different models utilizing the concept of utility analysis (Cascio, 2000). Also, the notion of putting a value on behavior change is a novel idea for many practitioners. With the increased interest in leadership behaviors and job competencies, the prospect of putting a value on those behaviors in the workplace has some appeal and explains the application of utility analysis in some situations. For example, the Eastman Chemical Company used this process to show the evaluation of an empowerment program for employees (Bernthal and Byham, 1997).

Utility analysis should be one of the tools considered in the ROI arsenal. In the framework presented in this book, it should be clearly understood that this is a Level 3 ROI analysis, which, in essence, is forecasting the value or impact based on the behavior change. This approach is covered in more detail in Chapter 9, *ROI Forecasting*.

CONSEQUENCES OF NOT TRAINING

For some organizations, the consequences of not training can be very serious. A company's inability to perform adequately might mean that it is unable to take on additional business or that it may lose existing business because of an untrained workforce. Training can also help avoid serious operational problems (accidents) or noncompliance issues (EEO violations). This method of calculating the return on training has received recent attention and involves the following steps:

☐ Recognize that there is a potential problem, loss, or negative consequence if the status quo is maintained.

☐ Isolate the potential problem linked to lack of performance, such as noncompliance issues, safety record, or the inability to take on additional business.

☐ Identify the specific measure that reflects the potential problem.

☐ Pinpoint the anticipated level of the measure if the status quo is maintained (industry average, benchmarking data, etc.).

☐ Calculate the difference in the measure from current levels desired and the potential problem level of the measure. This becomes the change that could occur if the program is not implemented.

☐ Develop the unit value of the measure using standard values, expert input, or external databases.

☐ Develop an estimate of the potential value. This becomes the total value of benefits derived from implementing the program.

☐ Estimate the total cost of training using the techniques outlined in Chapter 6.

☐ Compare benefits with costs.

An example can show how this process is used. An organization has an excellent record of discrimination lawsuits they want to maintain. The industry average shows discrimination charges at a ratio of 2:1000 employees per year. This company has a record average of only .25:1000—much below the industry average. The organization would like to implement a diversity program to continue to focus attention on this critical issue and ensure that the current, acceptable rate does not deteriorate. Thus, the first challenge is to identify the particular measure, which is the charges filed with the EEOC. The cost of a charge, derived from government and legal databases, set the value for a sexual harassment charge at $35,000. Using this as a measure, the payoff for the program is the funds lost if the organization's average migrated to the industry average. For 4000 employees, the difference is one complaint (the company's average) to eight complaints (the industry average). Thus, the value of seven complaints yields $245,000 (7 × $35,000). This is the potential savings of maintaining the current level of charges, assuming that the industry level is achieved if no program were implemented. Thus, the cost of the program can easily be compared with this monetary value to arrive at the potential payoff. In reality, the rate of charges may never reach the industry average because of company practices. If this is the situation, a discounted value could be developed. For example, 75% of the industry average could be used as the potential value achieved if no program were implemented.

This approach has some disadvantages. The potential loss of value (income or cost savings) can be highly subjective and difficult to measure. Because of these concerns, this approach to evaluating the return on training investments is limited to certain types of programs and situations.

This approach has some advantages, particularly with the focus on a variety of preventive programs. It provides a vehicle to use the ROI methodology in situations where the status quo is acceptable and often represents best practices. This approach can show the value of investing in new programs to maintain a good position. Essentially, the steps are the same. The challenge is to determine where the measure would be positioned, if the status quo were not maintained.

ROI, THE PROFIT CENTER, AND EVA

With the increased interest in converting the HRD function to the profit center concept, it is helpful to distinguish between the ROI methodology and the profit center strategy (Phillips, 1999). The ROI process described in this book shows the payoff of a specific program, or a group of programs, with highly integrated objectives. It is a micro-level process showing the economic value derived from these programs. The profit center concept usually applies to the entire HRD function. Under this concept, the HRD department operates as a privately owned business, with profit showing the true measure of economic success. Its customers, usually the key managers in the organization, have complete autonomy to use the internal services of the HRD function or to purchase those services externally. When the services are purchased internally, competitive prices are usually charged and transferred from the operating department to HRD. This serves as revenue to the HRD department. The department's expenses include salaries, office space, materials, fees, and services. Thus, the HRD department operates as a wholly owned subsidiary of the organization and with revenues for all the services and expenses representing the total expenses of the HRD staff. If the department realizes a profit, it means that the value received from the transfer of funds exceeds the costs. This approach holds much of the interest, particularly from senior executives who are seeking to bring complete accountability to this function. Also, this is a true test of the perceived value if managers have complete autonomy for using or not using the processes.

The profit center concept can be perceived to be a higher level of evaluation, as depicted in Figure 7-2, which shows the progression of eval-

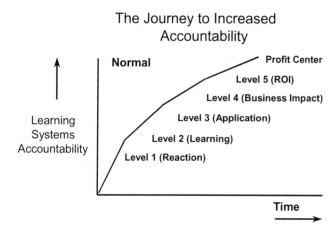

Figure 7-2. The progression of levels to the profit center.

uation levels to include the profit center. The figure illustrates the relative progression of these different levels of measurement. Level 1 has been used for many years and represents the most common and accepted evaluation data. Level 2 followed, as did Levels 3, 4, and now 5. The profit center concept is actually a higher level of accountability if it can be achieved. In essence, this is placing the value on the entire T&D function and can show the economic value added (EVA) to the organization. This is particularly important because of the recent emphasis on the EVA concept (Young and O'Byrne, 2001). This concept can be applied to departments generating revenue to offset expenses.

Figure 7-2 also underscores the fact that the previous levels of evaluation need to be in place before the next level will work. It is difficult for the profit center to be effective if Levels 4 and 5 evaluations have not become a routine part of the measurement scheme. Some of the organizations, that have failed in the move to the profit center concept, relied on their success with Levels 1 and 2 evaluation, skipping Levels 3, 4, and 5. Because participants reacted positively or developed skills, the HRD staff perceived that the program was adding value. Operating managers, on the other hand, were unable to see the value from this level of evaluation, and were reluctant to purchase the programs, when given an option. They were not convinced of the added value because they have not seen any data previously that showed the impact of the programs in their operating departments.

The profit center and EVA are excellent concepts for evaluating the impact of the entire training and development function. They are the goals of many training and development executives and managers. In reality, there are many barriers to making the process operational. Not every program should be optional; some programs and initiatives need to be consistent and the quality needs to be controlled in some way. Having managers opt out of programs and purchasing their own may develop a wide variety of programs that are not necessarily adding value. Also, some programs are necessary and should not be optional. Still, many HRD managers have this as a goal (Phillips, 1999).

ROI ISSUES

Cautions When Using ROI

Because of the sensitivity of the ROI process, caution is needed when developing, calculating, and communicating the return on investment. The implementation of the ROI process is a very important issue and a goal of many training and development departments. In addition to the guiding principles, a few issues should be addressed to keep the process from going astray. The following cautions are offered when using ROI.

Take a conservative approach when developing both benefits and costs. Conservatism in ROI analysis builds accuracy and credibility. What matters most is how the target audience perceives the value of the data. A conservative approach is always recommended for both the numerator of the ROI formula (benefits) and the denominator (program costs). The conservative approach is the basis for the guiding principles.

Use caution when comparing the ROI in training and development with other financial returns. There are many ways to calculate the return on funds invested or assets employed. The ROI is just one of them. Although the calculation for ROI in training and development uses the same basic formula as in other investment evaluations, it may not be fully understood by the target group. Its calculation method and its meaning should be clearly communicated. More importantly, it should be an item accepted by management as an appropriate measure for training program evaluation.

Involve management in developing the return. Management ultimately makes the decision if an ROI value is acceptable. To the extent possible, management should be involved in setting the parameters for calculations and establishing targets by which programs are considered acceptable within the organization.

Fully disclose the assumptions and methodology. When discussing the ROI methodology and communicating data, it is very important to fully disclose the process, steps, and assumptions used in the process. Strengths should be clearly communicated as well as weaknesses and shortcomings.

Approach sensitive and controversial issues with caution. Occasionally, sensitive and controversial issues will be generated when discussing an ROI value. It is best to avoid debates over what is measurable and what is not measurable unless there is clear evidence of the issue in question. Also, some programs are so fundamental to the survival of the organization that any attempt to measure it is unnecessary. For example, a program designed to improve customer service in a customer-focused company may escape the scrutiny of an ROI evaluation, on the assumption that if the program is well designed, it will improve customer service.

Teach others the methods for calculating the return. Each time an ROI is calculated, the training and development manager should use this opportunity to educate other managers and colleagues in the organization. Even if it is not in their area of responsibility, these individuals will be able to see the value of this approach to training and development evaluation. Also, when possible, each project should serve as a case study to educate the HRD staff on specific techniques and methods.

Recognize that not everyone will buy into ROI. Not every audience member will understand, appreciate, or accept the ROI calculation. For a variety of reasons, one or more individuals may not agree with the values. These individuals may be highly emotional about the concept of showing accountability for HRD. Attempts to persuade them may be beyond the scope of the task at hand.

Do not boast about a high return. It is not unusual to generate what appears to be a very high return on investment for an HRD program. Several examples in this book have illustrated the possibilities. An HRD manager who boasts about a high rate of return will be open to potential criticism from others, unless there are indisputable facts on which the calculation is based.

Choose the place for the debates. The time to debate the ROI methodology is not *during* a presentation (unless it can't be avoided). There are constructive times to debate the ROI process: in a special forum, among the HRD staff, in an educational session, in professional literature, on panel discussions, or even during the development of an ROI impact study. The time and place for debate should be carefully selected so as not to detract from the quality and quantity of information presented.

Do not try to use ROI on every program. As discussed earlier, some programs are difficult to quantify, and an ROI calculation may not be feasible. Other methods of presenting the benefits may be more appropriate. As discussed in Chapter 1, HRD executives are encouraged to set targets for the percent of programs in which ROIs are developed. Also, specific criteria should be established that select programs for ROI analysis, as briefly described.

ROI Myths

Although most practitioners recognize ROI as an important addition to measurement and evaluation, they often struggle with how to address the issue. Many professionals see the ROI methodology as a ticket to increased funding and prosperity for HRD. They believe that without it, they may be lost in the shuffle, and with it, they may gain the respect they need to continue moving the function forward. Regardless of their motivation for pursuing ROI, the key question is: "Is it a feasible process that can be implemented with reasonable resources, and will it provide the benefits necessary to make it a useful, routine tool?" The answer to this question may lead to debate, even controversy.

The controversy surrounding ROI stems from misunderstandings about what the process can and cannot do, and how it can or should be implemented in an organization. As a conclusion to the chapter, these misunderstandings are summarized as 15 myths about the ROI methodology. The myths are based on years of experience with ROI and the perceptions discovered during hundreds of consulting projects and workshops. Each myth is presented below, along with an appropriate explanation.

ROI is too complex for most users. This issue has been a problem because of a few highly complex models that have been presented publicly. Unfortunately, these models have done little to help users and have caused confusion about ROI. The ROI methodology is a basic financial formula for accountability that is simple and understandable: earnings are divided by investment; earnings equate to net benefits from the training program; and the investment equals the actual cost of the program. Straying from this basic formula can add confusion and create tremendous misunderstanding. The ROI model is simplified with a step-by-step, systematic process. Each step is taken separately and issues addressed for a particular topic; the decisions are made incrementally all the way through the process. This helps to reduce a complex process to a more simplified and manageable efforts.

ROI is expensive, consuming too many critical resources. The ROI process can become expensive if it is not carefully organized, controlled, and properly implemented. While the cost of an external ROI impact study can be significant, there are many actions that can be taken to keep costs down. Cost savings approaches to ROI are presented in Chapter 11.

If senior management does not require ROI, there is no need to pursue it. This myth captures the most innocent bystanders. It is easy to be lulled into providing evaluation and measurement that simply meets the status quo, believing that no pressure or requests means no requirement. The truth is that if senior executives have only seen Level 1 reaction data, they may not be asking for higher level data because they think it is not available. In some cases, training and development leaders have convinced top management that programs cannot be evaluated at the ROI level or that the specific impact of a program cannot be determined. Given these conditions, it comes as no surprise that some top managers are not asking for Level 5 (ROI) data.

There is another problem with this thinking. Paradigms are shifting—not only within the HRD context but within senior management teams as well. Senior managers are beginning to request this type of data. Changes in corporate leadership sometimes initiate important paradigm shifts. New leadership often requires proof of accountability. The process of integrating ROI into an organization takes time—about 12 to 18 months for many organizations. It is not a quick fix, and when senior executives suddenly ask the corporate university to produce this kind of data, they may expect the results to be produced quickly.

Because of this, training and performance improvement should initiate the ROI process and develop ROI impact studies long before senior management begins asking for ROI data.

ROI is a passing fad. Unfortunately, this comment does apply to many of the processes being introduced to organizations today. Accountability for expenditures will always be present, and the ROI provides the ultimate level of accountability. As a tool, ROI has been used for years. Previously, ROI has been used to measure the investment of equipment and new plants. Now it is being used in many other areas, including training, education, and learning solutions. With its rich history, ROI will continue to be used as an important tool in measurement and evaluation.

ROI is only one type of data. This is a common misunderstanding. The ROI calculation represents one type of data that shows the costs versus benefit for the program. However, six types of data are generated, representing both qualitative and quantitative data and often involves data from different sources, making the ROI methodology a rich source for a variety of data.

ROI is not future-oriented; it only reflects past performance. Unfortunately, many evaluation processes are past-oriented and reflect only what has happened with a program. This is the only way to have an accurate assessment of impact. However, the ROI methodology can easily be adapted to forecast the ROI, as described in Chapter 9, *ROI Forecasting*.

ROI is rarely used by organizations. This myth is easily dispelled when the evidence is fully examined. More than 1000 organizations use the ROI methodology, and there are at least 100 case studies published about the ROI methodology. Leading organizations throughout the world, including businesses of all sizes and sectors, use the ROI methodology to increase accountability and improve programs. This process is also being used in the nonprofit, educational, and government sectors. There is no doubt that it is a widely used process that is growing in use.

The ROI methodology cannot be easily replicated. This is an understandable concern. In theory, any process worthy of implementation is one that can be replicated from one study to another. For example, if two different people conducted an ROI impact study on the same program, would they obtain the same results? Fortunately, the ROI methodology is a systematic process with certain standards and guiding principles. The likelihood of two different evaluators obtaining the same results is quite high. Because it is a process that involves step-by-step procedures, it can also be replicated from one program to another.

ROI is not a credible process; it is too subjective. This myth has evolved because some ROI studies involving estimates have been publicized and promoted in literature and conferences. Many ROI studies have been conducted without the use of estimates. The problem with estimates often surfaces when attempting to isolate the effects of other factors. Using estimates from the participants is only one of several techniques used to isolate the effects of a program. Other techniques involve analytical approaches such as use of control groups and trend line analysis. Sometimes estimating is used in other steps of the process such as converting data to monetary values or estimating output in the data collection phase. In each of these situations, other options are often available, but for convenience or economics, estimation is often used. While estimations often represent the worst case scenario in ROI, they can be extremely reliable when they are obtained carefully, adjusted for error, and reported appropriately. The accounting, engineering, and technology fields routinely require the use of estimates—often without question or concern.

ROI is not possible for soft skills programs, only for production and sales. ROI often is most effective in soft skills programs. Soft skills training and learning solutions often drive hard data items such as output, quality, cost, or time. Case after case shows successful application of the ROI methodology to programs such as team building, leadership, communications, and empowerment. Additional examples of successful ROI application can be found in compliance programs such as diversity, sexual harassment prevention, and policy implementation. Any type of program or process can be evaluated at the ROI level. The issue surfaces when ROI is used for programs that should not be evaluated at this level. The ROI methodology should be reserved for programs that are expensive, address operational problems and issues related to strategic objectives, or attract the interest of management in terms of increased accountability.

ROI is for manufacturing and service organizations only. Although initial studies appeared in the manufacturing sector, the service sector quickly picked up the process as a useful tool. Then, it migrated to the nonprofit sector as hospitals and health care firms began endorsing and using the process. Next, ROI moved through government sectors around the world and, now, educational institutions are beginning to use the ROI methodology. Several educational institutions use ROI to measure the impact of their formal degree programs and less structured continuing education programs.

It is not always possible to isolate the influence of other factors. Isolating the effects of other factors is always achieved when using the ROI methodology. There are at least nine ways to isolate the influence of other factors, and at least one method will work in any given situation. The challenge is to select an appropriate isolation method for the resources and accuracy needed in a particular situation. This myth probably stems from an unsuccessful attempt at using a control group arrangement—a classic way of isolating the effect of a process, program, or initiative. In practice, a control group does not work in a majority of situations, causing some researchers to abandon the issue of isolating other factors. In reality, many other techniques provide accurate, reliable, and valid methods for isolating the effects.

Since there is no control over what happens after participants leave training, a process based on measuring on-the-job improvements should not be used. This myth is fading as organizations face the reality of implementing workplace learning solutions and realize the importance of measuring results. Although the HRD staff does not have direct control of what happens in the workplace, it does have influence on the process. A training or performance improvement program must be considered within the context of the workplace—the program is owned by the organization. Many individuals and groups are involved in training with objectives that push expectations beyond the classroom or keyboard. Objectives focus on application and impact data used in the ROI analysis. Also, the partnership often needed between key managers produces objectives that drive the program. In effect, HRD is a process with partnerships and a common framework to drive the results—not just classroom activity.

ROI is appropriate only for large organizations. While it is true that large organizations with enormous training budgets have the most interest in ROI, smaller organizations can also use the process, particularly when it is simplified and built into programs. Organizations with as few as 50 employees have successfully applied the ROI methodology, using it as a tool to bring increased accountability and involvement to training and development (Devaney, 2001).

There are no standards for the ROI methodology. An important problem facing measurement and evaluation is a lack of standardization or consistency. These questions are often asked: "What is a good ROI?" or, "What should be included in the cost so I can compare my data with other data?" or, "When should specific data be included in the ROI value instead of as an intangible?" While these questions are not easily answered, some help is on the way. Standards for the ROI methodology, using the guiding principles as a starting point, are under development. Also under development is a database that will share thousands of studies so that best practices, patterns, trends, and standards are readily available. For more information on these two issues, contact the author at roiresearch@mindspring.com.

FINAL THOUGHTS

After the program benefits are collected and converted to monetary values and the program costs are developed in a fully loaded profile, the ROI calculation becomes a very easy step. It is just a matter of plugging the values into the appropriate formula. This chapter has presented the two basic approaches for calculating the return—the ROI formula and the benefits/costs ratio. Each has its own advantages and disadvantages. Alternatives to ROI development were briefly discussed. Several examples were presented, along with key issues that must be addressed in ROI calculations. Cautions and myths surrounding the ROI capped off the chapter.

In conclusion, the ROI methodology is not for every organization or individual. The use of the ROI methodology represents a tremendous paradigm shift as an organization attempts to bring more accountability and results to the entire training and performance improvement process, from needs assessment to the development of an impact study. The ROI methodology brings a results-based focus to learning issues. This process is client-focused, requiring much contact, communication, dialogue, and agreement with the client group.

CASE STUDY—PART F, LINEAR NETWORK SYSTEMS

Costs

The costs to train 16 supervisors are:

Needs Assessment, Program Development, Facilitation	$51,000
Supplies and Materials ($185 × 16)	2,960
Food ($195 × 16)	3,120
Facilities (6 × 200)	1,200
Evaluation	10,000
Salaries and Benefits ($548 × 1.39 × 16)	12,188
Total	$80,468

The facilitation charge from the supplier, which totaled $51,000, includes the costs for needs assessment, program development, and facilitation. If the program had been developed internally, these three charges would need to be developed separately. The daily salary was developed by dividing the average salary ($47,500) by the total number of weekdays (52 × 5 = 260). To obtain the salaries and benefits costs for the 3-day workshop, this number is multiplied by 3, and adjusted upward by the benefits factor of 39%. (This is equivalent to multiplying by the average salary by 1.39.) The total for each participant is multiplied 16 to obtain the salaries and benefits for the group.

Follow-Up

Because management was interested in knowing the results of the program as soon as possible, a four-month evaluation period was used. Data for six months prior to and four months after the program are presented in Figures 7-3, 7-4, and 7-5, showing the productivity, turnover,

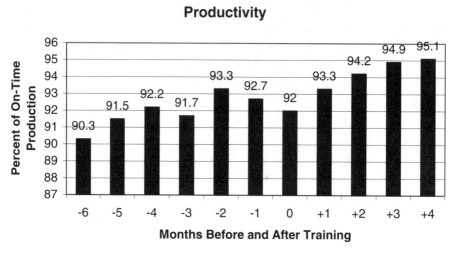

Figure 7-3. Productivity.

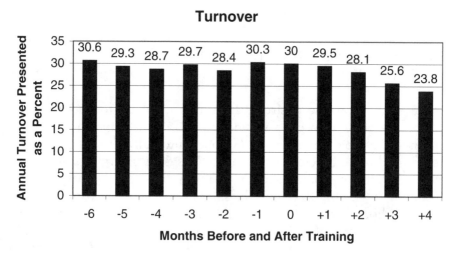

Figure 7-4. Turnover rates.

Absenteeism

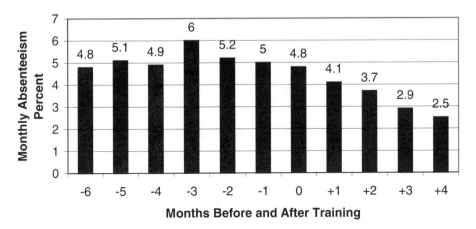

Figure 7-5. Absenteeism rates.

and absenteeism values for the plant. The training was conducted during a one-month period and no improvements were expected during that month. Consequently, the one-month training period was excluded from the analysis.

As Figure 7-3 shows, productivity was enhanced after the implementation of training. According to the records of the production control department, the average percent of on-time production for six months prior to training was 92%. A value of 95% was used as posttraining performance, which is the average of months three and four. Averaging the two monthly values avoids a spike in the calculations.

The plant's annual turnover rates averaged 29.5% for the six months prior to training and are presented in Figure 7-4. Turnover was calculated monthly and was reported as an annualized value for comparison (i.e., a 2% monthly turnover was reflected as a 24% annual turnover rate on the report). The average for months 3 and 4 yields a value of 24.7%.

The monthly absenteeism rates are shown in Figure 7-5. The absenteeism rate for the six months prior to training averaged 5.2% and was considered much too high by management. This figure includes only unexpected and unplanned absences. The average for months 3 and 4 yields a value of 2.7%.

Table 7-6. Contribution of Various Factors

	Training Program	TQM	Team Building	Total
Productivity (% of Schedule)	32%	49%	19%	100%
Turnover (Annualized)	72%	7%	21%	100%
Absenteeism (% Absence)	76%	4%	20%	100%

Table 7-7. Additional Benefits

Supervisor	Annual Improvement Value	Basis for Value	Isolation Factor	Confidence	Adjusted Value
#3	$36,000	Improvement in efficiency of group. $3,000/month × 12 (group estimate)	50%	85%	$15,300
#8	$24,000	Time savings: Improvement in customer response time (8 hours to 6 hours). Estimated value: $2,000/month	55%	60%	$7,920
#10	$8,090	Time savings: Team project completed 10 days ahead of schedule. Annual salaries #210,500 = $809/day × 10 days	45%	90%	$3,279
#15	$14,900	Direct cost savings	60%	90%	$7,830

Table 7-8. Improvement in Primary Measures

	Pretraining 6 Months Average	Posttraining, Months 3 and 4 Average	Prepost Differences	Participant's Estimate of Impact of Training	Unit Value	Annual Impact of Training (Estimates)
Productivity (% of Schedule)					$	$
Turnover (Annualized)					$	$
Absenteeism (% Absence)					$	$

In addition to action plans, supervisors completed a brief questionnaire where they estimated how much of the improvement in performance was related to each of the three factors influencing the output variables. The results are presented in Table 7-6.

Four of the supervisors submitted action plans focusing on measures other than productivity, turnover, or absenteeism. Three improvement areas were identified: time savings, efficiency, and direct cost savings. Table 7-7 shows a summary of these additional benefits.

Discussion Questions

1. Using the data in the case, complete Table 7-8.
2. What are the total benefits expected from the program using improvements in productivity, turnover, absenteeism (Table 7-8), and the additional benefits (Table 7-7)?
3. What are the benefits/costs ratio and the ROI for the program?

REFERENCES

Anthony, R.N., and J.S. Reece. *Accounting: Text and Cases*, 7th ed. Homewood, IL: Irwin, 1983.

Bernthal, P., and B. Byham. "Evaluation of Techniques for an Empowered Workforce," *In Action: Measuring Return on Investment*, vol. 2, J.J. Phillips (Ed.). Alexandria, VA: American Society for Training and Development, 1997, pp. 73–88.

Cascio, W.F. *Costing Human Resources: The Financial Impact of Behavior in Organizations*. Australia: South-Western College Publishing, 2000.

Devaney, M. "Measuring ROI of Computer Training in a Small to Medium-Sized Enterprise," *In Action: Measuring Return on Investment*, vol. 3, J.J. Phillips (Ed.). Alexandria, VA: American Society for Training and Development, 2001, pp. 185–196.

Horngren, C.T. *Cost Accounting*, 5th ed. Englewood Cliffs, NJ: Prentice-Hall, 1982.

Phillips, J.J. *HRD Trends Worldwide: Shared Solutions to Compete in a Global Economy*. Boston, MA: Butterworth–Heinemann, 1999.

Phillips, J.J., and D. Hill. "Preventing Sexual Harassment," The Human Resources Scores J.J. Phillips, R.D. Stone, and P.P. Phillips. Boston, MA:

Butterworth–Heinemann: American Society for Training and Development, 2001, pp. 354–372.

Phillips, J.J., and R.D. Stone, R.D. "Absenteeism Reduction Program," *In Action: Measuring ROI in the Public Sector*. Alexandria, VA: American Society for Training and Development, 2002, pp. 221–234.

Phillips, P.P. (Ed.) (2001). *In Action: Measuring Return on Investment*, vol. 3. Alexandria, VA: American Society for Training and Development.

Phillips, P.P., and J.J. Phillips. "Measuring Return on Investment on Interactive Selling Skills," *In Action: Measuring Return on Investment*, vol. 3, P.P. Phillips (Ed.). Alexandria, VA: American Society for Training and Development, 2001, pp. 233–249.

Schmidt, F.L., J.E. Hunter, and K. Pearlman. "Assessing the Economic Impact of Personnel Programs on Workforce Productivity," *Personnel Psychology*, vol. 35, 1982, pp. 333–347.

Seagraves, T.L. "Mission Possible: Selling Complex Services Over the Phone," *In Action: Measuring Return on Investment*, vol. 3, J.J. Phillips (Ed.). Alexandria, VA: American Society for Training and Development, 2001, pp. 65–79.

Young, S.D., and S.F. O'Byrne. *EVA® and Value-Based Management: A Practical Guide to Implementation*. New York, NY: McGraw-Hill, 2001.

FURTHER READING

Benson, D.K. *Return on Investment: Guidelines to Determine Workforce Development Impact*, 2nd ed. Peterborough, NH: Appropriate Solutions, Inc., 1999.

Chang, R.Y., and M.W. Morgan. *Performance Scorecards: Measuring the Right Things in the Real World*. San Francisco, CA: Jossey-Bass, 2000.

Eccles, R.G., R.H. Herz, E.M. Keegan, and D.M.H. Phillips. *The ValueReporting™ Revolution: Moving Beyond the Earnings Game*. New York, NY: John Wiley & Sons, Inc., 2001.

Epstein, M.J., and B. Birchard. *Counting What Counts: Turning Corporate Accountability to Competitive Advantage*. Reading, MA: Perseus, 1999.

Friedlob, G.T., and F.J. Plewa, Jr. *Understanding Return on Investment*. New York, NY: Wiley, 1991.

Gates, B., with Collins Hemingway. *Business @ the Speed of Thought: Using a Digital Nervous System*. New York, NY: Warner, 1999.

Marcum, D., S. Smith, and M. Khalsa. *businessThink: Rules for Getting It Right—Now, and No Matter What!* New York, NY: John Wiley & Sons, Inc., 2002.

Mitchell, D., C. Coles, and R. Metz. *The 2,000 Percent Solution: Free Your Organization from "Stalled" Thinking to Achieve Exponential Success.* New York, NY: AMACOM/American Management Association, 1999.

Price Waterhouse Financial & Cost Management Team. *CFO: Architect of the Corporation's Future.* New York, NY: Wiley, 1997.

Rasmussen, N., P.S. Goldy, and P.O. Solli. *Financial Business Intelligence: Trends, Technique, Softward Selection, and Implementation.* New York, NY: John Wiley & Sons, Inc., 2002.

Streeter, R. *Transforming Charity Toward a Results-Oriented Social Sector.* Indianapolis, IN: Hudson Institute, 2001.

Tesoro, F., and J. Tootson, J. *Implementing Global Performance Measurement Systems.* San Francisco, CA: Jossey-Bass/Pfeiffer, 2000.

Weddle, P.D. *ROI: A Tale of American Business.* McLean, VA: ProAction, 1989.

CHAPTER 8

Identifying Intangible Measures

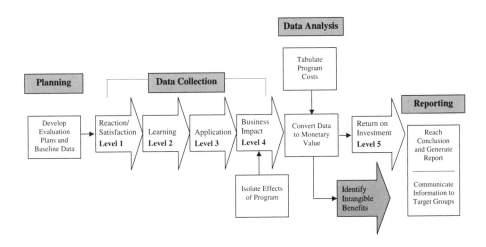

Intangible measures are the benefits or detriments directly linked to the training program, which cannot or should not be converted to monetary values. These measures are often monitored after the training program has been conducted and, although not converted to monetary values, they are still very important in the evaluation process. While the range of intangible measures is almost limitless, this chapter describes a few common measures, listed in Table 8-1, often linked with training.

Table 8-1. Typical Intangible Variables Linked with Training

☐ Attitude Survey Data	☐ Image
☐ Organizational Commitment	☐ Customer Satisfaction Survey Data
☐ Climate Survey Data	☐ Customer Complaints
☐ Employee Complaints	☐ Customer Retention
☐ Grievances	☐ Customer Response Time
☐ Discrimination Complaints	☐ Teamwork
☐ Stress Reduction	☐ Cooperation
☐ Employee Turnover	☐ Conflict
☐ Employee Absenteeism	☐ Decisiveness
☐ Employee Tardiness	☐ Communication
☐ Employee Transfers	☐ Innovation and Creativity
☐ Leadership	☐ Competencies

KEY ISSUES

Importance

Not all measures are in the tangible category. By design, some measures are captured and reported as intangible measures. Although they may not be perceived as valuable as the measures converted to monetary values, intangible measures are critical to the overall success of the organization (Oxman, 2002). In some programs, such as interpersonal skills training, team development, leadership, communications training, and management development, the intangible (nonmonetary) benefits can be more important than tangible (monetary) measures. Consequently, these measures should be monitored and reported as part of the overall evaluation. In practice, every project or program, regardless of its nature, scope, and content, will have intangible measures associated with it (Fitz-enz, 2001). The challenge is to efficiently identify and report them.

Perhaps the first step to understanding intangible is to clearly define the difference between tangible and intangible assets in a business organization. As presented in Table 8-2, tangible assets are required for business operations and are readily visible, rigorously quantified, and are represented as a line item on a balance sheet (Saint-Onge, 2000). The intangible assets are key to competitive advantage in the knowledge era and are invisible, difficult to quantify, and not tracked through traditional accounting practices. With this distinction, it is easier to

Table 8-2. Tangible and Intangible Comparisons

Tangible Assets Required for Business Operations	Intangible Assets Key to Competitive Advantage in the Knowledge Area
☐ Readily visible	☐ Invisible
☐ Rigorously quantified	☐ Difficult to quantify
☐ Part of the balance sheet	☐ Not tracked through accounting practices
☐ Investment produces known returns	☐ Assessment based on assumptions
☐ Can be easily duplicated	☐ Cannot be bought or imitated
☐ Depreciates with use	☐ Appreciates with purposeful use
☐ Has finite application	☐ Multiapplication without reducing value
☐ Best managed with "scarcity" mentality	☐ Best managed with "abundance" mentality
☐ Best leveraged through control	☐ Best leveraged through alignment
☐ Can be accumulated	☐ Dynamic: short shelf life when not in use

Table 8-3. Characteristics of Data

Hard Data	Soft Data
☐ Objectively based	☐ Subjectively based in many cases
☐ Easy to measure and quantify	☐ Difficult to measure and quantify, directly
☐ Relatively easy to assign monetary values	☐ Difficult to assign monetary values
☐ Common measures of organizational performance	☐ Less credible as a performance measure
☐ Very credible with management	☐ Usually behaviorally oriented

understand why intangible measures are difficult to convert to monetary values.

Another distinction between tangible and intangible is the concept of hard data versus soft data. This concept, discussed earlier, is perhaps more familiar to training and performance improvement practitioners. Table 8-3 shows the difference between hard and soft data, used earlier in this book. The most significant part of the definition is the difficulty in converting the data to monetary value. It is from this point that another guiding principle is derived.

Guiding Principle #11
Intangible measures are defined as measures that are purposely not converted to monetary values.

Using this simple definition avoids confusion of whether a data item should be classified as hard data or soft data. It is considered soft data if a credible, economically feasible process is unavailable for conversion. The ROI methodology discussed throughout this book will utilize this definition of intangibles.

Identification of Measures

Intangible measures can be identified from different sources representing different time frames, as illustrated in Figure 8-1. First, they can be uncovered early in the process, during the needs assessment. Once identified, the intangible data are planned for collection as part of the overall data collection strategy. For example, a team leader training program has several hard data measures linked to the program. An intangible measure, such as employee satisfaction, is identified and monitored with no plans to convert it to a monetary value. Thus, from the beginning, this measure is destined to be a nonmonetary benefit reported along with the ROI results.

A second way an intangible benefit is identified is during discussions with clients or sponsors about the impact of training. Clients can usually

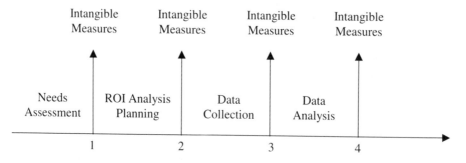

Figure 8-1. Identifying intangible measures.

identify intangible measures that are expected to be influenced by the program. For example, a management development program in a large multinational company was conducted, and an ROI analysis was planned. During the ROI planning session, program developers, instructors, a sample of participants' managers, and a senior executive identified potential intangible measures that were perceived to be influenced by the program. These measures are included on the ROI analysis planning document.

A third way an intangible measure is identified is during a follow-up evaluation. Although the measure was not expected or anticipated in the initial program design, the measure surfaces on a questionnaire, in an interview, or during a focus group. Questions are often asked about other improvements linked to the training program. Several intangible measures are usually provided and there are no planned attempts to place a value on the actual measure. For example, in an innovation and creativity training program, participants were asked specifically what had improved in their work as a result of the program. The participants provided several intangible measures, which managers perceived to be linked to the program.

The fourth way an intangible measure is identified is during an attempt to convert the data to monetary values. If the process loses credibility, the measure should be reported as an intangible benefit. For example, in a selling skills program, customer satisfaction is identified early in the process as one of the measures of training success. A conversion of the data to monetary values was attempted. However, the process of assigning a value to the data lost credibility; therefore, customer satisfaction was reported as an intangible benefit.

Is It Measurable?

Sometimes a debate will erupt over whether a particular item perceived as intangible (soft) can actually be measured. In reality, anything that represents the outcome of training can be measured. (The measure may have to be a perception of the issue taken from a particular stakeholder involved in the process, but it is still a measure.) The ROI methodology rests on the assumption that anything can be measured. In the mind of the sponsor or senior executive, if an intangible (soft) item cannot be measured, why bother? The state of that situation or issue will never be known. Thus, on a practical basis, any intangible can be measured— some, precisely; others not precisely. For example, team conflicts is a measure that can be captured and categorized precisely. Every conflict observer is recorded and the types of conflicts are placed in categories. However, to place a value on having fewer conflicts may cause the data item to be intangible if there is not a credible, economically feasible way to convert the measure to monetary value.

Can It Be Converted?

Chapter 5 focuses on different ways to convert data to monetary values. The philosophy taken is simple: Any data item can be converted to monetary value (i.e., there is no measure that can be presented to which a monetary value cannot be assigned). The key issue is credibility. Is it a believable value? Is the process to convert it to monetary value credible? Does it cost too much to convert it? Is that value stable over time? These are critical issues that will be explored mentally by senior executives when they examine the conversion of data to monetary value. For tangible data conversion, the issue is of little concern. Tangible data items are easily converted, such as increased output, reduction in rejects, and time savings. However, the soft measures (stress, complaints, and attitudes) often lose credibility in the process. Table 8-4 shows a four-part test for converting intangibles to monetary values. The test was described on an operational basis in Chapter 5 and is repeated here because this is the test that often leads to the classification of data as intangible. The ultimate test is #4. If the converted value cannot be communicated to the management group and secure their buy-in in two minutes, the data should be listed as intangible. This is a practical test that protects the credibility of the impact study and also allows for consistency from one

Table 8-4. Test for Converting Intangibles to Monetary Values

Tangible versus Intangible

1. Does an acceptable, standard monetary value exist for the measure? If yes, use it; if not, go to the next step.
2. Is there a method that *can* be used to convert the measure to money? If not, list it as an intangible; if yes, go to the next step.
3. Can the conversion be accomplished with minimum resources? If not, list it as an intangible; if yes, go to the next step.
4. Can the conversion process be described to an executive audience *and* secure their buy-in in two minutes? If yes, use it in the ROI calculation; if not, list it as an intangible.

study to another. The ROI methodology would be unreliable if one evaluator converted a particular data item to monetary value whereas another evaluator did not. This is an important part of building the standards necessary for the ROI methodology.

Intangible Measures versus Intellectual Capital

With the attention given to the concept of intellectual capital in recent years, and the value of intangible assets in organizations, it is helpful to distinguish between the intangible measures from a training or performance improvement program and those that might appear in a variety of measures in intellectual capital. Figure 8-2 shows the categories of intangible assets and their relationship to intellectual capital. Intellectual capital typically involves customer capital, human capital, and structural capital (Saint-Onge, 2000). Most of the HRD programs are driving measures in the human capital area, which includes the capability of individuals to provide solutions. More specifically, Table 8-5 offers the common human capital measures tracked by organizations as part of

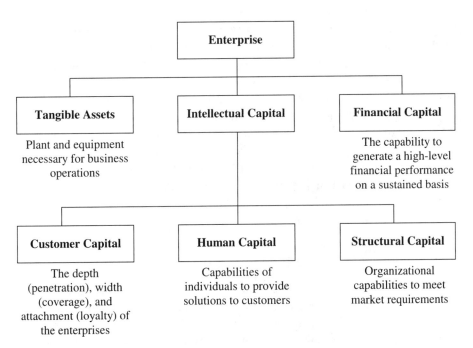

Figure 8-2. Tangible versus intangible assets.

Table 8-5. Common Human Capital Measures

☐ Innovation	☐ Learning	
☐ Employee satisfaction	☐ Competencies	
☐ Organizational commitment	☐ Educational level	
☐ Turnover	☐ HR investment	
☐ Tenure	☐ Leadership	
☐ Experience	☐ Productivity	

their human capital monitoring processes (Phillips, 2002). Many of these measures are driven by the training and performance improvement programs and are often considered intangible. Some of these will be described in this chapter.

Analysis

For most intangible data, no specific analysis is planned. Previous attempts to convert intangible data to monetary units resulted in aborting the process, thus no further data analysis is conducted. In some cases, there may be attempts to isolate the effects of training using one or more of the methods outlined in Chapter 4. This step is necessary when there is a need to know the specific amount of change in the intangible measure that is linked to the program. In many cases, however, the intangible data reflect evidence of improvement. Neither the precise amount of the improvement nor the amount of improvement related directly to the training is needed. Since the value of this data is not placed in the ROI calculation, intangible measures are not normally used to justify additional training or continuation of existing training. Consequently, a detailed analysis is not justified. Intangible benefits are viewed as supporting evidence of the programs success and are presented as qualitative data.

TYPICAL INTANGIBLE MEASURES

Most of the remainder of the chapter focuses on typical intangible measures. These measures are often presented as intangibles in impact studies. For each individual measure, there may be exceptions where organizations *can* convert the data to monetary value. Three notable exceptions are offered. Retention (employee turnover) is now converted to monetary value in most cases and presented as a tangible. Reliable ways are available to arrive at the value for absenteeism without exhausting resources. Also, recent developments in the measurement of customer satisfaction include ways to convert these critical measures to monetary value. These three, plus others, are described in more detail in this section.

Employee Satisfaction

Employee satisfaction is perhaps one of the most important intangible measures. Some HRD programs are designed to improve employee satisfaction. Attitude surveys are conducted to measure the extent to which employees are satisfied with the organization, their jobs, their supervisor, coworkers, and a host of other job related factors. Attitude survey data is usually linked to training results when specific issues on the survey are related to training. For example, in a diversity training program conducted for all employees at a television station, the annual attitude survey contained five questions directly tied to perceptions and attitudes influenced by the training program.

Because attitude surveys are usually taken annually, survey results may not be in sync with the timing of the training program. When job satisfaction is one of the program objectives, and is a critical outcome, some organizations conduct surveys at a prescribed time frame after training, and design the survey instrument around issues related to the training program. This approach, however, is very expensive.

While employee satisfaction has always been an important issue in employee relations, in recent years it has taken on new importance because of the key relationships of job satisfaction to other measures. A classical relationship with employee satisfaction is in the area of employee recruitment and retention. Firms with excellent employee satisfaction ratings are often attractive to potential employees. It becomes a subtle but important recruiting tool. "Employers of Choice" and "Best Places to Work," for example, often have high levels of employee satisfaction ratings, which attract employees. There is also a relationship between employee satisfaction and employee turnover. This relationship has taken on a new meaning as turnover and retention have become critical issues in the last decade and are projected to continue to be critical in the future. Today these relationships are often easily developed as many of the human resource information systems have modules to calculate the correlation between the turnover rates and the employee satisfaction scores for the various job groups, divisions, departments, etc.

Employee satisfaction has taken on new meanings in connection with customer service. Hundreds of applied research projects are beginning to show a very high correlation between employee satisfaction scores and customer satisfaction scores. Intuitively, this seems obvious—a more satisfied employee is likely to provide more productive, friendly, and appropriate customer service. Likewise, a disgruntled employee will provide poor service. These links, often referred to as a service-profit-chain, create a promising way to identify important relationships between attitudes and profits in an organization.

Even with these developments, most organizations do not, or cannot, place credible values on employee satisfaction data. The trend is definitely in that direction, but until that occurs, job satisfaction is usually listed as an intangible benefit in most impact studies.

Organizational Commitment

In recent years, organizational commitment (OC) measures have complemented or replaced job satisfaction measures. OC measures go beyond employee satisfaction and include the extent to which the employees identify with organizational goals, mission, philosophy, value, policies, and practices. The concept of involvement and becoming a part of the organization is the key issue. OC is a measure that more closely correlates with productivity and other performance improvement measures, while employee satisfaction does not always correlate with improvements in productivity. As OC scores improve (taken on a standard index), there should be corresponding improvement in productivity. The OC is often measured the same way as attitude surveys, using a five- or seven-point scale taken directly from employees or groups of employees.

Organizational commitment is rarely converted to monetary value. Although some relationships have been developed to link it to more tangible data, this research is still in the developing stage. For most studies, organizational commitment would be listed as an intangible.

Climate Survey Data

Some organizations conduct climate surveys, which reflect work climate changes such as communication, openness, trust, and quality of feedback. Closely related to organizational commitment, climate surveys are more general and often focus on a range of workplace issues and environmental enablers and inhibitors. Climate surveys conducted before and after training may reflect the extent to which training has changed these intangible measures.

Employee Complaints

Some organizations record and report specific employees' complaints. These feedback mechanisms are usually highly visible with catchy names such as "Speak Out," "Talk Back," or "Hey, Mike" (in an organization where the CEO's first name is Mike). A reduction of employee complaints is sometimes directly related to training and performance improvement, such as a team-building program. Consequently, the level of complaints is used as a measure of the program's success and is usually reported as an intangible measure. Because of the difficulty in converting complaints to monetary values, this measure is almost always listed as an intangible benefit.

Grievances

In both union and nonunion organizations, grievances often reflect the level of dissatisfaction or disenchantment with a variety of factors in their organization. Sometimes, training and performance improvement programs, such as labor–management cooperation, are designed to reduce the number of grievances when they are considered excessive. An improvement in the grievance level may reflect the success of the programs. The impact of grievances can be significant—affecting a variety of cost categories. While this measure may be converted to a monetary value, it may be reported as an intangible measure.

Discrimination Complaints

Employee dissatisfaction shows up in different types of discrimination complaints, ranging from informal complaints to external charges and even litigation against the organization. Training programs, such as a sexual harassment prevention workshop, may be designed to prevent complaints or to reduce the current level of complaint activity. This measure can be devastating in organizations. However, the success of the program, in terms of complaint reduction, is sometimes not converted to monetary values because of the various assumptions and estimations involved in the process. When this is the case, these measures are reported as intangible program benefits.

Stress Reduction

Training programs such as time management, personal productivity, or conflict resolution, can reduce work-related stress by preparing participants to identify and confront stress factors, to improve job performance, accomplish more in a workday, and relieve tension and anxiety. The subsequent reduction in stress may be directly linked to the program. Although excessive stress may be directly linked to other, easy to convert data, such as productivity, absenteeism, and medical claims, it is usually listed as an intangible benefit.

Employee Retention

When job satisfaction deteriorates to the point where employees withdraw from work or the organization, either permanently or temporarily, the results can be disastrous. Perhaps the most critical employee withdrawal variable is employee turnover (or employee retention). An extremely costly variable, turnover, can have devastating consequences on organizations when it is excessive. Few measures have attracted so much attention as employee turnover. Fueled, in part, by low unemployment rates in North America and industrialized countries, retention has become a strategic issue. The survival of some firms depends on low turnover rates for critical job groups. Not only is turnover compared to historical rates, but it is often compared to best practice firms.

The good news is that many firms have made important strides in maintaining low turnover even in high turnover industries such as retail, hotel, and restaurant. Turnover is defined as the number of employees leaving in a month divided by the average number of employees in the month. This is a standard turnover rate that includes all individuals leaving. A more appropriate measure would be to include only turnover considered to be avoidable, usually referring to employees who voluntarily leave or those whose departure could have been prevented. For example, if an employee is terminated for poor performance in the first six months of employment, something went wrong that could have been prevented. Avoidable turnover is an important issue.

Many supervisor and team leader training programs are designed to reduce employee turnover in their work units. In many situations, turnover is actually converted to monetary values, using one of the methods described in Chapter 5. However, because of the multitude of costs and assumptions involved in developing the value, some organizations prefer not to convert turnover to a monetary value. In this case, turnover is reported as an intangible benefit, reflecting the success of the training or performance improvement program.

Employee Absenteeism

Unplanned absenteeism is another disruptive and costly variable. Many training programs are designed to reduce absenteeism; the amount of absenteeism reduction related to training can usually be pinpointed. Although the cost of absenteeism can be developed, the variety of costs—direct and indirect—necessary for a fully loaded cost impact make the process difficult. Consequently, the conversion process is not credible enough for some audiences and absenteeism changes are reported as intangible benefits.

Employee Tardiness

Some organizations actually monitor tardiness, especially in highly focused work and tightly contained work environments, such as call centers. Tardiness is an irritating work habit problem that can cause inefficiencies and delays. Electronic and computerized time reporting is used to pinpoint the problem area. A few training programs are designed to reduce or prevent it. Tardiness is very difficult to convert to a monetary value because of the many aspects of the impact of the unacceptable work habit. Consequently, when tardiness is presented as an improvement from a training program, it is usually listed as an intangible benefit.

Employee Transfers

Another way for employees to withdraw is to request a transfer to another section, department, or division of the organization. Requests for transfers often reflect dissatisfaction with a variety of issues, including management, policies, and practices in the organization. Transfers are essentially internal turnover. Training programs are sometimes designed to reduce or remove these unpleasant environmental influences. In these situations, requests for transfers are monitored and reported as an intangible benefit of training. Although it is possible to place a value on this internal turnover, usually no attempt is made to assign monetary values to transfers.

Innovation and Creativity

For many progressive organizations, innovation is important to success in creation. A variety of innovation and creativity training programs are implemented to make improvement in this critical area. Innovation is both easy and difficult to measure. It is easy to measure outcomes in areas such as copyright, patents, inventions, and employee suggestions. It is more difficult to measure the creative spirit and behavior of employees. Perhaps the most obvious measure is tracking the patents and trademarks that are not only used internally but are licensed for others to use through a patent and license exchange website.

An employee suggestion system, a longtime measure of the innovative and creative processes of an organization, still flourishes today in many firms. Employees are rewarded for their suggestions if they are approved and implemented. Tracking the suggestion rates and comparing them with other organizations is an important benchmarking item for innovation and creative capability. Other measures, such as the number of new projects, products, processes, and strategies, can be monitored and measured in some way. Subjectivity often enters the measurement process with these issues. Some organizations will actually measure the creative capability of employees using inventories and instruments. Comparing actual scores of groups of employees over time reflects the degree to which employees are improving innovativeness and creativity in the workplace. Having consistent and comparable measures is still a challenge. Because of the difficulty of converting data to monetary values, these measures are usually listed as intangibles.

Competencies

Organizations are interested in developing key competencies in particular areas such as the core mission, key product lines, and important processes. Core competencies are often identified and implemented in critical job groups. Competencies are measured with self-assessments from the individual employee as well as assessments from the supervisor. In some cases, other inputs may be important or necessary to measure. That approach goes beyond just learning new skills, processes, or knowledge to using a combination of skills, knowledge, and behavior on the job to develop an acceptable level of competence to meet competitive challenges.

Leadership

Perhaps the most difficult measure is leadership, yet leadership can make the difference in the success or failure of an organization. Without the appropriate leadership behaviors throughout the organization, the other resources can be misapplied or wasted. Measuring leadership can be accomplished in many different ways.

One of the most common methods is known as a 360-degree feedback. Here, a prescribed set of leadership behaviors desired in an organization is assessed by different sources to provide a composite of the overall leadership capability. The sources often come from the immediate manager of the leader, a colleague in the same area, the employees under the direct influence of the leader, internal or external customers, and through a self-assessment. These assessments come from different directions, forming a 360-degree circle. The measure is basically an observation captured in a survey, often reported electronically. This 360-degree feedback has been growing rapidly in North America, Europe, and Asia as an important way to capture overall leadership behavior change.

Customer Satisfaction

Because of the importance of building and improving customer service, a variety of measures are often monitored and reported as a payoff of training. A variety of customer service training programs have a direct influence on these measures. One of the most important measures is survey data showing the degree to which customers are pleased with the products and services. These survey values, reported as absolute data or as an index, represent important data from which to compare the success of a customer service training program.

As described earlier, customer satisfaction data is achieving a lot of interest and its value is often connected with linkages to other measures such as revenue growth, market share, and profits. Several models are available to show what happens when customers are dissatisfied, along with the economic impact of those decisions. In the health care area, researchers show linkages between patient satisfaction and customer retention. Still others are showing relationships between customer satisfaction, innovation, product development, and other tangible measures.

Techniques are available to convert survey data to monetary values, but in most situations, the conversion is rarely attempted. Consequently, customer satisfaction improvements at the present time are usually reported as intangible benefits.

Customer Complaints

Most organizations monitor customer complaints. Each complaint is recorded along with the disposition and the time required to resolve the complaint, as well as specific costs associated with the complaint resolution. Organizations sometimes design training programs to reduce the number of customer complaints. The total cost and impact of a complaint has three components: the time it takes to resolve the complaint, the cost of making restitution to the customer, and the ultimate cost of ill-will generated by the dissatisfaction (lost future business). Because of the difficulty in assigning an accurate monetary value to a customer complaint, the measure usually becomes a very important intangible benefit.

Customer Loyalty

Customer retention is a critical measure that is sometimes linked to sales, marketing, and customer service training and performance improvement programs. Long-term, efficient, and productive customer relationships are important to the success of an organization. While the importance of customer retention is understood, it is not always converted to monetary value. Specific models have been developed to show the value of a customer and how to keep customers over a period of time. For example, the average tenure of a customer can translate directly into a bottom-line savings.

Tied very closely with customer loyalty is the rate at which customers leave the organization. The churn rate is a critical measure that can be costly, not only in lost business (profits from lost customers), but the cost necessary to generate a new customer. Because of the difficulty of converting directly to a specific monetary value, customer loyalty is listed as an intangible benefit.

Customer Response Time

Providing prompt customer service is a critical issue in most organizations. Consequently, the time it takes to respond to specific customer service requests or problems is recorded and monitored. Response time reduction is sometimes an objective of training programs, although the reduction is not usually converted to monetary values. Thus, customer response time becomes an important intangible benefit.

Other Customer Responses

A variety of other types of customer responses can be tracked such as creativity with customer response, responsiveness to cost and pricing issues, and other important issues customers may specify or require. Monitoring these variables can provide more evidence of the training program's results when the program influences particular variables. And because of the difficulty of assigning values to the items, they are usually reported as intangible measures.

Teamwork

A variety of measures are often monitored to reflect how well teams are working. Although the output of teams and the quality of their work are often measured as hard data and converted to monetary values, other interpersonal measures may be monitored and reported separately. Sometimes organizations survey team members before and after training to determine if the level of teamwork has increased. Using a variable scale, team members provide a perception of improvement. The monetary value of increased teamwork is rarely developed and consequently, it is reported as an intangible benefit.

Cooperation

The success of a team often depends on the cooperative spirit of team members. Some instruments measure the level of cooperation before and after training, using a perception scale. Because of the difficulty of converting this measure to a monetary value, it is almost always reported as an intangible benefit.

Conflict

In team environments, the level of conflict is sometimes measured. A reduction in conflict may reflect the success of training. Although conflict reduction can be measured by perception or numbers of conflicts, the monetary value is an illusive figure. Consequently, in most situations, a monetary value is not placed on conflict reduction, and it is reported as an intangible benefit.

Decisiveness

Teams make decisions, and the timing of the decision-making process often becomes an issue. Consequently, decisiveness is sometimes measured in terms of the speed at which decisions are made. Some training programs are expected to influence this process. Survey measures may reflect the perception of the team or, in some cases, may monitor how quickly decisions are made. Although reductions in the timing of decisions can be converted to monetary values, improvements are usually reported as intangible benefits.

Communication

A variety of communication instruments reflect the quality and quantity of communication within a team. Improvement in communications effectiveness, or perceptions of effectiveness, driven by a training program is not usually converted to monetary values and is reported as an intangible benefit.

FINAL THOUGHTS

A variety of available intangible measures reflect the success of training and performance improvement programs. Although they may not be perceived as valuable as specific monetary measures, they nevertheless are an important part of an overall evaluation. Intangible measures should be identified, explored, examined, monitored, and analyzed for changes when they are linked to the program. Collectively, they add a unique dimension to the overall program results since most, if not all, programs have intangible measures associated with them. While some of the most common intangible measures were covered in this chapter, the coverage was not meant to be complete. The number of intangible measures is almost unlimited.

CASE STUDY—PART G, LINEAR NETWORK SYSTEMS

The tabulations of the benefits for the program for the primary measures are shown in Tables 8-6, 8-7, and 8-8.

Table 8-6. Annual Monetary Values for Primary Measures

	Pretraining, 6 Month Average	Posttraining Months 3 and 4 Average	Prepost Differences	Participant's Estimate of Impact of Training	Unit Value	Annual Impact of Training (Estimates)
Productivity (% of Schedule)	92%	95%	3%	.96% (3% × 32%)	$21,000 for 1%	$20,160
Turnover (Annualized)	29.5%	24.7%	4.8%	3.46% (4.8% × 72%)	$24,800 for each turnover	$330,360
Absenteeism (% Absence)	5.2%	2.7%	2.5%	1.9% (2.5% × 76%)	$98 for each absence	$163,446

Calculations

Productivity:

Savings = .96 × $21,000 = $20,160

Turnover:

Change in number leaving in a year = 385 × 3.46% = 13.3

Savings = 13.3 × $24,800 = $330,360

Absenteeism:

Change in absences (Incidents) = 385 × 228 × 1.9% = 1668

Savings = 1668 × $98 = $163,446

Table 8-7. Summary of Primary Monetary Values

Measures	Benefits
Increase in Productivity	$20,160
Reduction in Employee Turnover	$330,360
Reduction in Absenteeism	$163,446
Total	$513,966

Table 8-8. Summary of Other Monetary Values

Measures	Benefits
Efficiency	$15,300
Time Savings (participant 1)	$7,920
Time Savings (participant 2)	$3,279
Direct Cost Savings	$7,830
Total	$34,329

ROI and BCR Calculations

Total Benefits: $513,966 + $34,329 = $548,295

$$\text{BCR} = \frac{\$548,295}{\$80,468} = 6.81$$

$$\text{ROI (\%)} = \frac{\$548,295 - \$80,468}{\$80,468} \times 100 = 581\%$$

Discussion Questions

1. Are these numbers lower or higher than you expected? Comment.
2. How do you think these estimates would compare with the values at six months after the program is conducted? One year?
3. How could the ROI process be improved?
4. What are the potential intangible benefits from this program?

REFERENCES

Chang, R.Y., and M.W. Morgan, *Performance Scorecards: Measuring the Right Things in the Real World*. San Francisco, CA: Jossey-Bass, 2000.

Denzin, M.K., and Y.S. Lincoln (Eds.), *Handbook of Qualitative Research*. Thousand Oaks, CA: Sage Publications, 1994.

Fitz-enz, J. *The ROI of Human Capital: Measuring the Economic Value of Employee Performance*. New York, NY: American Management Association, 2001.

Fitz-enz, J., and B. Davison, *How to Measure Human Resources Management*, 3rd ed. New York, NY: McGraw-Hill, 2002.

Gummesson, E. *Qualitative Methods and Management Research* (revised ed.). Thousand Oaks, CA: Sage Publications, 1991.

Oxman, J.A. "The Hidden Leverage of Human Capital," *MIT Sloan Management Review*, Summer 2002.

Phillips, P.P. (Ed.). *In Action: Measuring Intellectual Capital*. Alexandria, VA: American Society for Training and Development, 2002.

Saint-Onge, H. "Shaping Human Resource Management within the Knowledge-Driven Enterprise." *Leading Knowledge Management and Learning*, edited by Dede Bonner. Alexandria, VA: American Society for Training and Development, 2000.

FURTHER READING

Badaracco, Jr., J.L. "We Don't Need Another Hero," *Harvard Business Review*, September 2001, p. 121.

Baynton, D. "America's $60 Billion Problem," *Training*, May 2001, p. 51.

Caudron, S. "How HR Drives Profits," *Workforce*, December 2001, p. 26

Collins, J. "Good to Great," *Fast Company*, October 2001, p. 90.

Deming, W.E. "Implementing a Global Performance Measurement System," *Performance Improvement*, vol. 40, No. 6, September 2001, p. 17.

Richard, L., C. Nimmy, and G.F. Walker. "HR Metrics Measured," *Globalhr*, December/January 2002, pp. 22–25.

Selden, L., and Colvin, G. "A Measure of Success," *Business 2.0*, November 2001, p. 59.

Ulwick, A.W. "Turn Customer Input into Innovation," *Harvard Business Review*, January 2002, p. 91.

CHAPTER 9

ROI Forecasting

Sometimes there is confusion about when it is appropriate to develop the ROI. The traditional and recommended approach, described in the previous chapters of this book, is to base ROI calculations strictly on business impact data obtained after the program has been implemented. In the approach, business performance measures (Level 4 data) are easily converted to a monetary value, which is necessary for an ROI calculation. Sometimes these measures are not yet available, and it is usually assumed that an ROI calculation is out of the question. This chapter will illustrate that ROI calculations are possible at a variety of time frames using a variety of data. Preprogram ROI forecasts are possible, as well as forecasts with reaction data (Level 1), learning data (Level 2), and application data (Level 3).

WHY FORECAST ROI?

Although the most accurate way to assess and develop an ROI calculation is based on postprogram data, sometimes it is important to know the forecast before the final results are tabulated. Forecasting ROI during the project, or in some cases, even before the program is pursued, is an important issue. Critical reasons drive the need for a forecasted ROI. Collectively, the five reasons, described in this section, are causing more organizations to examine ROI forecasts so that the client or sponsor will have some estimate of the expected payoff.

Reduce Uncertainty

Reducing uncertainty in a proposed program is sometimes critical. In a perfect world, the client or sponsor of a new program would like to know the expected payoff before any action is taken. Realistically, knowing the exact payoff may be impossible and, from a practical standpoint, it may not be feasible to obtain. However, there is still the desire to take the uncertainty out of the equation and act on the best data available, sometimes pushing the project to a forecasted ROI before any resources are expended. Some managers will simply not budge without a preproject forecast; they need some measure of expected success before allocating any resources to the project.

New Programs Are too Expensive to Pursue without Supportive Data

In some cases even a pilot program is not practical until some analysis has been conducted to examine the potential ROI. For example, if the program involves a significant amount of work in design, development, and delivery, a client may not want to expend the resources, even for a pilot program, unless there is some assurance of a positive ROI. Although there may be tradeoffs with a lower-profile and lower-cost pilot program, the preprogram ROI, nevertheless, becomes an important issue, prompting some sponsors to stand firm until an ROI forecast is produced.

Compare with Post Data

Whenever there is a plan to collect data on the success of the training application, impact, and ROI, it is helpful to compare actual results to preprogram expectations. In an ideal world, a forecasted ROI should have a defined relationship with the actual ROI, or they should be very similar. One important reason for forecasting ROI is to see how well the forecast holds up under the scrutiny of postprogram analysis.

Save Costs

There are several cost-saving issues prompting the use of ROI forecasting. First, developing the forecast itself is often a very inexpensive process because it involves estimations and many different assumptions. Second, if the forecast becomes a reliable predictor of the postprogram analysis, the forecasted ROI might substitute for the actual ROI, at least with some adjustments. This could save money on the postprogram analysis. Finally, the forecasted ROI data might be used for comparisons in other areas, at least as a beginning point for other types of programs. Thus, there may be the potential to transfer the forecasted ROI to other specific programs.

Comply with Policy

More organizations are developing policy statements requiring a fore-casted ROI before major projects are undertaken. For example, in one organization, any project exceeding $300,000 must have a forecasted ROI before it can be approved. In the United States, federal government units are required to show a preprogram cost benefit analysis (ROI) for selecting new programs. In one country, an organization can receive partial payments for a training project if the ROI forecast is positive and likely to enhance the organization. This formal policy and legal structure is becoming a more frequent reason for developing the ROI forecast.

THE TRADE-OFFS OF FORECASTING

ROI can be developed at different times using different levels of data. Unfortunately, the ease, convenience, and low cost involved in captur-ing a forecasted ROI create trade-offs in accuracy and credibility. As shown in Figure 9-1, there are five distinct time intervals during the implementation of a program when the ROI can actually be developed. The relationship with credibility, accuracy, cost, and difficulty is also shown in this figure.

The time intervals are:

1. A preprogram forecast can be developed using estimates of the impact of the training and performance improvement program. This approach lacks credibility and accuracy, but it is also the least expensive and least difficult ROI to calculate. There is value in developing the ROI on a preprogram basis. This will be discussed in the next section.
2. Reaction and satisfaction data can be extended to develop an anticipated impact, including the ROI. In this case, participants actually anticipate the chain of impact as a program is applied,

ROI with:	Data Collection Timing (Relative to Program Implementation)	Credibility	Accuracy	Cost to Develop	Difficulty
1. Preprogram Data	Before Program	Not Very Credible	Not Very Accurate	Inexpensive	Not Difficult
2. Reaction and Satisfaction Data	During Program				
3. Learning Data	During Program				
4. Application and Implementation	After Program				
5. Business Impact Data	After Program	Very Credible	Very Accurate	Expensive	Very Difficult

Figure 9-1. ROI at different times and levels.

implemented, and influences specific business measures. While the accuracy and credibility are greater than for the preprogram forecast, this approach still lacks the credibility and accuracy desired in most situations.

3. Learning data in some programs can be used to forecast the actual ROI. This approach is applicable only when formal testing shows a relationship between acquiring certain skills or knowledge and subsequent business performance. When this correlation is available (it is usually developed to validate the test), test data can be used to forecast subsequent performance. The performance can then be converted to monetary impact and the ROI can be developed. This has less potential as an evaluation tool due to the lack of situations in which a predictive validation can be developed.

4. In some situations, when frequency of skills and actual use of skills are critical, the application and implementation of those skills or knowledge can be converted to a value using employee compensation as a basis. This is particularly helpful in situations where competencies are being developed and values are placed on improving competencies, even if there is no immediate increase in pay.

5. Finally, the ROI can be developed from business impact data converted directly to monetary values and compared to the cost of the program. This is not a forecast. This postprogram evaluation is the basis for the other ROI calculations in this book and has been the principal approach used in previous chapters. It is the preferred approach, but because of the pressures outlined above, it is critical to examine ROI calculations at other times and with data other than Level 4.

This chapter will discuss in detail preprogram evaluation and the ROI calculations based on reactions. To a lesser degree, the ROI calculations developed from learning and application data will be discussed.

PREPROGRAM ROI FORECASTING

Perhaps one of the most useful steps in convincing a sponsor that a training expense is appropriate is to forecast the ROI for the project. The process is very similar to the postprogram analysis, except that the extent of the impact must be estimated along with the forecasted cost.

Basic Model

Figure 9-2 shows the basic model for capturing the necessary data for a preprogram forecast. This model is a modification of the postprogram ROI model, except that data are projected instead of being collected during different time frames. In place of the data collection is an estimation of the change in impact data expected to be influenced by the training program. Isolating the effects of the training becomes a nonissue, as the estimation is focused on the anticipated impact of training only, not considering other factors that may come into play.

The method to covert data to monetary values is the same as in postprogram ROI because the data items examined in a pre- and postprogram analysis should be the same. Estimating the program's cost should be an easy step, as costs can easily be anticipated based on previous projects using reasonable assumptions about the current project. The anticipated intangibles are merely speculation in forecasting but can be reliable indicators of which measures may be influenced in addition to those included in the ROI calculation. The formula used to calculate the ROI is the same as in the postprogram analysis. The amount of monetary value from the data conversion is included as the numerator, while the estimated cost of the training program is inserted as the denominator. The projected benefits/costs analysis can be developed along with

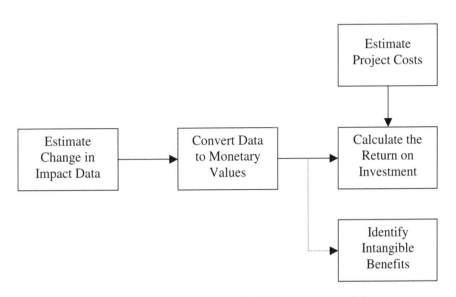

Figure 9-2. Preprogram ROI forecast model.

the actual ROI. The steps to actually develop the process are detailed next.

Steps to Develop the ROI

The detailed steps to develop the preprogram ROI forecast are presented in simplified form below:

1. Develop the Levels 3 and 4 objectives with as many specifics as possible. Ideally, these should be developed from the initial needs analysis and assessment. They detail what will change in the work setting and identify which measures will be influenced. If these are not known, the entire forecasting process is in jeopardy. There must be some assessment of which measures will change as a result of the training, and someone must be able to provide the extent to which the measures will change.
2. Estimate or forecast the monthly improvement in the business impact data. This is considered to be the amount of change directly related to the intervention and is denoted by ΔP. This is the most difficult step and is examined in more detail in the next section.
3. Convert the business impact data to monetary values using one or more of the methods described in Chapter 5. These are the same techniques, using the same processes as a postprogram analysis; V denotes this value.
4. Develop the estimated annual impact for each measure. In essence, this is the first-year improvement from the training program, showing the value for the change in the business impact measures directly related to the training program. In formula form this is $\Delta I = \Delta P \times V \times 12$.
5. Factor additional years into the analysis if a program will have a significant useful life beyond the first year. When this is the case, these values may be discounted to reflect a diminished benefit in subsequent years. The sponsor or owner of the program should provide some indication as to the amount of the reduction and the values developed for years two, three, etc. However, it is helpful to be conservative by using the smallest numbers possible.
6. Estimate the fully loaded cost of the program. Using all of the cost categories contained in Chapter 6, the fully loaded cost will be estimated and projected for the program. This is denoted as C.

Again, all direct and indirect costs should be included in the calculation.

7. Calculate the forecasted ROI using the total projected benefits and the estimated cost in the standard ROI formula:

$$\text{ROI}(\%) = \frac{\Delta I - C}{C} \times 100$$

8. Use sensitivity analysis to develop several potential ROI values with different levels of potential improvements (ΔP). When more than one measure is changing, that analysis would perhaps be performed using a spreadsheet showing different possible scenarios for output and the subsequent ROI.
9. Identify potential intangible benefits by obtaining input from those most knowledgeable of the situation. These are only anticipated and are based on assumptions from previous experience with this type of program implementation.
10. Communicate the ROI projection and anticipated intangibles with much care and caution. The target audience must clearly understand that this is based on several assumptions (clearly defined), and that the values are the best possible estimates. However, there is still room for error.

These ten steps enable an individual to forecast the ROI. The most difficult part of the process is the initial estimate of performance improvement. Several sources of data are available for this purpose, as described next.

Forecasting/Estimating Performance Improvement

When attempting to estimate the actual performance improvement that will be influenced by the training program, multiple sources for input should be considered. The following important possibilities should be explored:

1. Experience in the organization with previous training or similar programs can help form the basis of the estimate. Adapting that breadth of experience can be an important factor as comparisons are rarely, if ever, exact.

2. Data sources may have experience with similar programs in other organizations or in other situations. Here, the experience of the designers, developers, and implementers involved in the program will be helpful as they reflect on their experiences with other organizations.

3. The input of external experts who have worked in the field or addressed similar programs in other organizations can be extremely valuable. These may be consultants, suppliers, designers, or others who have earned a reputation as knowledgeable about this type of process in this type of situation.

4. Estimates can be obtained directly from a subject matter expert (SME) in the organization. This is an individual who is very familiar with the internal processes being altered, modified or improved by the training. Internal SMEs are very knowledgeable and sometimes the most favored source for obtaining conservative estimates.

5. Estimates can be obtained directly from the program sponsor. This is the individual who is ultimately making the purchasing decision and is providing data or input on the anticipated change in a measure linked to the training program. This influential position makes him or her a very credible source.

6. Individuals who are directly involved in the training, often labeled participants, are sometimes in a position to know how much of a measure can be changed or improved with a particular type of program. These individuals understand the processes, procedures, and performance measurements being influenced. Their close proximity to the situation makes them highly credible and often the most accurate sources for estimating the amount of change.

Collectively, these sources provide an appropriate array of possibilities to help estimate the value of an improvement. This is the weakest link in the ROI forecasting process and deserves the most attention. It is important that the target audience understands where the estimates came from, as well as who provided them. Even more important, the target audience must view the source as credible. Otherwise, the forecasted ROI will have no credibility.

Case Example

It may be helpful to illustrate how a forecasted ROI can be developed using the processes explained here. A global financial services company was interested in developing relationship selling skills to enable its relationship managers to meet the needs of customers. According to the needs assessment and initial analysis, there was a need for the program. A training/performance improvement program would involve further detailing of the exact needs, training on appropriate skills, and implementing the skills along with appropriate job aids. However, before the program could be pursued, a forecasted ROI was needed. Following the steps outlined earlier in this chapter, it was determined that four business impact measures would be influenced by the implementation of this project:

1. Increase in sales to existing customers
2. Reduction in customer complaints due to missed deadlines, late responses, and failure to complete transactions
3. Reduction in the response time for customer inquiries and requests
4. Increase in customer satisfaction composite survey index

In examining the potential problem, several individuals provided input. With comprehensive relationship selling skills in place, relationship managers would benefit from effective customer communication and persuasive selling skills. To determine the extent to which the measures would change, input was collected from four sources:

1. Internal developers, with expertise in various sales skills applications, provided input on expected changes in each of the measures.
2. Relationship managers provided input on expected changes in the variables if the skills were used regularly.
3. The program sponsor provided input on what could be expected from the program.
4. Finally, a brief survey of internal facilitators provided some input.

When input is based on estimates, the results may differ significantly. However, this program sponsor was interested in a forecast based on very limited analysis but strengthened with the best expert opinions available. After some discussion of the availability of data and examining the techniques to convert data to monetary values, the following conclusions were reached:

☐ The increase in sales could easily be converted to a monetary value as the margin for this particular project is applied directly.

☐ The cost of a customer complaint could be based on a discounted internal value currently in use, thus providing a generally accepted cost of a complaint.

☐ Customer response time was not tracked accurately, nor was the value of this measure readily available. Consequently, it was anticipated that this would be an intangible benefit.

☐ There is no generally accepted value for increasing customer satisfaction, so customer satisfaction impact data would be listed as a potential intangible.

The forecasted ROI calculation was developed for a single division in the organization. After reviewing the possible scenarios, a range of possibilities was offered for increasing sales and reducing complaints. The sales increase should be in the range of 3–9%. Thus, three scenarios were developed using 3, 6, and 9% as the increase in sales. Complaint reduction was expected to be in the range of 10–30%, so three scenarios were developed for the reduction in actual complaints, using 10, 20, and 30% in the ROI calculation. More detailed groupings could be developed, but three were considered appropriate.

The increase in sales was converted to monetary values using the margin rates, and the reduction in customer complaints was converted, using the discounted value for a customer complaint. The cost for the project was easily estimated, based on input from those who examined the situation. The total cost was developed to include development costs, materials, facilitators, facilities for meetings, lost time for learning activities, and coordination and evaluation. This fully loaded projected cost, when compared to the benefits, yielded a range of expected ROI values. Table 9-1 shows a matrix of the nine possible scenarios using payoffs on the two measures. This is a sensitivity analysis of expected ROI values. The ROI values range from a low of 60% to a high of 180%. With these values in hand, the decision to move forward was a relatively easy one, as even the worst-case scenarios were very positive, and the best case was approximately three times that amount. As this simple example illustrates, the process needs to be kept simple, using the most credible resources available to quickly arrive at estimates for the process. Recognizing this is an estimate, its advantage is simplicity and low cost, two factors that should be considered when developing the process.

FORECASTING WITH A PILOT PROGRAM

Although the steps listed above provide a process for estimating the ROI when a pilot program is not conducted, the more favorable approach is

Table 9-1. Sensitivity Analysis for Expected
ROI Values

Potential Sales Increase (Existing Customers, %)	Potential Compliant Reduction (Monthly Reduction)	Expected ROI (%)
3	10	60
3	20	90
3	30	120
6	10	90
6	20	120
6	30	150
9	10	120
9	20	150
9	30	180

to develop a small-scale pilot project and develop the ROI based on post-program data. This scenario involves the following five steps:

1. As in the previous process, develop Levels 3 and 4 objectives.
2. Initiate the program on a very small-scale sample as a pilot program, without all the bells and whistles. This keeps the cost extremely low without sacrificing the fundamentals of the project.
3. Fully implement the program with one or more of the typical groups of individuals who can benefit from the program.
4. Develop the ROI using the ROI model for postprogram analysis. This is the ROI process used in the previous chapters.
5. Finally, decide whether to implement the program throughout the organization based on the results of the pilot program.

Postprogram evaluation of a pilot program provides much more accurate information by which to base decisions regarding full implementation of the program. Using this scenario, data can be developed using all six types of measures outlined in this book.

FORECASTING ROI WITH REACTION DATA

When reaction data includes planned applications of training, this important data can ultimately be used in forecasting ROI. Detailing how

Planned Improvements

■ As a result of this program what specific actions will you attempt as you apply what you have learned?
   1. _____
   2. _____
   3. _____

■ Please indicate what specific measures, outcomes, or projects will change as a result of your actions.

   1. _____
   2. _____
   3. _____

■ As a result of the anticipated changes in the above, please estimate (in monetary values) the benefits to your organization over a period of one year._____

■ What is the basis of this estimate?
   _____
   _____

■ What confidence, expressed as a percentage, can you put in your estimate?
   (0% = No Confidence; 100% = Certainty) _____%

Figure 9-3. Important questions to ask on feedback questionnaires.

participants plan to use what they have learned and the results that they expect to achieve, more valuable evaluation information can be developed. The questions presented in Figure 9-3 illustrate how data are collected with an end-of-program questionnaire for a supervisory training program. Participants are asked to state specifically how they plan to use the program material and the results they expect to achieve. They are asked to convert their accomplishments to an annual monetary value and to show the basis for developing the values. Participants can moderate their responses with a confidence estimate to make the data more credible while allowing participants to reflect their uncertainty with the process.

When tabulating data, the confidence level is multiplied by the annual monetary value, which yields a conservative estimate for use in the data analysis. For example, if a participant estimated that the monetary impact of the program would be $10,000, but was only 50% confident, a $5000 value is used in the calculations.

To develop a summary of the expected benefits, several steps are taken. First, any data that are incomplete, unusable, extreme, or unrealistic is discarded. (This is Guiding Principle #8.)

Next, an adjustment is made for the confidence estimate as previously described. Individual data items are then totaled. Finally, as an optional exercise, the total value is adjusted again by a factor that reflects the subjectivity of the process and the possibility that participants will not achieve the results they anticipate. In many training programs, the participants are very enthusiastic about what they have learned and may be overly optimistic about expected accomplishments. This figure adjusts for this overestimation and can be developed with input from management or established by the training and development staff. In one organization, the benefits are multiplied by 50% to develop an even more conservative number to use in the ROI equation. Finally, the ROI is developed, using the net program benefits divided by the program costs. This value, in essence, becomes the expected return on investment, after the two adjustments for accuracy and subjectivity.

Perhaps this process can be best described using an actual case. M&H Engineering and Construction Company is involved in the design and construction of large commercial projects such as plants, paper mills, and municipal water systems. Safety is always a critical issue at M&H and usually commands much management attention. To improve the current level of safety performance, a two-day safety awareness program was developed for project engineers and construction superintendents. The program focused on safety leadership, safety planning, safety training, safety meetings, accident investigation, safety policy and procedures, safety standards, and workers' compensation. After completing this training program, participants were expected to improve the safety performance of their specific construction projects. A dozen safety performance measures used in the company (usually Level 4 impact data) were presented and discussed during the program. At the end of the two-day program, participants completed a comprehensive reaction questionnaire, which probed into specific action items planned as a result of this program and the monetary value of the completed items. In addition, participants explained the basis for estimates and placed a confidence level on their estimates. Table 9-2 presents data provided by the first group of participants. Only 18 of the 24 participants supplied data (based on the author's experience, approximately 50–70% of participants will provide usable data on this series of questions). The total cost

Table 9-2. Level 1 Data for ROI Calculations

Participant No.	Estimated Value	Basis	Confidence Level
1	$80,000	Reduction in Accidents	90%
2	90,000	OSHA Reportable Injuries	80%
3	50,000	Accident Reduction	100%
4	10,000	First Aid Visits/Visits to Doctor	100%
5	50,000	Reduction in Lost Time Injuries	95%
6	Millions	Total Accident Cost	100%
7	75,000	Workers' Compensation	80%
8	7,500	OSHA Citations	75%
9	50,000	Reduction in Accidents	100%
10	30,000	Workers Compensation	80%
11	150,000	Reduction in Total Accident Costs	90%
12	20,000	OSHA Fines/Citations	70%
13	40,000	Accident Reductions	100%
14	4,000,000	Total Cost of Safety	95%
15	65,000	Total Workers' Compensation	50%
16	Unlimited	Accidents	100%
17	45,000	Injuries	90%
18	2,000	Visits to Doctor	100%

of the program, including participants' salaries, was $29,000. Prorated development costs were included in the cost figure.

The monetary value of the planned improvements is extremely high, reflecting the participants' optimism and enthusiasm at the end of a very effective program. As a first step in the analysis, extreme data items are omitted. Data such as millions, unlimited, and $4 million are discarded, and each remaining value is multiplied by the confidence value and totaled. This adjustment reduces these estimates and increases the credibility of the values. The resulting tabulations yielded a total improvement of $655,125. Because of the subjectivity of the process, the values were adjusted by 50%, an arbitrary discount suggested by the HRD manager, but supported by the program sponsor. This "adjusted" value is $327,563 or $328,000 with rounding. The projected ROI, based on the end-of-program questionnaire, is as follows:

$$\text{ROI} = \frac{\$328,000 - \$29,000}{\$29,000} \times 100 = 1,031\%$$

The HRD manager communicated these projected values to the CEO but cautioned that the data was very subjective, although it had been adjusted downward twice. The HRD manager also emphasized that the participants in the program, who should be aware of what they could accomplish, generated the forecasted results. In addition, she mentioned that a follow-up was planned to determine the results that were actually delivered by the group.

A word of caution is in order when using Level 1 ROI data. These calculations are highly subjective and do not reflect the extent to which participants actually apply what they have learned to achieve results. A variety of influences in the work environment can enhance or inhibit the participants' attainment of performance goals. Having high expectations at the end of the program is no guarantee that those expectations will be met. Disappointments are documented regularly in programs throughout the world and are reported in research findings (Kaufman, 2002).

While this process is subjective and possibly unreliable, it does have some usefulness. First, if evaluation must stop at this level, this approach provides more insight into the value of the program than the data from typical reaction questionnaires. Managers will usually find this data more useful than a report stating, "40% of participants rated the program above average." Unfortunately, a high percentage of evaluations stop at this first level of evaluation (Van Buren, 2002). The majority of HRD programs do not enjoy rigorous evaluations at Levels 3 and 4. Reporting Level 1 ROI data is a more useful indication of the potential impact of the program than the alternative of reporting attitudes and feelings about the program and facilitator.

Second, ROI forecast data can form a basis for comparison of different presentations of the same program. If one program forecasts an ROI of 300%, whereas another projects 30%, it appears that one program may be more effective than the other. The participants in the first program have more confidence in the planned application of the program material.

Third, collecting this type of data brings increased attention to program outcomes. Participants leave the program with an understanding that specific behavior change is expected, which produces results for the organization. This issue becomes very clear to participants as they anticipate results and convert them to monetary values. Even if this pro-

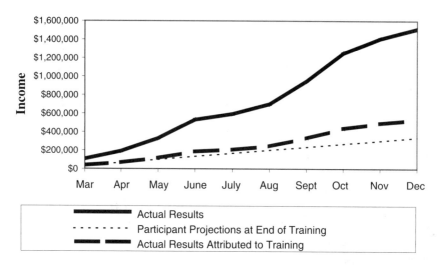

Figure 9-4. Forecasted versus actual data.

jected improvement is ignored, the exercise is productive because of the important message sent to participants. It helps to change mindsets about the value, impact, and importance of training.

Fourth, if a follow-up is planned to pinpoint postprogram results, the data collected in the Level 1 evaluation can be very helpful for comparison. This end-of-program data collection helps participants plan the implementation of what they have learned. For example, in a products training program for Wachovia Bank, the results after training are compared to the forecasted results (Wallace, 2001). Figure 9-4 shows the results of training, the participant's projections at the end of training, and the results attributed to the training. As the figure illustrates, the forecasts are lower than the results attributed to training. This comparison begins to build credibility in a forecasting method and, in this case, revealed that forecasting was actually more conservative than the actual results.

The use of Level 1 ROI is increasing, as more organizations base a larger part of ROI calculations on Level 1 data. Although it may be very subjective, it does add value, particularly when it is included as part of a comprehensive evaluation system.

FORECASTING ROI WITH LEARNING DATA

Testing for changes in skills and knowledge in HRD programs is a very common technique for learning evaluation (Level 2). In many situations,

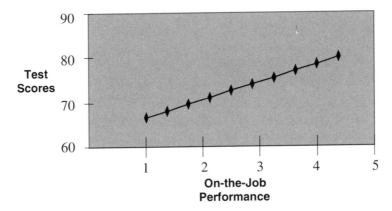

Figure 9-5. Relationship between test scores and performance.

participants are required to demonstrate their knowledge or skills at the end of the program, and their performance is expressed as a numerical value. When this type of test is developed and utilized, it must be reliable and valid. A reliable test is one that is stable over time with consistent results. A valid test is one that measures what it purports to measure. Since a test should reflect the content of the HRD program, successful mastery of program content should be related to improved job performance. Consequently, there should be a relationship between test scores and subsequent on-the-job performance. Figure 9-5 illustrates a perfect correlation between test scores and job performance. This relationship, expressed as a correlation coefficient, is a measure of validity of the test.

This testing situation provides an excellent opportunity for an ROI calculation with Level 2 data using test results. When there is a statistically significant relationship between test scores and on-the-job performance, and the performance can be converted to monetary units, then it is possible to use test scores to estimate the ROI from the program, using the following steps:

☐ Ensure that the program content reflects desired on-the-job performance.
☐ Develop an end-of-program test that reflects program content.
☐ Establish a statistical relationship between test data and output performance for participants.
☐ Predict performance levels of each participant with given test scores.

☐ Convert performance data to monetary value.
☐ Compare total predicted value of program with program costs.

An example illustrates this approach. Consumer Products Marketing (CPM) is the marketing division of a large consumer products company. Sales representatives for CPM make frequent sales calls to large retail food and drug companies with the objective of increasing sales and market share of CPM products. Sales representatives must ensure that retailers understand the advantages of CPM products, provide adequate space for their products, and assist in promotional and advertising efforts.

CPM has developed a very strong sales culture and recruits highly capable individuals for sales representative assignments. Newly recruited sales representatives rotate through different divisions of the company in a two-month assignment to learn where and how the products are made and their features and benefits, as well as specific product marketing strategies. This initial assignment culminates with an intensive one-week Professional Marketing Training Program, which focuses on sales techniques, marketing strategies, and customer service skills. At the end of the one-week program, participants complete a comprehensive exam which reflects the knowledge and skills taught in the program. As part of the exam, participants analyze specific customer service and sales situations and decide on specific actions. Also, the test covers product features, policies, and marketing practices.

To validate the test, CPM developed correlations between test scores and actual on-the-job performance measured by sales volumes, sales growth, and market shares for sales representatives six months after completing the program. The correlations were statistically significant with each variable. As a quick way of calculating the expected ROI for a program, CPM estimates output levels for each item using the test scores, converts them to monetary values, and calculates the ROI forecast.

As with the previous ROI estimate with end-of-program questionnaires, some cautions are in order. This is a forecast of the ROI and not the actual value. Although participants acquired the skills and knowledge from the program, there is no guarantee that they will apply the techniques and processes successfully and that the results will be achieved. This process assumes that the current group of participants has the same relationship to output performance as previous groups. It ignores a variety of environmental influences, which can alter the situation entirely. Finally, the process requires calculating the initial correlation coefficient, which may be difficult to develop for most tests.

Although this approach develops an estimate, based on historical relationships, it can be useful in a comprehensive evaluation strategy and it has several advantages. First, if postprogram evaluations (Level 4) are not planned, this process will yield more information about the projected value of the program than what would be obtained from the raw test scores. This process represents an expected return on investment based on the historical relationships involved. Second, by developing individual ROI measurements, and communicating them to participants, the process has reinforcement potential. It communicates to participants that increased sales and market share are expected through the applications of what was learned in the program. Third, this process can have considerable credibility with management and can preclude expensive follow-ups and postprogram monitoring. If these relationships are statistically sound, the estimate should have credibility with the target group.

FORECASTING ROI WITH SKILLS AND COMPETENCIES

In almost every HRD program, participants are expected to change their on-the-job behaviors by applying the program materials. On-the-job applications are very critical to program success. Although the use of the skills on the job is no guarantee that results will follow, it is an underlying assumption for most programs that if the knowledge and skills are applied, then results will follow. Some of the most prestigious training organizations, such as Motorola University, base their ultimate evaluation on this assumption. A few organizations attempt to take this process a step further and measure the value of on-the-job behavior change and calculate the ROI. In these situations, estimates are taken from individual participants, their supervisors, the management group, or experts in the field. This is a forecast of the impact, based on the change in behavior on the job immediately after the program. The following steps are used to develop the ROI:

1. Develop competencies for the target job.
2. Indicate percentage of job success that is covered in the training program.
3. Determine monetary value of competencies using salaries and employee benefits of participants.

4. Compute the worth of pre- and postprogram skill levels.
5. Subtract postprogram values from preprogram values.
6. Compare the total added benefits with the program costs.

This analysis was described in Chapter 7 as utility analysis. It is attempting to place a value on the improvement of an individual. The concept ignores the consequence of this improvement, but examines the behavior change and factors the monetary value relative to the salary of the individual. This is referred to as a Level 3 ROI forecast because it takes the change in behavior and converts it to monetary value using salaries of participants as a base.

Perhaps an example will illustrate one technique to measure the value of on-the-job applications. The U.S. government redesigned its Introduction to Supervision course, a five-day training program for newly appointed supervisors (Broad, 1994). The program focused on eight competencies:

1. role and responsibilities of the supervisor;
2. communications;
3. planning, assigning, controlling, and evaluating work;
4. ethics;
5. leadership and motivation;
6. analyzing performance problems;
7. customer service; and
8. managing diversity.

The immediate managers of the new supervisors indicated that these eight competencies accounted for 81% of first-level supervisors' jobs. For the target group being evaluated, the average annual salary plus benefits for the newly appointed supervisors was $42,202. Thus, multiplying this figure by the amount of job success accounted for by the competencies (81%), yielded a dollar value of $34,184 per participant. If a person were performing successfully in these eight competencies for one year, the value to the agency would be $34,184. Of course, this assumes that employees are paid an amount equal to their contribution, when they are fully competent.

Using a scale of 0–9, managers rated the skills for each of the competencies before the program was conducted. The average level of skills required to be successful in the job was rated at 6.44. The skill ratings, prior to the program, were 4.96, which represented 77% of the 6.44 (i.e., participants were performing at 77% of the level to be successful in the competencies). After the program, the skill rating was 5.59, representing 87% of the level to be successful.

Monetary values were assigned based on the participants' salaries. Performance at the required level of success was worth $34,184 (at the 6.44 rating). At a 77% proficiency level, the new supervisors were performing at a contribution value of $26,322 (77% of $34,184). After training, this value had reached 87%, representing a contribution value of $29,740 (87% of $34,184). The difference in these values ($3418) represents the gain per participant attributable to training. The program cost was $1368 per participant. Thus, the ROI is:

$$\text{ROI} = \frac{\$3418 - \$1368}{\$1368} = \frac{2050}{1368} \times 100 = 150\%$$

As with other estimates, a word of caution is in order. These results are subjective because the rating systems used are subjective and may not necessarily reflect an accurate assessment of the value of the program. This is a Level 3 ROI forecast. Since training is usually implemented to help the organization achieve its objectives, some managers insist on tangible changes in business impact data such as output, quality, cost, and time. For them, a Level 3 ROI forecast is not always an acceptable substitute for Level 4 (business impact) data.

Although this process is subjective, it has several useful advantages. First, if there are no plans to track the actual impact of the program in terms of specific measurable business impact (Level 4), this approach represents a credible substitute. In many programs—particularly skill-building and competency programs for supervisors—it may be difficult to identify tangible changes on the job. Therefore, alternative approaches to determine the worth of a program are needed. Second, this has been developed in the literature as utility analysis and has some support from researches. Third, this approach develops data that may be credible with the management group if they understand how it is developed and the assumptions behind it. An important point is that the data on the changes in competence level came from the managers who have rated their supervisors. In this specific project, the numbers were large enough to make the process statistically significant.

FORECASTING GUIDELINES

With the four different time frames for forecasting outlined in this chapter, a few guidelines may help drive the forecasting possibilities within an organization. These guidelines are based on experience in forecasting a variety of processes along with training and performance improvement (Bowers, 1997).

1. **If you must forecast, forecast frequently.** Forecasting is a process that is both an art and a science and it needs to be pursued regularly to build comfort, experience, and history with the process. Also, those who use the data need to see forecasting frequently, to further integrate it as part of the training evaluation mix.
2. **Consider forecasting an essential part of the evaluation mix.** This chapter began with a listing of reasons why forecasting is essential. The concept is growing in use and is being demanded by many executives. It can be a very effective and useful tool when used properly and in conjunction with other types of evaluation data. Some organizations have targets for the use of forecasting (e.g., if a project exceeds a certain cost, it will always require a preprogram forecast). Others will target a certain number of programs for a forecast based on reaction data and use that data in the manner described here. Others will have some low-level targets for forecasting at Levels 2 and 3. The important point is to plan for the forecast, and let it be a part of the evaluation mix, working it regularly.
3. **Forecast different types of data.** Although most of this chapter focuses on how to develop a forecasted ROI using the standard ROI formula, it is helpful to forecast the value of other data. A useable, helpful forecast will include predictions around reaction and satisfaction, the extent of learning, and the extent of application and implementation. These types of data are very important in anticipating movements and shifts, based on the planned program. It is not only helpful in developing the overall forecast, but important in understanding the total anticipated impact of the project.
4. **Secure input from those who know the process best.** As forecasts are developed, it is essential to secure input from individuals who understand the dynamics of the workplace and the measures being influenced by the project. Sometimes the participants in training or the immediate managers are best. In other situations, it is the variety of analysts who are aware of the major influences in the workplace and the dynamics of those changes. The important point is to go to the experts. This will increase not only the accuracy of the forecast, but also the credibility of the final results.

5. **Long-term forecasts will usually be inaccurate.** Forecasting works much better in a short time frame. For most short-term scenarios, it is possible to have a better grasp of the influences that might drive the measure. On a long-term basis, a variety of new influences, unforeseen now, could enter the process and drastically change the impact measures. If a long-term forecast is needed, it should be updated regularly to become a continuously improving process.

6. **Expect forecasts to be biased.** Forecasts will consist of data coming from those who have an interest in the issue. Some will want the forecast to be optimistic; others will have a pessimistic view. Almost all input is biased in one way or another. Every attempt should be made to minimize the bias, adjust for the bias, or adjust for the uncertainty in the process. Still, the audience should recognize that it is a biased prediction.

7. **Serious forecasting is hard work.** The value of forecasting often depends on the amount of effort put into the process. High-stakes programs need to have a serious approach, collecting all possible data, examining different scenarios, and making the best prediction available. It is in these situations that mathematical tools can be most valuable.

8. **Review the success of forecasting routinely.** As forecasts are made, it is imperative to revisit the forecast with actual postprogram data to check the success of the forecast. This can aid in the continuous improvement of the processes. Sources could prove to be more credible or less credible, specific inputs may be more biased or less biased, certain analyses may be more appropriate than others. It is important to constantly improve the ideal methods and approaches for forecasting within the organization.

9. **The assumptions are the most serious error in forecasting.** Of all the variables that can enter into the process, the greatest opportunity for error are the assumptions made by the individual providing the forecast. It is important for the assumptions to be clearly understood and communicated. When there are multiple inputs, each forecaster should use the same set of assumptions, if possible.

10. **Utility is the most important characteristic of forecasting.** The most important use of forecasting is the information and input for the decision maker. Forecasting is a tool for those attempting to make a decision about training or performance improvement. It is not a process that is trying to maximize the output or minimize any particular variable. It is not a process that is attempting to

dramatically change the way in which the program is implemented. It is a process to provide data for decisions—that's the greatest utility of forecasting.

FINAL THOUGHTS

This chapter illustrates that ROI forecasts can be developed at different time frames. Although most practitioners and researchers use application and impact data for ROI calculations, there are situations when Level 3 and Level 4 data are not available or evaluations at those levels are not attempted or planned. ROI forecasts, developed before the program is implemented, can be very useful and helpful to management and the HRD staff, while at the same time focusing attention on the potential economic impact of training. Forecasts are also possible with reaction and learning data. Be aware that using ROI forecasts may provide a false sense of accuracy. As would be expected, ROI forecasts on a preprogram basis are the lowest in credibility and accuracy, but have the advantage of being inexpensive and relatively easy to conduct. On the other hand, ROI calculations using Level 4 data are highest in credibility and accuracy, but are more expensive and difficult to develop.

Although ROI calculations with impact data (Level 4) are preferred, ROI forecasts at other times are an important part of a comprehensive and systematic evaluation process. This usually means that targets for evaluation should be established.

CASE STUDY—PART H, LINEAR NETWORK SYSTEMS

ROI Analysis

The values presented in this study were much higher than management anticipated. In discussions held before implementation, the senior management team (president, director of manufacturing, and plant manager) agreed that for the program to be successful, the payoff would have to be in productivity. This senior management group even suggested that absenteeism and turnover be considered intangible data and reported as additional improvements without a conversion to monetary values. Thus, in early discussions, absenteeism and turnover, although linked directly to the skills training, were considered to be potentially low impact variables. If the original suggestion had been followed, the program would have generated a negative ROI. An important lesson was learned. Behaviorally driven Level 4 data, although considered to be soft in nature, can have a tremendous impact in the organization. And in this situation, the impact would have been considerably enhanced if more appropriate values were used for the monetary conversion of absenteeism and turnover. (Instead, lower, more conservative values were used.)

An important issue evolved concerning the projection of output data six months to one year after the program. It was clear that the output was moving in the right direction and it appeared that further improvement was in store. While it is tempting to assume the variables will continue to improve, in reality, other variables usually enter the analysis and a deterioration of the output variables may be realized, unless additional training or other interventions are implemented. This is what happened in this case. Each data item continued to improve for the six months. Absenteeism tapered off and then increased slightly, turnover remained fairly constant, while productivity continued to improve, perhaps driven by the TQM and team building sessions.

As part of the evaluation process, the evaluation team (consultant, facilitators, HRD manager, and department heads) explored ways in which the process could be improved. The team discussed several issues. First, because the control group strategy most accurately isolates the effects of training, the team thought it would have been better to initiate this program in a plant that could be compared to another location in a control group arrangement. This strategy will often develop more confidence in the process and will build a more convincing case for a high impact ROI.

A second issue was the needs assessment. The team thought it was important to have sufficient evidence of a direct connection between the Level 4 business impact measures and the planned training program. However, some team members wanted to see more evidence of how this was accomplished so that they would be more convinced about the direct linkage.

The third issue was the early follow-up. The consultants wanted to wait six months to capture the improvement, although management insisted on making a decision in four months. Perhaps a compromising solution is to capture data at four months, make the decision based on the apparent high impact level, and continue to capture data for another two months and develop an ROI impact study with six months of data, which would then be communicated to the target audience.

The fourth issue involved the apparent lack of a comprehensive evaluation at Level 3. Some team members wanted a more comprehensive assessment of actual behavior changes, which would convince them that the supervisors were actually operating differently. While this is an important issue, it was a trade-off process. A comprehensive Level 3 evaluation is time consuming and costly. When a Level 4 evaluation was planned with a specific technique to isolate the effects of training, other team members felt that a more comprehensive Level 3 was unnecessary.

Overall, the evaluation team perceived this to be an excellent ROI analysis. The process was credible with an acceptable level of accuracy.

Intangible Benefits

Other potential intangible benefits were identified including improved job satisfaction of first level managers, improved overall job satisfaction, reduction in stress for supervisors, and an increase in the bonus for supervisors (bonus pay is linked to productivity). While these items were considered to be important benefits of the program, they were not measured because of the additional effort required for monitoring and analysis. When intangible benefits are important and influential to the target audience, they should be monitored and analyzed in a more comprehensive way. Interestingly, the management group initially proposed absenteeism and turnover measures as intangible benefits. If this suggestion had been followed, the improvements in absenteeism and turnover would have been presented as intangible benefits, resulting in a negative ROI. The team learned a valuable lesson. There should be an attempt to convert each intangible measure that is monitored and isolated. If the conversion process becomes unmanageable, inaccurate, or not very credible, then a data item is listed as an intangible benefit and reported without any further analysis. (Guiding Principle #11)

Discussion Questions
1. Although the ROI analysis plan is usually completed prior to pursuing the evaluation process, please take a few minutes to complete the plan shown in Figure 9-6.
2. Could the ROI forecast be developed on a preprogram basis? Please explain.
3. Is a forecast with reaction data possible? Please explain.
4. Would an ROI forecast with Level 2 or 3 data be possible? Please explain.
5. How should the results of this study be communicated? Please explain.

ROI ANALYSIS PLAN

Program: ______________________ **Responsibility:** ______________________ **Date:** __________

Data Items (Usually Level 4)	Methods for Isolating the Effects of the Program/ Process	Methods of Converting Data to Monetary Values	Cost Categories	Intangible Benefits	Communication Targets for Final Report	Other Influences/ Issues During Application	Comments

Figure 9-6. ROI analysis plan.

REFERENCES

Bishop, P. "Thinking Like a Futurist," *The Futurist,* June–July 1998, p. 42.

Bowers, D.A. *Forecasting for Control and Profit.* Menlo Park, CA: Crisp Publications, 1997.

Broad, M. "Built-in Evaluation," *In Action: Measuring Return on Investment,* vol. 1, J.J. Phillips (Ed.). Alexandria, VA: American Society for Training and Development, 1994, pp. 55–70.

Dixon, N.M., "The Relationship between Trainee Responses on Participant Reaction Forms and Post-test Scores," *Human Resource Development Quarterly,* 1(2), pp 129–137.

Kaufman, R. "Resolving the (Often-Deserved) Attacks on Training," *Performance Improvement,* vol. 41, No. 6, 2002.

Van Buren, M. *ASTD Report.* Alexandria, VA: American Society for Training and Development, 2002.

Wallace, D. "Partnering to Achieve Measurable Business Results in the New Economy," *In Action: Measuring Return on Investment,* vol. 3, Phillips (Ed.). Alexandria, VA: American Society for Training and Development, 2001, pp. 81–104.

FURTHER READING

Armstrong, J.S. *Principles of Forecasting: A Handbook for Researchers and Practitioners,* Boston, MA: Kluwer Academic Publishers, 2001.

Burke, W.W., and W. Trahant, with R. Koonce. *Business Climate Shifts: Profiles of Change Makers.* Boston, MA: Butterworth–Heinemann, 2000.

Farrell, W. *How Hits Happen: Forecasting Predictability in a Chaotic Marketplace.* London, England: Texere, 2000.

Franses, P.H. *Time Series Models for Business and Economic Forecasting.* London, England: Cambridge University Press, 1998.

Harmon, F. *Business 2010: Five Forces That Will Reshape Business—And How to Make Them Work for You.* Washington, DC: Kiplinger Books, 2001.

Jarrett, J. *Business Forecasting Methods.* Oxford, England: Basil Blackwell, 1991.

Marcum, D., S. Smith, and M. Khalsa. *businessThink: Rules for Getting It Right—Now, and No Matter What!* Hoboken, NJ: John Wiley & Sons, Inc., 2002.

Mazarr, M.J. *Global Trends 2005: An Owner's Manual for the Next Decade.* New York, NY: Palgrave, 1999.

Modis, T. *Conquering Uncertainty: Understanding Corporate Cycles and Positioning Cycles and Positioning Your Company to Survive the Changing Environment.* New York, NY: McGraw-Hill, 1998.

Swanson, R.A., and D.B. Gradous. *Forecasting Financial Benefits of Human Resource Development.* San Francisco, CA: Jossey-Bass Publishers, 1988.

Weisbord, M., and S. Janoff. *Future Search: An Action Guide to Finding Common Ground in Organizations and Communities*, 2nd ed. San Francisco, CA: Berrett-Koehler Publishers, 2000.

How to Communicate Results

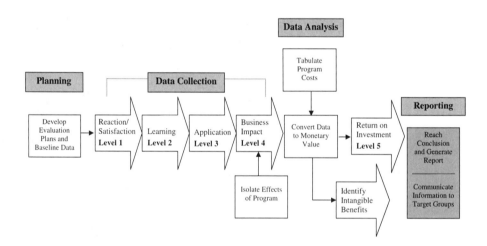

With data in hand, what's next? Should the data be used to modify the program, change the process, show the contribution, justify new programs, gain additional support, or build goodwill? How should the data be presented? Who should present the data? Where should the data be communicated? These and other questions are examined in this chapter. The worst course of action is to do nothing. Communicating results is as important as achieving them. Using many examples, this chapter provides useful information to help present evaluation data to the various audiences using both oral and written reporting methods.

The Importance of Communication

Communicating results is a critical issue in the ROI methodology. While it is important to communicate achieved results to interested stakeholders after the project is complete, it is important to communicate throughout the training program as well. This ensures that information is flowing so adjustments can be made and all stakeholders are aware of the success and issues surrounding the program. There are at least five key reasons for being concerned about communicating results. Collectively, these reasons, described next in this section, make communication a critical issue, although it is often overlooked or underestimated in training and performance improvement projects. This chapter builds on this important issue and shows a variety of techniques for accomplishing all types of communication for various target audiences.

Measurement and Evaluation Mean Nothing without Communication

Measuring success and collecting evaluation data mean nothing unless the findings are communicated promptly to the appropriate audiences so that they will be aware of what is occurring and can take action if necessary. Communication allows a full loop to be made from the program results to necessary actions based on those results.

Communication Is Necessary to Make Improvements

Because information is collected at different points during the process, the communication or feedback to the various groups that will take action is the only way adjustments can be made. Thus, the quality and timeliness of communication become critical issues for making necessary adjustments or improvements. Even after the project is completed, communication is necessary to make sure the target audience fully understands the results achieved and how the results could either be enhanced in future projects or in the current project, if it is still operational. Communication is the key to making these important adjustments at all phases of the program.

Communication Is Necessary for Explaining Contributions

The contribution of the training program explained with six major types of measures is a confusing issue, at best. The different target audiences will need a thorough explanation of the results. A communication strategy including techniques, media, and the overall process will determine the extent to which they understand the contribution. Communicating results, particularly with business impact and ROI, can quickly become confusing for even the most sophisticated target audiences. Communication must be planned and implemented with the goal of making sure the audiences understand the full contribution.

Communication Is a Sensitive Issue

Communication is one of those important issues that can cause major problems. Because the results of a program can be closely linked to the performance of others and the political issues in an organization, communication can upset some individuals while pleasing others. If certain individuals do not receive the information, or it is delivered inconsistently from one group to another, problems can quickly surface. Not only is it an understanding issue, it is also a fairness, quality, and political correctness issue to make sure communication is properly constructed and effectively delivered to all key individuals who need the information.

A Variety of Target Audiences Need Different Information

Because there are so many potential target audiences for receiving communication on the success of a program, it is important for the communication to be tailored directly to their needs. A varied audience will command varied needs. Planning and effort are necessary to make sure the audience receives all of the information it needs, in the proper format, and at the proper time. A single report for all audiences may not be appropriate. The scope, size, media, and even the actual information of different types and different levels will vary significantly from one group to another, making the target audience the key to determining the appropriate communication process.

PRINCIPLES OF COMMUNICATING RESULTS

The skills required to communicate results effectively are almost as delicate and sophisticated as those needed to obtain results. The style is as important as the substance. Regardless of the message, audience, or medium, a few general principles apply and are explored next. These general principles are important to the overall success of the communication effort. They should serve as a checklist for the HRD team when disseminating program results.

Communication Must Be Timely

Usually, results should be communicated as soon as they are known. From a practical standpoint, it may be best to delay the communication until a convenient time, such as the publication of the next newsletter or the next general management meeting. Timing issues must be addressed. Is the audience ready for the results in light of other things that may have happened? Is it expecting results? When is the best time for having the maximum effect on the audience? Are there circumstances that dictate a change in the timing of the communication?

Communication Should Be Targeted to Specific Audiences

Communication will be more effective if it is designed for a particular group. The message should be specifically tailored to the interests, needs, and expectations of the target audience.

The results described in this chapter reflect outcomes at all levels, including the six types of data developed in this book. Some of the data are developed earlier in the project and communicated during the project. Other data are collected after implementation and communicated in a follow-up study. Thus, the results, in their broadest sense, may involve early feedback in qualitative terms to ROI values in varying quantitative terms.

Media Should Be Carefully Selected

For particular groups, some media may be more effective than others. Face-to-face meetings may be better than special bulletins. A memo distributed exclusively to top management may be more effective than the company newsletter. The proper method of communication can help improve the effectiveness of the process.

Communication Should Be Unbiased and Modest

It is important to separate fact from fiction and accurate statements from opinions. Various audiences may accept communication from the HRD staff with skepticism, anticipating biased opinions. Boastful statements sometimes turn off recipients, and most of the content is lost. Observable, believable facts carry far more weight than extreme or sensational claims. Although such claims may get audience attention, they often detract from the importance of the results.

Communication Must Be Consistent

The timing and content of the communication should be consistent with past practices. A special communication at an unusual time during the training program may provoke suspicion. Also, if a particular group, such as top management, regularly receives communication on outcomes, it should continue receiving communication—even if the results are not positive. If some results are omitted, it might leave the impression that only positive results are reported.

Testimonials Are More Effective Coming from Individuals the Audience Respects

Opinions are strongly influenced by others, particularly those who are respected and trusted. Testimonials about results, when solicited from individuals respected by others in the organization, can influence the effectiveness of the message. This respect may be related to leadership ability, position, special skills, or knowledge. A testimonial from an individual who commands little respect and is regarded as a substandard performer can have a negative impact on the message.

The Audience's Opinion of the HRD Staff and Function Will Influence the Communication Strategy

Opinions are difficult to change, and a negative opinion of the HRD group may not change with the mere presentation of facts. However, the presentation of facts alone may strengthen the opinions held by those who already agree with the results. It helps reinforce their position and provides a defense in discussions with others. An HRD group with a high level of credibility and respect may have a relatively easy time communicating results. Low credibility can create problems when trying to be persuasive. The reputation of the HRD group is an important consideration in developing the overall strategy.

Analyzing the Need for Communication

Because there are many reasons for communicating results, a list should be tailored to the situation and project. The specific reasons depend on the project, the setting, and the unique needs of the sponsor. The most common reasons are:

☐ **To secure approval for the project and allocate resources of time and money.** The initial communication presents a proposal, projected ROI, or other data that are intended to secure the project approval. This communication may not have very much data but rather anticipates what is to come.

☐ **To gain support for the project and its objectives.** It is important to have support from a variety of groups. This communication is intended to build the necessary support to make the project work successfully.

☐ **To secure agreement on the issues, solutions, and resources.** As the program begins, it is important for all those directly involved to have some agreement and understanding of the important elements and requirements surrounding the program.

☐ **To build credibility for the HRD group, its techniques, and the finished products.** It is important early in the process to make sure that those involved understand the approach and reputation of the HRD staff, and, based on the approach taken, the commitments made by all parties.

☐ **To reinforce the processes.** It is important for key managers to support the program and reinforce the various processes used in design, development, and delivery. This communication is designed to enhance those processes.

☐ **To drive action for improvement in the project.** This early communication is designed as a process improvement tool to effect changes and improvements as the needs are uncovered and various individuals make suggestions.

☐ **To prepare participants for the program.** It is necessary for those most directly involved in the program, the participants, to be prepared for learning, application, and responsibilities that will be required of them as they bring success to the project.

☐ **To enhance results throughout the project and the quality of future feedback.** This communication is designed to show the status of the project and to influence decisions, seek support, or communicate events and expectations to the key stakeholders. In addition, it will enhance both the quality and quantity of information as stakeholders see the feedback cycle in action.

☐ **To show the complete results of the training program.** This is perhaps the most important communication, where all of the results involving all six types of measures are communicated to the appropriate individuals so they have a full understanding of the success or shortcomings of the project.

☐ **To underscore the importance of measuring results.** Some individuals need to understand the importance of measurement and evaluation and see the need for having important data on different measures.

☐ **To explain techniques used to measure results.** The program sponsor and support staff need to understand the techniques used in measuring results. In some cases, these techniques may be transferred internally to use with other projects. In short, these individuals need to understand the soundness and theoretical framework of the process used.

☐ **To stimulate desire in participants to be involved in the program.** Ideally, participants want to be involved in the program. This communication is designed to pique their interest in the program and inform them of its importance.

☐ **To stimulate interest in the HRD function.** From an HRD perspective, some communications are designed to create interest in all of the products and services based on the results obtained by the current programs.

☐ **To demonstrate accountability for expenditures.** It is important for a broad group to understand the need for accountability and the approach of the HRD staff. This ensures accountability for expenditures on the project.

☐ **To market future projects.** From an HRD perspective, it is important to build a database of successful projects to use in convincing others that the training and performance improvement can add value.

Although this list is comprehensive, there may be other reasons for communicating results. The situation context should be considered when developing others.

Planning the Communication

Any successful activity must be carefully planned for it to produce the maximum results. This is a critical part of communicating the results of major programs. The actual planning of the communications is important to ensure that each audience receives the proper information at the right time and that appropriate actions are taken. Three separate issues are important in planning the communication of results, as presented next.

Communication Policy Issues

In examining the overall HRD process, policy issues need to be developed around the communication of results. These range from providing feedback during a project to communicating the ROI from an impact study. Seven different areas will need some attention as the policies are developed:

1. **What will actually be communicated?** It is important to detail the types of information communicated throughout the project—not only the six types of data from the ROI model, but the overall progress with HRD may be a topic of communications as well.
2. **When will the data be communicated?** With communications, timing is critical. If adjustments in the program need to made, the information should be communicated quickly so that swift actions can be taken.
3. **How will the information be communicated?** This shows the preferences toward particular types of communication media. For example, some organizations prefer to have written documents sent out as reports, while others prefer face-to-face meetings, and still others want electronic communications utilized as much as possible.
4. **The location for communication.** Some prefer that the communication take place close to the sponsor; others prefer the HRD offices. The location can be an important issue in terms of convenience and perception.
5. **Who will communicate the information?** Will the HRD staff, an independent consultant, or an individual involved from the sponsor's office communicate the information? The person communicating must have credibility so that the information is believable.

6. **The target audience.** Identify specific target audiences that should always receive information and others that will receive information when appropriate.
7. **The specific actions that are required or desired.** When information is presented, in some cases no action is needed; in others, changes are desired and sometimes even required.

Collectively these seven issues frame the policy around communication as a whole.

Planning the Communication around the Complete Project

When a major project is approved, the communication plan is usually developed. This details how specific information is developed and communicated to various groups and the expected actions. In addition, this plan details how the overall results will be communicated, the time frames for communication, and the appropriate groups to receive information. The HRD team and sponsor need to agree on the extent of detail in the plan. Additional information on this type of planning is provided later.

Planning the Communication of an Impact Study

A third issue is the plan aimed at presenting the results of an impact study. This occurs when a major program is completed and the detailed results are known. One of the major issues is who should receive the results and in what form. This is more specialized than the plan for the entire project because it involves the final study from the project. Table 10-1 shows the communication plan for communicating the results of a major stress reduction program. Teams were experiencing high levels of stress and, through a variety of activities and behavior changes, stress began to diminish among the teams.

Five different communication pieces were developed for different audiences. The complete report was an ROI impact study, a 75-page report that served as the historical document for the project. It went to the sponsor, the HRD staff, and the particular manager of each of the teams involved in the studies. An executive summary, a much smaller document, went to some of the higher-level executives. A general interest overview and summary without the ROI calculation went to the participants. A general-interest article was developed for company

Table 10-1. Communication Plan for a Major Stress Reduction Program

Communication Document	Communication Target(s)	Distribution Method
Complete Report with Appendices (75 pages)	☐ Program sponsor ☐ HRD Staff ☐ Intact Team Manager	Distribute and Discuss in a Special Meeting
Executive Summary (8 pages)	☐ Senior Management in the Business Units ☐ Senior Corporate Management	Distribute and Discuss in Routine Meeting
General Interest Overview and Summary without the Actual ROI Calculation (10 pages)	☐ Participants	Mail with Letter
General Interest Article (1 page)	☐ All Employees	Publish in Company Publication
Brochure highlighting program, objectives, and specific results	☐ Team Leaders with an Interest ☐ in the Program ☐ Prospective sponsors	Include with Other Marketing Materials

publications, and a brochure was developed to show the success of the program. That brochure was used in marketing the same process internally to other teams and served as additional marketing material for the HRD staff. This detailed plan may be part of the overall plan for the assignment but may be fine-tuned during the actual process.

Collectively, these three issues and plans underscore the importance of organizing the communication strategy for a particular program or the overall HRD process in an organization.

SELECTING THE AUDIENCE FOR COMMUNICATIONS

Preliminary Issues

When approaching a particular audience, the following questions should be asked about each potential group:

- ☐ Are they interested in the project?
- ☐ Do they really want to receive the information?
- ☐ Has someone already made a commitment to them regarding communication?
- ☐ Is the timing right for this audience?
- ☐ Are they familiar with the project?
- ☐ How do they prefer to have results communicated?
- ☐ Do they know the team members?
- ☐ Are they likely to find the results threatening?
- ☐ Which medium will be most convincing to this group?

For each target audience, three actions are needed:

1. To the greatest extent possible, the HRD staff should know and understand the target audience.
2. The HRD staff should find out what information is needed and why. Each group will have its own needs relative to the information desired. Some want detailed information while others want brief information. Rely on the input from others to determine audience needs.
3. The HRD staff should try to understand audience bias. Each will have a particular bias or opinion. Some will quickly support the results, whereas others may be against them or be neutral. The staff should be empathetic and try to understand differing views. With this understanding, communications can be tailored to each group. This is especially critical when the potential exists for the audience to react negatively to the results.

Basis for Selecting the Audience

The potential target audiences to receive information on results are varied in terms of job levels and responsibilities. Determining which groups will receive a particular communication piece deserves careful thought, as problems can arise when a particular group receives inappropriate information or when another is omitted altogether. A sound basis for proper audience selection is to analyze the reason for communication, as discussed in an earlier section. Table 10-2 shows common target audiences and the basis for selecting the audience.

Perhaps the most important audience is the sponsor, the individual, or team supporting the ROI study. This group (or individual) initiates the project, reviews data, and weighs the final assessment of the effectiveness of the project. Another important target audience is the top management group. This group is responsible for allocating resources to the program and needs information to help justify expenditures and gauge the effectiveness of the efforts.

Selected groups of managers (or all managers) are also important target audiences. Management's support and involvement in the process

Table 10-2. Rationale for Specific Target Audiences

Reason for Communication	Primary Target Audiences
To secure approval for the project	Sponsor, Top Executives
To gain support for the project	Immediate Managers, Team Leaders
To secure agreement with the issues	Participants, Team Leaders
To build credibility for HRD	Top Executives
To enhance reinforcement of the processes	Immediate Managers
To drive action for improvement	Sponsor, HRD Staff
To prepare participants for the project	Team Leaders
To enhance results and quality of future feedback	Participants
To show the complete results of the project	Sponsor
To underscore the importance of measuring results	Sponsor, HRD Staff
To explain techniques used to measure results	Sponsor, Support Staff
To create desire for a participant to be involved	Team Leaders
To stimulate interest in the HRD staff	Top Executives
To demonstrate accountability for expenditures	All Employees
To market future projects	Prospective Sponsors

and the department's credibility are important to success. Effectively communicating program results to management can increase both support and credibility.

Communicating with the participants' team leaders or immediate managers is essential. In many cases, they must encourage participants to implement the project. Also, they often support and reinforce the objectives of the program. An appropriate return on investment improves the commitment to training and provides credibility for the HRD staff.

Occasionally, results are communicated to encourage participation in the program. This is especially true for those programs offered on a volunteer basis. The potential participants are important targets for communicating results.

Participants need feedback on the overall success of the effort. Some individuals may not have been as successful as others in achieving the desired results. Communicating the results adds additional pressure to effectively implement the program and improve results for the future. For those achieving excellent results, the communication will serve as a reinforcement of the training. Communicating results to participants is often overlooked, with the assumption that since the program is complete, they do not need to be informed of its success.

The HRD staff must receive information about program results. Whether for small projects where the HRD staff receives an update, or for larger projects where a complete team is involved, those who design, develop, facilitate, and implement the program must be given information on the program's effectiveness. Evaluation information is necessary so adjustments can be made if the program is not as effective as it could be.

The support staff should receive detailed information about the process to measure results. This group provides support services to the HRD team, usually in the department.

Company employees and stockholders may be less likely targets. General interest news stories may increase employee respect. Goodwill and positive attitudes toward the organization may also be by-products of communicating results. Stockholders, on the other hand, are more interested in the return on their investment.

While Table 10-2 shows the most common target audiences, there can be others in a particular organization. For instance, management or employees could be subdivided into different departments, divisions, or even subsidiaries of the organization. The number of audiences can be large in a complex organization.

> **Guiding Principle #12**
> The results from the ROI methodology must be communicated to all key stakeholders.

At a minimum, four target audiences are always recommended: a senior management group, the participants' immediate manager or team leader, the participants, and the HRD staff. The first four levels of data should be communicated to these groups. ROI data should be communicated, if the audience understands ROI. Sometimes, participants may not fully understand the concept.

DEVELOPING THE INFORMATION: THE IMPACT STUDY

The type of formal evaluation report depends on the extent of detailed information presented to the various target audiences. Brief summaries of results with appropriate charts may be sufficient for some communication efforts. In other situations, particularly with a significant program requiring extensive funding, the amount of detail in the evaluation report is more crucial. A complete and comprehensive impact study report may be necessary. This report can then be used as the basis of information for specific audiences and various media. The report may contain the following major sections.

Executive Summary

The executive summary is a brief overview of the entire report, explaining the basis for the evaluation and the significant conclusions and recommendations. It is designed for individuals who are too busy to read a detailed report. It is usually written last but appears first in the report for easy access.

Background Information

The background information provides a general description of the project. If applicable, the needs assessment that led to the implementation of the project is summarized. The program is fully described, including the events that led to the intervention. Other specific items necessary to provide a full description of the project are included. The extent of detailed information depends on the amount of information the audience needs.

Objectives

The objectives for both the impact study and the actual training program are outlined. Sometimes they are the same, but they may be different. The report details the particular objectives of the study itself so that the reader clearly understands the rationale for the study and how the data will be used. In addition, specific objectives of the training program are detailed, as these are the objectives from which the different types or levels of data will be collected.

Evaluation Strategy/Methodology

The evaluation strategy outlines all of the components that make up the total evaluation process. Several components of the results-based model and the ROI methodology presented in this book are discussed in this section of the report. The specific purposes of evaluation are outlined, and the evaluation design and methodology are explained. The instruments used in data collection are also described and presented as exhibits. Any unusual issues in the evaluation design are discussed. Finally, other useful information related to the design, timing, and execution of the evaluation is included.

Data Collection and Analysis

This section explains the methods used to collect data as outlined in earlier chapters. The data collected are usually presented in the report in summary form. Next, the methods used to analyze data are presented with interpretations.

Program Costs

Program costs are presented in this section. A summary of the costs by category is included. For example, analysis, development, implementation, and evaluation costs are recommended categories for cost presentation. The assumptions made in developing and classifying costs are discussed in this section of the report.

Reaction and Satisfaction

This section details the data collected from key stakeholders, particularly the participants involved in the process, to measure reactions to the program and levels of satisfaction with various issues and parts of the process. Other input from the sponsor or managers may be included to show the levels of satisfaction.

Learning

This section shows a brief summary of the formal and informal methods for measuring learning. It explains how participants have learned new processes, skills, tasks, procedures, and practices.

Application and Implementation

This section shows how the project was actually implemented and the success with the application of new skills and knowledge. Implementation issues are addressed, including any major success and/or lack of success.

Business Impact

This section shows the actual business impact measures representing the business needs that initially drove the project. This shows the extent to which performance has changed during the implementation of the program.

Return on Investment

This section actually shows the ROI calculation along with the benefits/costs ratio. It compares the value to what was expected and provides an interpretation of the actual calculation.

Intangible Measures

This section shows the various intangible measures directly linked to the training program. Intangibles are those measures not converted to monetary values or included in the actual ROI calculation.

Barriers and Enablers

The various problems and obstacles affecting the success of the project are detailed and presented as barriers to implementation. Also, those factors or influences that had a positive effect on the project are included as enablers. Together, they provide tremendous insight into what can hinder or enhance projects in the future.

Conclusions and Recommendations

This section presents conclusions based on all of the results. If appropriate, brief explanations are presented on how each conclusion was reached. A list of recommendations or changes in the program, if appropriate, is provided with brief explanations for each recommendation. It is important that the conclusions and recommendations are consistent with one another and with the findings described in the previous section.

The above components make up the major parts of a complete evaluation report.

Developing the Report

Table 10-3 shows the table of contents from a typical evaluation report for an ROI evaluation. While this report is an effective, professional way to present ROI data, several cautions need to be followed. Since this document reports the success of groups of employees, complete credit for the success must go to the participants and their immediate leaders. Their performance generated the success. Another important caution is to avoid boasting about results. Although the ROI methodology may be accurate and credible, it still may have some subjective issues. Huge claims of success can quickly turn off an audience and interfere with the delivery of the desired message.

A final caution concerns the structure of the report. The methodology should be clearly explained, along with assumptions made in the analysis. The reader should readily see how the values were developed and how the specific steps were followed to make the process more conservative, credible, and accurate. Detailed statistical analyses should be placed in the appendix.

SELECTING THE COMMUNICATION MEDIA

There are many options available to communicate program results. In addition to the impact study report, the most frequently used media are

Table 10-3. Outline of Impact Study

- ☐ Executive Summary
- ☐ General Information
    - ☐ Background
    - ☐ Objectives of Study
- ☐ Methodology for Impact Study
    - ☐ Levels of Evaluation
    - ☐ ROI Process
    - ☐ Collecting Data
    - ☐ Isolating the Effects of Training
    - ☐ Converting Data to Monetary Values
    - ☐ Assumptions

    } Builds credibility for the process

- ☐ Data Analysis Issues
- ☐ Program Costs
- ☐ Results: General Information
    - ☐ Response Profile
    - ☐ Success with Objectives
- ☐ Results: Reaction and Satisfaction
    - ☐ Data Sources
    - ☐ Data Summary
    - ☐ Key Issues
- ☐ Results: Learning
    - ☐ Data Sources
    - ☐ Data Summary
    - ☐ Key Issues
- ☐ Results: Application and Implementation
    - ☐ Data Sources
    - ☐ Data Summary
    - ☐ Key Issues
- ☐ Results: Business Impact
    - ☐ General Comments
    - ☐ Linkage with Business Measures
    - ☐ Key Issues
- ☐ Results: ROI and Its Meaning
- ☐ Results: Intangible Measures

    } The results with six measures: Levels 1, 2, 3, 4, 5, and Intangibles

- ☐ Barriers and Enablers
    - ☐ Barriers
    - ☐ Enablers
- ☐ Conclusions and Recommendations
    - ☐ Conclusions
    - ☐ Recommendations

meetings, interim and progress reports, the organization's publications, e-mail, brochures, and case studies.

Meetings

In addition to the meeting with the sponsor to discuss results, other meetings are fertile opportunities for communicating program results. All organizations have a variety of meetings and, in each, the proper context and consulting results are an important part. A few examples illustrate the variety of meetings.

STAFF MEETINGS

Throughout the chain of command, staff meetings are held to review progress, discuss current problems, and distribute information. These meetings can be an excellent forum for discussing the results achieved in a major training program when it relates to the group's activities. Program results can be sent to executives for use in staff meetings, or a member of the HRD team can attend the meeting to make the presentation.

MANAGER MEETINGS

Routine meetings with the first-level management group are quite common. Typically, items are discussed that will possibly help their work units. A discussion of a training program and the subsequent results can be integrated into the regular meeting format.

BEST PRACTICES MEETINGS

Some organizations have best practices meetings or videoconferences to discuss recent successes and best practices. This is an excellent opportunity to learn and share methodologies and results.

BUSINESS UPDATE MEETINGS

A few organizations have initiated a periodic meeting for all members of management, in which the CEO reviews progress and discusses plans for the coming year. A few highlights of major program results can be integrated into the CEO's speech, showing top executive interest, commitment, and support. Results are mentioned along with operating profit, new facilities and equipment, new company acquisitions, and next year's sales forecast.

Interim and Progress Reports

Although usually limited to large projects, a highly visible way to communicate results is through interim and routine memos and reports. Published or disseminated via the intranet on a periodic basis, they usually have several purposes:

- ☐ To inform management about the status of the project
- ☐ To communicate the interim results achieved in the program
- ☐ To activate needed changes and improvements

A more subtle reason for the report is to gain additional support and commitment from the management group and to keep the project intact. This report is produced by the HRD staff and distributed to a select group of managers in the organization. Format and scope vary considerably. Common topics are presented here.

- ☐ **Schedule of Activities.** A schedule of planned steps/activities should be an integral part of this report. A brief description should be presented.
- ☐ **Reactions from Participants.** A brief summary of reaction evaluations may be appropriate to report initial success. Also, brief interviews with participants might be included.
- ☐ **Results.** A key focus of this report is the results achieved from the program. Significant results that can be documented should be presented in an easily understood format. The method(s) of evaluation should be briefly outlined, along with the measurement data.
- ☐ **Change in Responsibility.** Occasionally, people involved in planning, developing, implementing, or evaluating the program are reassigned, transferred, or promoted. It is important to communicate how these changes affect responsibilities and the program.
- ☐ **Participant Spotlight.** A section that highlights a participant can focus additional attention on results. This is an opportunity to recognize outstanding participants responsible for excellent results and bring attention to unusual achievements.

While the previous list may not be suited for every report, it represents topics that should be presented to the management group. When produced in a professional manner, the report can improve management support and commitment to the effort.

The Organization's Publications and Standard Communication Tools

To reach a wide audience, the HRD staff can use in-house publications. Whether a newsletter, magazine, newspaper, or electronic file, these types of media usually reach all employees. The information can be quite effective if communicated appropriately. The scope should be limited to general interest articles, announcements, and interviews. Following are types of issues that should be covered in these publications.

☐ **Program Results.** Results communicated through these types of media must be significant enough to arouse general interest. For example, a story with the headline, "Safety Training Program Helps Produce One Million Hours without a Lost-Time Accident," will catch the attention of many people because they may have participated in the program and can appreciate the significance of the results. Reports on the accomplishments of a small group of participants may not create interest unless the audience can relate to the accomplishments.

For many training implementations, results are achieved weeks or even months after the project is completed. Participants need reinforcement from many sources. If results are communicated to a general audience, including the participant's subordinates or peers, there is additional pressure to continue the project or similar ones in the future.

☐ **Participant Recognition.** General audience communication can bring recognition to participants, particularly those who excel in some aspect of the project. When participants deliver unusual performance, public recognition can enhance their self-esteem.

☐ **Human Interest Stories.** Many human interest stories can come out of major training programs. A rigorous program with difficult requirements can provide the basis for an interesting story on participants who implement the program.

In one organization, the editor of the company newsletter participated in a very demanding training program and wrote a stimulating article about what it was like to be a participant. The article gave the reader a tour of the entire program and its effectiveness in terms of the results achieved. It was an interesting and effective way to communicate about a challenging activity.

The benefits are many and the opportunities endless for HRD staff to utilize in-house publications and company-wide intranets to let others know about the success of programs.

E-Mail and Electronic Media

Internal and external web pages on the Internet, company-wide intranets, and e-mail are excellent vehicles for releasing results, promoting ideas, and informing employees and other target groups about results. E-mail, in particular, provides a virtually instantaneous means with which to communicate and solicit response from large numbers of people.

Brochures and Pamphlets

A brochure might be appropriate for programs conducted on a continuing basis, where participants have produced excellent results. It should be attractive and present a complete description of the program, with a major section devoted to results obtained with previous participants, if available. Measurable results and reactions from participants, or even direct quotes from individuals, could add spice to an otherwise dull brochure.

Case Studies

Case studies represent an effective way to communicate the results of a training program. Consequently, it is recommended that a few evaluation projects be developed in a case format. A typical case study describes the situation, provides appropriate background information (including the events that led to the intervention), presents the techniques and strategies used to develop the study, and highlights the key issues in the program. Case studies tell an interesting story of how the evaluation was developed and the problems and concerns identified along the way.

Case studies have many useful applications in an organization. First, they can be used in group discussions, where interested individuals can react to the material, offer different perspectives, and draw conclusions about approaches or techniques. Second, the case study can serve as a self-teaching guide for individuals trying to understand how evaluations are developed and utilized in the organization. Finally, case studies provide appropriate recognition for those involved in the actual case. More important, they recognize the participants who achieved the results, as well as the managers who allowed the participants to be involved in the program. The case study format has become one of the most effective ways to learn about project evaluation.

A Case Example

These various methods for communicating HRD program results can be creatively combined to fit any situation. Here is an effective example utilizing three approaches: a case study, management meetings, and a brochure.

The production unit had achieved outstanding results through the efforts of a team of two supervisors. The results were in the form of key bottom-line measures, such as absenteeism, turnover, lost-time accidents, grievances, scrap rate, and unit hour. The unit hour was a basic measure of individual productivity.

These results were achieved through the efforts of the supervisors applying the basic skills taught in a supervisor-training program. This fact was discretely mentioned at the beginning of a presentation made by the supervisors. In a panel discussion format with a moderator, the two supervisors outlined how they achieved results. It was presented in a question-and-answer session at a monthly meeting for all supervisors. They mentioned that many of the skills were acquired in the training program.

The comments were published in a brochure and distributed to all supervisors through their department managers. The title of the publication was "Getting Results: A Success Story." On the inside cover, specific results were detailed, along with additional information on the supervisors. A close-up photograph of each supervisor, taken during the panel discussion, was included on this page. The next two pages presented a summary of the techniques used to secure the results. The pamphlet was used in staff meetings as a discussion guide to cover the points from the panel discussion. Top executives were also sent copies. In addition, the discussion was videotaped and used in subsequent training programs as a model of application of skills. The pamphlet served as a handout.

The communication effort was a success. Favorable responses were received from all levels of management. Top executives asked the HRD department to prepare and conduct similar meetings. Other supervisors began to use more of the skills and techniques presented by the two supervisors.

COMMUNICATING THE INFORMATION

Perhaps the greatest challenge of communication is the actual delivery of the message. This can be accomplished in a variety of ways and settings, based on the target audience and the media selected for the message. Three particular approaches deserve additional coverage. The first is providing insight into how to give feedback throughout the project to make sure information flows so changes can be made. The second is presenting an impact study to a senior management team. This may be one of the most challenging tasks for the evaluator. The third is communicating regularly and routinely with the executive management group. Each of these three approaches is explored in more detail.

Providing Feedback

One of the most important reasons for collecting reaction, satisfaction, and learning data is to provide feedback so adjustments or changes can be made throughout the program. In most training programs, data is routinely collected and quickly communicated to a variety of groups. Table 10-4 shows a comprehensive feedback action plan designed to provide information to several feedback audiences using a variety of media. This type of process is only necessary for large projects.

As the plan in Table 10-4 shows, data are collected during the project at four specific time intervals and communicated back to at least four audiences—and sometimes six. Some of these feedback sessions result in identifying specific actions that need to be taken. This process becomes comprehensive and needs to be managed in a very proactive way. The following steps are recommended for providing feedback and managing the feedback process (Block, 2000).

- ☐ **Communicate quickly.** Whether the news is good or bad, it is important to let individuals involved in the project have the information as soon as possible. The recommended time for providing feedback is usually a matter of days; certainly no longer than a week or two after the results are known.
- ☐ **Simplify the data.** Condense data into an understandable, concise presentation. This is not the format for detailed explanations and analysis.

Table 10-4. Feedback Action Plan

Data Collection Item	Timing	Feedback Audience	Media	Timing of Feedback	Action Required
1. ☐ Preprogram Survey Climate/Environment ☐ Issue Identification	Beginning of the Project	Participants Team Leaders HRD Staff	Meeting Survey Summary Survey Summary Meeting	One Week Two Weeks Two Weeks One Week	None None Communicate Feedback Adjust Approach
2. Implementation Survey ☐ Reaction to Plans ☐ Issue Identification	Beginning of Actual Implementation	Participants Team Leaders HRD Staff	Meeting Survey Summary Survey Summary Meeting	One Week Two Weeks Two Weeks One Week	None None Communicate Feedback Adjust Approach
3. Implementation Reaction Survey/Interviews ☐ Reaction to Solution ☐ Suggested Changes	One Month into Implementation	Participants Support Staff Team Leaders Immediate Managers HRD Staff	Meeting Study Summary Study Summary Study Summary Study Summary Meeting	One Week Two Weeks Two Weeks Two Weeks Three Weeks Three Days	Comments None None Support Changes Support Changes Adjust Approach
4. Implementation Feedback Questionnaire ☐ Reaction (Satisfaction) ☐ Barriers ☐ Projected Success	End of Implementation	Participants Support Staff Team Leaders Immediate Managers HRD Staff	Meeting Study Summary Study Summary Study Summary Study Summary Meeting	One Week Two Weeks Two Weeks Two Weeks Three Weeks Three Days	Comments None None Support Changes Support Changes Adjust Approach

☐ **Examine the role of the HRD staff and the sponsor in the feedback situation.** Sometimes the HRD staff member is the judge, and sometimes the jury, prosecutor, defendant, or witness. On the other hand, sometimes the sponsor is the judge, jury, prosecutor, defendant, or witness. It is important to examine the respective roles in terms of reactions to the data and the actions that need to be taken.

☐ **Use negative data in a constructive way.** Some of the data will show that things are not going so well, and the fault may rest with the HRD staff or the sponsor. In either case, the story basically changes from "Let's look at the success we've made" to "Now we know which areas to change."

☐ **Use positive data in a cautious way.** Positive data can be misleading and if they are communicated too enthusiastically, they may create expectations beyond what may materialize later. Positive data should be presented in a cautious way—almost in a discounting mode.

☐ **Choose the language of the meeting and communication very carefully.** Use language that is descriptive, focused, specific, short, and simple. Avoid language that is too judgmental, macro, stereotypical, lengthy, or complex.

☐ **Ask the sponsor for reactions to the data.** After all, the sponsor is the customer, and the sponsor's reaction is critical.

☐ **Ask the sponsor for recommendations.** The sponsor may have some very good recommendations of what needs to be changed to keep a project on track or put it back on track if it derails.

☐ **Use support and confrontation carefully.** These two issues are not mutually exclusive. There may be times when support and confrontation are needed for the same group. The sponsor may need support and yet be confronted for lack of improvement or sponsorship. The HRD staff may be confronted on the problem areas that are developed but may need support as well.

☐ **React and act on the data.** Weigh the different alternatives and possibilities to arrive at the adjustments and changes that will be necessary.

☐ **Secure agreement from all key stakeholders.** This is essential to make sure everyone is willing to make adjustments and changes that seem necessary.

☐ **Keep the feedback process short.** Don't let it become bogged down in long, drawn-out meetings or lengthy documents. If this occurs, stakeholders will avoid the process instead of being willing to participate in the future.

Following these steps will help move the project forward and provide important feedback, often ensuring that adjustments are supported and made.

Presenting Impact Study Data to Senior Management

Perhaps one of the most challenging and stressful company communications is presenting an impact study to the senior management team, which also serves as the sponsor on a project. The challenge is convincing this highly skeptical and critical group that outstanding results have been achieved (assuming they have), in a very reasonable time frame, addressing the salient points, and making sure the managers understand the process. Two particular issues can create challenges. First, if the results are very impressive, it may be difficult to make the managers believe the data. On the other extreme, if the data are negative, it will be a challenge to make sure managers don't overreact to the negative results and look for someone to blame. Following are guidelines that can help make sure this process is planned and executed properly:

☐ Plan a face-to-face meeting with senior team members for the first one or two major impact studies, as detailed in Figure 10-1. If they

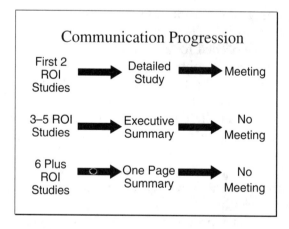

Figure 10-1. Communication Strategy.

are unfamiliar with the ROI methodology, a face-to-face meeting is necessary to make sure they understand the process. The good news is that they will probably attend the meeting because they have not seen ROI data developed for training or performance improvement. The bad news is that it takes a lot of time, usually an hour for this presentation.

☐ After a group has had a face-to-face meeting with a couple of presentations, an executive summary may suffice for the next 3–9 studies. At this point they understand the process, so a shortened version may be appropriate.

☐ After the target audience is familiar with the process, a brief version may be necessary, which will involve a one- to two-page summary with charts or graphs showing all six types of measures. Table 10-5 shows a sample of a one-page summary.

☐ When making the initial presentation, distribution of the results should be saved until the end of the session. This will allow enough time to present the process and obtain reaction to it before the target audience sees the actual ROI number.

☐ Present the process step-by-step, showing how the data were collected, when they were collected, who provided the data, how the data were isolated from other influences, and how they were converted to monetary values. The various assumptions, adjustments, and conservative approaches are presented along with the total cost of the program. The costs are fully loaded so that the target audience will begin to buy into the process of developing the actual ROI.

☐ When the data are actually presented, the results are presented step-by-step, starting with Level 1, moving through Level 5, and ending with the intangibles. This allows the audience to see the chain of impact with reaction and satisfaction, learning, application and implementation, business impact, and ROI. After some discussion on the meaning of the ROI, the intangible measures are presented. Allocate time to each level, as appropriate, for the audience. This helps overcome the potentially negative reactions to a very positive or negative ROI.

☐ Show the consequences of additional accuracy if it is an issue. The trade-off for more accuracy and validity often means more expense. Address this issue whenever necessary, agreeing to add more data if required.

☐ Collect concerns, reactions, and issues for the process and make adjustments accordingly for the next presentation.

Table 10-5. A One Page Summary of Impact Study

ROI Impact Study

Program Title: Preventing Sexual Harassment at Healthcare, Inc.
Target Audience: First and Second Level Managers (655); Secondary: All employees through group meetings (6844).
Duration: 1 day, 17 sessions
Technique to Isolate Effects of Program: Trend analysis; participant estimation
Technique to Convert Data to Monetary Value: Historical costs: internal experts
Fully-Loaded Program Costs: $277,987

Results

Level 1: Reaction	Level 2: Learning	Level 3: Application	Level 4: Impact	Level 5: ROI	Intangible Benefits
93% provided action items	65% increase posttest versus pretest Skill practice demonstration	96% conducted meetings and completed meeting record 4.1 out of 5 on behavior change survey 68% report all action items complete 92% report some action items complete	Turnover reduction: $2,840,632 Complaint reduction: $360,276 Total improvement: $3,200,908	1051%	Job satisfaction Reduced absenteeism Stress reduction Better recruiting

Collectively, these steps will help prepare for and present one of the most critical meetings in the ROI process.

Routine Communication with Executive Management and Sponsors

No group is more important than top executives when it comes to communicating results. In many situations, this group is also the sponsor. Improving communications with this group requires developing an overall strategy, which may include all or part of the actions outlined next.

☐ **Strengthen the relationship with executives.** An informal and productive relationship should be established between the HRD manager (responsible for the project evaluation) and the top executive at the location where the project is taking place. Each should feel comfortable discussing needs and project results. One approach is to establish frequent, informal meetings with the executive to review problems with current projects and discuss other performance problems/opportunities in the organization. Frank and open discussions can provide the executive with insight not possible from any other source. Also, it can be very helpful to the HRD manager to determine the direction.

☐ **Show how training programs have helped solve major problems.** While hard results from recent projects are comforting to an executive, solutions to immediate problems may be more convincing. This is an excellent opportunity to discuss possible future programs for ROI evaluation.

☐ **Distribute memos on project results.** When an intervention has achieved significant results, make appropriate top executives aware of them. This can easily be done with a brief memo or summary outlining what the project was supposed to accomplish, when it was implemented, who was involved, and the results achieved. This should be presented in a for-your-information format that consists of facts rather than opinions. A full report may be presented later.

All significant communications on training evaluation projects, plans, activities, and results should include the executive group. Frequent information on the projects, as long as it is not boastful, can reinforce credibility and accomplishments.

☐ **Ask executives to be involved in a review.** An effective way to enhance commitment from top executives is to ask them to serve on a training review committee. A review committee provides input and advice to the HRD staff on a variety of issues, including needs, problems with the present project, and project evaluation issues. This committee can be helpful in letting executives know what the projects are achieving.

ANALYZING REACTIONS TO COMMUNICATION

The best indicator of how effectively the results of a training program have been communicated is the level of commitment and support from the management group. The allocation of requested resources and strong commitment from top management are tangible evidence of management's perception of the results. In addition to this macro-level reaction, there are a few techniques the HRD staff can use to measure the effectiveness of their communication efforts.

Whenever results are communicated, the reaction of the target audiences can be monitored. These reactions may include nonverbal gestures, oral remarks, written comments, or indirect actions that reveal how the communication was received. Usually, when results are presented in a meeting, the presenter will have some indication of how the results were received by the group. The interest and attitudes of the audience can usually be quickly evaluated.

During the presentation, questions may be asked or, in some cases, the information is challenged. In addition, a tabulation of these challenges and questions can be useful in evaluating the type of information to include in future communications. Positive comments about the results are desired and, when they are made—formally or informally— they should also be noted and tabulated.

HRD staff meetings are an excellent arena for discussing the reaction to communicating results. Comments can come from many sources depending on the particular target audiences. Input from different members of the staff can be summarized to help judge the overall effectiveness.

When major program results are communicated, a feedback questionnaire may be used for an audience or a sample of the audience. The purpose of this questionnaire is to determine the extent to which the audience understood and/or believed the information presented. This is practical only when the effectiveness of the communication has a significant impact on future actions.

Another approach is to survey the management group to determine its perceptions of the results. Specific questions should be asked about results. What does the management group know about the results? How believable are the results? What additional information is desired about the project? This type of survey can help provide guidance in communicating results.

The purpose of analyzing reactions is to make adjustments in the communication process—if adjustments are necessary. Although the reactions may involve intuitive assessments, a more sophisticated analysis will provide more accurate information to make these adjustments. The net result should be a more effective communication process.

Final Thoughts

This chapter presented the final step in the ROI model. Communicating results is a crucial step in the overall evaluation process. If this step is not taken seriously, the full impact of the results will not be realized. The chapter began with general principles for communicating program results. A communications framework was presented which can serve as a guide for any significant communication effort. The various target audiences were discussed and, because of its importance, emphasis was placed on the executive group. A suggested format for a detailed evaluation report was also provided. Much of the remainder of the chapter included a detailed presentation of the most commonly used media for communicating program results, including meetings, publications, and electronic media. Numerous examples illustrated these concepts.

Case Study—Part I, Linear Network Systems

ROI Analysis Plan

Figure 10-2 shows the ROI analysis plan for the leadership development program. Each decision and strategy outlined in the various parts of this case is reflected on this form. This document is a decision-making tool for ROI analysis and is used to make specific plans for the analysis to be complete. It is completed before beginning the evaluation process.

Date:_____

ROI Analysis Plan

Data Items	Methods of Isolating the Effects of the Program	Methods of Converting Data	Cost Categories	Intangible Benefits	Communication Targets	Other Influences/Issues
Productivity % of Shipments Met	• Participant Estimates	• Direct Conversion— Company Standard Value	• Program Fee from Consulting Company • Program Materials	• Improved Supervisor Job Satisfaction • Improved Employee Job Satisfaction	• Participants • Managers of Participants • Senior Management • Training and HR Staff	• Team building was in process • Total Quality Management program has been launched
Turnover (Quits and Discharges)	• Participant Estimates	• External Studies • Senior Management Estimate	• Food and Refreshments • Facilities • Evaluation Costs	• Stress Reduction • Increase in Bonus Pay	• Other Plant Managers • Potential Clients	• Management support is good • Management is very anxious to see results
Absenteeism	• Participant Estimates	• External Studies • Participant Estimate	• Salaries and Benefits of Participants			

Figure 10-2. ROI analysis plan.

Level 1 ROI Forecast

Although it was not attempted in this case, it is possible and perhaps instructive to develop a Level 1 ROI forecast. With this process, a series of potential impact questions could be asked where participants anticipate potential changes and estimate the particular impact of changes for each of the three variables (productivity, turnover, and absenteeism). Estimates could be provided on other measures that may be driven by the program. First year values could be developed, along with a confidence percentage obtained from participants reflecting their level of certainty with the process. The data could be adjusted with this confidence level to provide a forecast of the benefit and the calculation of the ROI. Although this ROI value is subjective and often inflated, this analysis would provide some insight into the relationship between the projections at the end of the program and the actual performance four months later. Also, it may actually enhance the results because participants who make projections of performance may be motivated to meet those projections.

Levels 2 and 3 ROI Forecast

At LNS, it was impossible to capture data for a Level 2 ROI forecast. For this forecast to be possible, a validated instrument must be developed to measure the performance of first level managers in the program and have it correlated with subsequent on-the-job performance. This was not feasible in this situation.

A Level 3 ROI forecast was not considered because of the concern over the subjective assessments that must be made converting Level 3 data to monetary values. Also, the client was very bottom-line oriented and preferred to discuss performance in terms of Level 4 measures (productivity, turnover, absenteeism, etc.). While management recognized that skills must be acquired and behavior must be changed, they were less interested in discussing the extent to which changes have occurred and the value of the change. Thus, a Level 3 ROI forecast would have provided little value for the client.

Communication of Results

Communication of results from an ROI impact study is very crucial to the ROI methodology. Three documents were created: a detailed impact study, an executive summary, and brief summary, with a little more detail than the executive summary. Although there can be many target audiences, six audiences received the study results at LNS:

1. The participants (first level managers) were provided a brief summary of the study results revealing what they had accomplished, collectively. The brief summary of the impact study showed how the ROI was developed.
2. The managers of the participants (middle level managers) received a summary of the study with an appropriate explanation. These department heads for the various production and support departments were aware of the ROI impact study and were anticipating the results.
3. Senior management received executive summaries and copies of the detailed study. At LNS, this group included the president, director of manufacturing (for all plants), and the plant manager. In addition, this group received a briefing on the study results and discussed how it was developed along with its interpretation. This step is important to ensure that there is a complete understanding of the ROI methodology.
4. The training and HR staff received copies of the complete study so that they could understand how the ROI methodology is applied to this type of program. This ROI study was part of an ongoing effort to build skills and develop strategies to increase accountability of HR programs.
5. Plant managers for the other locations received copies of the executive summary to show what can be accomplished with this type

of training. Essentially, this communication served as an internal marketing tool to convince others that leadership development can improve their plants.

6. Potential clients for the consulting firm received brief summary copies of the study. This target group was unique to the consulting firm. With permission of the company, the study summary was used by the consulting firm to convince other prospective clients that leadership development can produce high impact. The name of the organization was disguised and sensitive data was slightly altered to protect the identity of the company.

Collectively, these six target audiences received information on the ROI impact study, ensuring that all important audiences understand the results and the process.

Discussion Questions

1. How can the results of this study be used to generate additional funding for measurement and evaluation?
2. How should the ROI methodology by transferred internally in terms of responsibilities and skills?
3. How should management support for ROI be enhanced?
4. What other steps should be taken to implement the ROI methodology at LNS?

REFERENCES

Block, P. *Flawless Consulting,* 2nd ed. San Francisco, CA: Jossey-Bass/Pfeiffer, 2000.

Phillips, J.J. *The Consultant's Scorecard: Tracking Results and Bottom-Line Impact of Consulting Projects,* New York, NY: McGraw-Hill, 2000.

Phillips, P.P., and H. Burkett. "Managing Evaluation Shortcuts," *Info-line.* Alexandria, VA: American Society for Training and Development, November 2001.

Rae, L. *Using Evaluation in Training and Development,* London, England: Kogan Page, 1999.

Sanders, J.R. *The Program Evaluation Standards: How to Assess Evaluations of Educational Programs,* 2nd ed. Thousand Oaks, CA: Sage Publications, 1994.

Torres, R.T., H.S. Preskill, and M.E. Piontek. *Evaluation Strategies for Communicating and Reporting: Enhancing Learning in Organizations.* Thousand Oaks, CA: Sage Publications, 1996.

FURTHER READING

Bleech, J.M., and D.G. Mutchler. *Let's Get Results, Not Excuses!* Hollywood, FL: Lifetime Books Inc., 1995.

Fuller, J. *Managing Performance Improvement Projects: Preparing, Planning, and Implementing.* San Francisco, CA: Pfeiffer & Co., 1997.

Hale, J. *The Performance Consultant's Fieldbook: Tools and Techniques for Improving Organizations and People.* San Francisco, CA: Jossey-Bass/Pfeiffer, 1998.

Knox, A.B. *Evaluation for Continuing Education.* San Francisco, CA: Jossey-Bass, 2002.

Labovitz, G., and V. Rasansky. *The Power of Alignment: How Great Companies Stay Centered and Accomplish Extraordinary Things.* New York, NY: John Wiley & Sons, Inc., 1997.

Langdon, Danny G. *The New Language of Work.* Amherst, MA: HRD Press, Inc., 1995.

Patton, M.Q. *Utilization-Focused Evaluation: The New Century Text*, 4th ed. Thousand Oaks, CA: Sage Publications, 2002.

Russ-Eft, D., and H. Preskill. *Evaluation in Organizations: A Systematic Approach to Enhancing Learning Performance, and Change*, Cambridge, MA: Perseus Publishing, 2001.

Sujansky, J.C. *The Power of Partnering.* San Diego, CA: Pfeiffer & Co., 1991.

Tufte, E.R. *Envisioning Information.* Cheshire, CT: Graphics Press, 1990.

Zelazny, G. *Say It with Charts: The Executive's Guide to Visual Communication*, 3rd ed. New York, NY: McGraw-Hill, 1996.

CHAPTER 11

Implementation Issues

The best designed model or technique will be worthless unless it is integrated efficiently and effectively in the organization. Although the ROI methodology presented in this book is a step-by-step, methodical, and simplistic procedure, it will fail even in the best organizations if it is not integrated into the mainstream of activity and fully accepted and supported by those who should make it work in the organization. This chapter focuses on the critical issues involved in implementing the ROI methodology in the organization.

OVERCOMING THE RESISTANCE TO ROI

With any new process or change, there is resistance. Resistance shows up in many ways—negative comments, inappropriate actions, or dysfunctional behaviors. Table 11-1 shows some comments that reflect open resistance to the ROI methodology, based on a decade of implementation experience of the author, his partner, and associates. Each represents an issue that must be resolved or addressed in some way. A few of the comments are based on realistic barriers, while others are based on myths that must be dispelled. Sometimes, resistance to ROI reflects underlying concerns. The individuals involved may have fear of losing control and others may feel that they are vulnerable to actions that may be taken if their programs are not successful. Still others may be concerned about any process that requires additional learning and actions.

Resistance can appear in all major audiences addressed in this book. It can appear in the HRD staff as they resist ROI and openly make

Table 11-1. Typical Objections to the ROI Methodology

---

1. It costs too much.
2. It takes too much time.
3. Who is asking for this?
4. It is not in my job duties.
5. I did not have input on this.
6. I do not understand this.
7. What happens when the results are negative?
8. How can we be consistent with this?
9. The ROI process is too subjective.
10. Our managers will not support this.
11. ROI is too narrowly focused.
12. This is not practical.

---

comments similar to those listed in Table 11-1. Heavy persuasion and evidence of tangible benefits may be needed to convince those individuals that this is a process that should be implemented—because it is in their best interest. Another major audience, the sponsor, will also experience resistance. Although most sponsors would want to see the results of an ROI project, they may have concerns about the quality and accuracy of data. Also, they may be concerned about the time commitments and costs of the ROI.

The managers of participants in programs may develop resistance. They may have concerns about the information they are asked to provide and about whether their performance is being judged along with the evaluation of the participants. In reality, they may express the same fears listed in the Table 11-1.

The challenge is to implement the process in organizations methodically and consistently so that it becomes a routine and standard process built into training and performance improvement programs. Implementation is a plan for overcoming resistance. There are four key reasons why there should be a detailed plan for overcoming resistance:

1. Resistance is always present
2. Implementation is key
3. Consistency is needed
4. Efficiency

Resistance Is Always Present

There is always resistance to change. Sometimes there are good reasons for resistance, but often it exists for the wrong reasons. The important point is to sort out both types and try to dispel the myths. When legitimate barriers are the basis for resistance, trying to minimize or remove them altogether is the task.

Implementation Is Key

As with any process, effective implementation is the key to its success. This occurs when the new technique or tool is integrated into the routine framework. Without effective implementation, even the best process will fail. A process that is never removed from the shelf will never be understood, supported or improved. There must be clear-cut steps for designing a comprehensive implementation process that will overcome resistance.

Consistency Is Needed

As this process is implemented from one impact study to another, consistency is an important consideration. With consistency comes accuracy and reliability. The only way to make sure consistency is achieved is to follow clearly defined processes and procedures each time the ROI is tackled. Proper implementation will ensure that this occurs.

Efficiency

Cost control and efficiency will always be an issue in any major undertaking, and the ROI methodology is no exception. Implementation must ensure that tasks are completed efficiently as well as effectively. It will help ensure that the process cost is kept to a minimum, that time is utilized appropriately, and that the process remains affordable.

The implementation necessary to overcome resistance covers a variety of areas. Figure 11-1 shows actions outlined in this chapter that are presented as building blocks to overcoming resistance. They are all necessary to build the proper base or framework to dispel myths and remove or minimize actual barriers. The remainder of this chapter presents specific strategies and techniques around each of the building blocks identified in Figure 11-1.

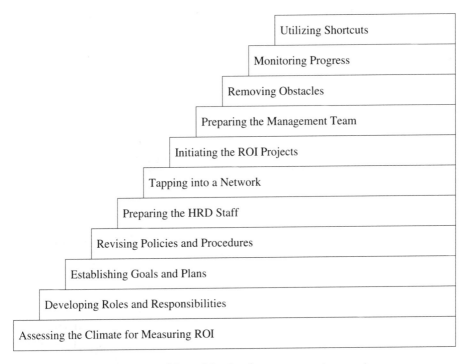

Figure 11-1. Building blocks for overcoming resistance.

PLANNING THE IMPLEMENTATION

Few initiatives will be effective without proper planning and the ROI methodology is no exception. Planning is synonymous with success. Several issues are fundamental to preparation for ROI and positioning the ROI methodology as an essential component of the training and development process.

Identifying a Champion

As a first step in the process, one or more individuals should be designated as the internal leader for ROI. As in most change efforts, someone must take the responsibility for ensuring that the process is implemented successfully. This leader serves as a champion for ROI and is usually the one who understands the process best and sees the vast potential for the contribution of the process. More important, this leader is willing to show and teach others.

Table 11-2. Potential Roles of Implementation Leader

Technical expert	Cheerleader
Consultant	Communicator
Problem solver	Process monitor
Initiator	Planner
Designer	Analyst
Developer	Interpreter
Coordinator	Teacher

The ROI leader is usually a member of the HRD training staff who usually has this responsibility full-time in larger organizations or part-time in smaller organizations. The typical job title for a full time ROI leader is manager or leader of measurement and evaluation. Some organizations assign this responsibility to a team and empower them to lead the ROI effort. For example, Nortel Networks selected five individuals to lead this effort as a team. All five received certification in the ROI methodology.

Developing the ROI Leader

In preparation for this assignment, individuals usually obtain special training to build specific skills and knowledge in the ROI process. The role of the implementation leader is very broad and serves a variety of specialized duties. The leader can take on many roles, as shown in Table 11-2.

At times, the ROI implementation leader serves as technical expert, giving advice and making decisions about some of the issues involved in evaluation design, data analysis, and presentation. As an initiator, the leader identifies programs for ROI analysis and takes the lead in conducting a variety of ROI studies. When needed, the implementation leader is a cheerleader, bringing attention to the ROI methodology, encouraging others to become involved, and showing how value can be added to the organization. Finally, the implementation leader is a communicator—letting others know about the process and communicating results to a variety of target audiences. All the roles can come into play at one time or another as the leader implements ROI in the organization.

Table 11-3. Skill Areas for Certification

1. Planning for ROI calculations
2. Collecting evaluation data
3. Isolating the effects of training
4. Converting data to monetary values
5. Monitoring program costs
6. Analyzing data including calculating the ROI
7. Presenting evaluation data
8. Implementing the ROI process
9. Providing internal consulting on ROI
10. Teaching others the ROI process

It is a difficult and challenging assignment that will need special training and skill building. In the past, there have been only a few programs available that help build these skills. Now there are many available and some are quite comprehensive. For example, a program has been developed by the author to certify the individuals who are assuming a leadership role in the implementation of ROI. The process involves prework and preparation prior to attending a one-week workshop and project follow-up 3–6 months later. The comprehensive workshop is designed to build ten essential skills, listed in Table 11-3, required to apply and implement the ROI methodology.

During the workshop, the participants plan a project for ROI evaluation, develop the data collection and ROI analysis plans for the project, and present them to the team for feedback. In addition, they develop and present a plan to show how they will help implement the ROI methodology in their organization, addressing the issues under their control. The typical participant is charged with the responsibility of implementing ROI, or a part of it, in his or her division or organization. Sometimes, participants are part of a team and the entire team attended.

A public version was first offered in 1995 when it became apparent that many organizations wanted to send one or two individuals to this type of session—to develop the skills to lead the implementation of ROI—but did not have the resources to send the entire team to an internal certification workshop.

To date, over 2000 individuals have attended a certification workshop, representing 500 organizations in 35 countries. Table 11-4 shows

Table 11-4. Sample of Organizations Participating in Certifications

- ☐ Air Canada
- ☐ Accenture
- ☐ Aetna
- ☐ Allstate Insurance Company
- ☐ amazon.com
- ☐ AmSouth Bank
- ☐ Apple Computer
- ☐ Asia Pacific Breweries
- ☐ AT&T
- ☐ Bank of America
- ☐ Banner Health Care
- ☐ Baptist Health Systems
- ☐ Bell South
- ☐ Blue Cross & Blue Shield of Maryland
- ☐ BP Amoco
- ☐ Bristol-Myers Squibb
- ☐ Caltex–Pacific
- ☐ Canadian Imperial Bank of Commerce
- ☐ Canadian Tire
- ☐ Chevron/Texaco
- ☐ Commonwealth Edison
- ☐ Deloitte & Touche
- ☐ Delta Airlines
- ☐ DHL Worldwide Express
- ☐ Duke Energy
- ☐ Eli Lilly
- ☐ Entergy Corporation
- ☐ Eskom (South Africa)
- ☐ Federal Express
- ☐ First American Bank
- ☐ Ford Motor Company
- ☐ Georgia Pacific
- ☐ GlaxoSmithKline
- ☐ Guthrie Healthcare Systems
- ☐ Harley Davidson
- ☐ Hewlett-Packard
- ☐ Home Depot
- ☐ Hong Kong Bank
- ☐ IBM
- ☐ Illinois Power
- ☐ Intel
- ☐ Lockheed Martin
- ☐ M&M Mars
- ☐ Mead
- ☐ Microsoft
- ☐ Motorola
- ☐ NCR
- ☐ Nextel
- ☐ Nortel Networks
- ☐ Novus Services
- ☐ Olive Garden Restaurants
- ☐ Overseas–Chinese Banking Corp
- ☐ Pfizer
- ☐ Price WaterhouseCoopers
- ☐ Raytheon
- ☐ Rolls Royce
- ☐ Singapore Airlines
- ☐ Singapore Technologies
- ☐ Sprint
- ☐ Toronto Dominion Bank
- ☐ United Parcel Service
- ☐ UNOCAL
- ☐ Verizon Communications
- ☐ Vodafone
- ☐ Volvo of North America
- ☐ Wachovia Bank
- ☐ Waste Management Company
- ☐ Wells Fargo
- ☐ Whirlpool
- ☐ Xerox

a small sample of the organizations participating in certification. Almost one-third of this group had an internal team certified. Others sent one or two individuals to a public workshop. The adoption has been widespread with certification conducted on several continents. Certification is unique and no other process is available to satisfy these critical needs. It still enjoys internal and public success. For more information on the certification, contact the author.

Assigning Responsibilities

Determining the specific responsibilities is a critical issue because there can be confusion when individuals are unclear about their specific assignments in the ROI process. Responsibilities apply to two broad groups. The first is the measurement and evaluation responsibility for the entire training and development staff. It is important for all of those involved in designing, developing, delivering, coordinating, and supporting programs to have some responsibility for measurement and evaluation. These responsibilities include providing input on the design of instruments, planning a specific evaluation, collecting data, and interpreting the results. Typical responsibilities include:

- ☐ Ensuring that the needs assessment includes specific business impact measures.
- ☐ Developing specific application objectives (Level 3) and business impact objectives (Level 4) for each program.
- ☐ Focusing the content of the program on performance improvement, ensuring that exercises, tests, case studies, and skill practices relate to the desired objectives.
- ☐ Keeping participants focused on application and impact objectives.
- ☐ Communicating rationale and reasons for evaluation.
- ☐ Assisting in follow-up activities to capture application and business impact data.
- ☐ Providing assistance for data collection, data analysis, and reporting.
- ☐ Developing plans for data collection and analysis.
- ☐ Presenting evaluation data to a variety of groups.
- ☐ Assisting with the design of instruments

While it may be inappropriate to have each member of the staff involved in all of these activities, each individual should have at least one or more responsibilities as part of their routine job duties. This assignment of responsibility keeps the ROI process from being disjointed and separate from major training and development activities. More importantly, it brings accountability to those who develop, deliver, and implement the programs.

The second issue involves the technical support function. Depending on the size of the HRD staff, it may be helpful to establish a group of technical experts to provide assistance with the ROI process. When this group is established, it must be clear that the experts and are not there to relieve others of evaluation responsibilities, but to supplement technical expertise. Some firms have found this approach to be effective. At one time, Accenture had a measurement and evaluation staff of 32 individuals to provide technical support for the evaluation of internal professional education. When this type of support is developed, responsibilities revolve around eight key areas:

1. designing data collection instruments;
2. providing assistance for developing an evaluation strategy;
3. coordinating a major evaluation project;
4. analyzing data, including specialized statistical analyses;
5. interpreting results and making specific recommendations;
6. developing an evaluation report or case study to communicate overall results;
7. presenting results to critical audiences; and
8. providing technical support in any phase of the ROI process.

The assignment of responsibilities for evaluation is also an issue that needs attention throughout the evaluation process. Although the HRD staff must have specific responsibilities during an evaluation, it is not unusual to require others in support functions to have responsibility for data collection. These responsibilities are defined when a particular evaluation strategy plan is developed and approved.

Tapping into a Network

Because the ROI methodology is new to many individuals, it is helpful to have a peer group experiencing similar issues and frustrations. Tapping into an international network (already developed), joining or creating a local network, or building an internal network are all possible ways to utilize the resources, ideas, and support of others.

ASTD ROI Network

In 1996, the ROI network was created to exchange information among the graduates of the certification workshop. During certification the participants bond and freely exchange information with each other. The ROI network is an attempt to provide a permanent vehicle of information and support.

The ROI Network is a professional organization, which claims about 400 members. It is now affiliated with ASTD and is poised for growth. The network operates through a variety of committees and communicates with members through newsletters, websites, listservers, and annual meetings. The ROI network represents an opportunity to build a community of practice around the ROI methodology. To learn more about the ASTD ROI network, visit www.ASTD.org.

Creating a Local Network

In some situations, it may be appropriate, and feasible, to develop a group of local individuals who have the same interest and concerns about ROI methodology. When this is the case, a local network may be feasible. For some occasions, this is a country (such as the Australian ROI Network); in other situations it is a more confined area (such as the Puerto Rico ROI network). In Puerto Rico, a group of 30 individuals, who participated in the certification process, challenge each other to remain as an intact group to discuss issues and report progress. Members come from a wide variety of backgrounds, but meet routinely to present progress, discuss problems, barriers, and issues, and plan next steps. This is a very active group, typical of what can develop if the individuals are willing to share the information and support each other.

Building an Internal Network

One way to integrate the information needs of HRD practitioners for an effective ROI evaluation process is through an internal ROI network. The experience with networks—in organizations where the idea has been tried—shows that these communities of practice are powerful tools for both accelerating evaluation skill development and cultivating a new culture of accountability.

The concept of a network is simplicity itself. The idea is to bring people who are interested in ROI together throughout the organization to work under the guidance of trained ROI evaluators. Typically, advocates within the HRD department see both the need for beginning networks and the potential of ROI evaluation to change how the department does its work. Interested network members learn by designing and executing real evaluation plans. This process generates commitment for accountability as a new way of doing business for the HRD department (Phillips and Pulliam, 1999).

Developing Evaluation Targets

As presented earlier, establishing specific targets for evaluation levels is an important way to make progress with measurement and evaluation. Targets enable the staff to focus on the improvements needed with specific evaluation levels. In this process, the percent of courses or programs planned for evaluation at each level is developed. The first step is to assess the present situation. The number of all courses (or programs), including repeated sections of a course, is tabulated along with the corresponding level(s) of evaluation presently conducted for each course. Next, the percent of courses using Level 1 reaction questionnaires is calculated. The process is repeated for each level of the evaluation. The current percentages for Levels 3, 4, and 5 are usually low.

After detailing the current situation, the next step is to determine a realistic target for each level within a specific time frame. Many organizations set annual targets for changes. This process should involve the input of the entire HRD staff to ensure that the targets are realistic and that the staff is committed to the process and targets. If the training and development staff does not develop ownership for this process, targets will not be met. The improvement targets must be achievable, while at the same time, challenging and motivating. Table 11-5 shows the targets

Table 11-5. Evaluation Targets for Wachovia Bank

Level of Evaluation	Percent of Programs Evaluated at this Level
Level 1—Reaction	100%
Level 2—Learning	50%
Level 3—Application	30%
Level 4—Business Results	10%
Level 5—ROI	5%

initially established for Wachovia Bank, a large financial services company with hundreds of programs.

Using this as an example, 100% of the programs are measured at Level 1, which is consistent with many other organizations. Only half of the programs are measured at Level 2 using a formal method of measurement. At this organization, informal methods are not counted as a learning measure. At Level 3, application represents a 30% follow-up. In essence, this means that almost one third of the programs will have some type of follow-up method implemented—at least for a small sample of those programs. Ten percent are planned for business impact and half of those for ROI. These percentages are typical and often recommended. The Level 2 measure may increase significantly in groups where there is much formal testing, or if informal measures (e.g., self assessment) are included as a learning measure. There is rarely a need to go beyond 10 and 5% for Levels 4 and 5, respectively.

Table 11-6 shows current percentages and targets for five years in a large Asia Pacific multinational company. This table reflects the gradual improvement of increasing evaluation activity at Levels 3, 4, and 5; year 0 is the current status.

Target setting is a critical implementation issue. It should be completed early in the process with full support of the entire HRD staff. Also, if practical and feasible, the targets should have the approval of the key management staff, particularly the senior management team.

Developing a Project Plan for Implementation

An important part of the planning process is to establish timetables for the complete implementation process. This document becomes a master

Table 11-6. Gradual Implementation of ROI Methodology

	Percent of Courses Evaluated at Each Level					
	Year 0	Year 1	Year 2	Year 3	Year 4	Year 5
Reaction and Planned Action	85%	90%	95%	100%	100%	100%
Learning	30%	35%	40%	45%	50%	60%
Job Application	5%	10%	15%	20%	25%	30%
Business Results	2%	4%	5%	9%	12%	15%
ROI	0%	2%	4%	6%	8%	10%

	J	F	M	A	M	J	J	A	S	O	N	D	J	F	M	A	M	J	J	A	S	O	N
Team Formed	■																						
Policy Developed		■	■	■																			
Targets Set	■	■																					
Network Formed			■																				
Workshops Developed			■	■	■	■	■																
ROI Project (A)					■	■	■	■															
ROI Project (B)							■	■	■	■													
ROI Project (C)										■	■	■	■										
ROI Project (D)												■	■	■	■	■	■						
HRD Staff Trained								■	■	■													
Suppliers Trained															■	■	■						
Managers Trained																	■	■	■				
Support Tools Developed				■	■	■																	
Evaluation Guidelines Developed		■	■	■																			

Figure 11-2. ROI implementation project plan for a large petroleum company.

plan for the completion of the different elements presented in this chapter, beginning with assigning responsibilities and concluding with meeting the targets previously described. Figure 11-2 shows an ROI implementation project plan for a large petroleum company.

From a practical basis, this schedule is a project plan for transition from the present situation to a desired future situation. The items on the schedule include, but are not limited to, developing specific ROI projects, building staff skills, developing policy, teaching managers the process, analyzing ROI data, and communicating results. The more detailed the document, the more useful it will become. The project plan is a living long-range document that should be reviewed frequently and adjusted as necessary. More importantly, it should always be familiar to those who are routinely working with the ROI methodology.

Revising/Developing Policies and Procedures

Another key part of planning is revising (or developing) the organization's policy concerning measurement and evaluation, often a part of policy and practice for developing and implementing training and development programs. The policy statement contains information developed specifically for the measurement and evaluation process. It is frequently developed with the input of the HRD staff, key managers or sponsors, and the finance and accounting staff. Sometimes policy issues are addressed during internal workshops designed to build skills with measurement and evaluation. Figure 11-3 shows the topics in the measurement and evaluation policy for a large firm in South Africa.

1. Purpose

2. Mission

3. Evaluate all programs which will include the following levels:

   a. Participant satisfaction (100%)

   b. Learning (no less than 70%)

   c. Job applications (50%)

   d. Results (usually through sampling) (10%) (highly visible, expensive)

   e. ROI (5%)

4. Evaluation support group (corporate) will provide assistance and advice in Measurement & Evaluation, Instrument Design, Data Analysis, and Evaluation Strategy.

5. New programs are developed following logical steps beginning with needs analysis and ending with communicating results.

6. Evaluation instruments must be designed or selected to collect data for evaluation. They must be valid, reliable, economical, and subject to audit by evaluation support group.

7. Responsibility for HRD program results rests with trainers, participants, and supervisors of participants.

8. An adequate system for collecting and monitoring HRD costs must be in place. All direct costs should be included.

9. At least annually the management board will review the status and results of HRD. The review will include HRD plans, strategies, results, costs, priorities, and concerns.

Figure 11-3. Results-based internal HRD policy (excerpts from actual policy for a large firm in South Africa).

10. Line management shares in the responsibility for HRD programs. Evaluation through follow-up, preprogram commitments, and overall support.

11. Managers/Supervisors must declare competence achieved through training and packaged programs. When not applicable, HRD staff should evaluate.

12. External HRD consultants must be selected based on previous evaluation. Central data/resource base should exist. All external HRD programs of over one day in duration will be subjected to evaluation procedures. In addition, participants will assess the quality of external programs.

13. HRD program results must be communicated to the appropriate target audience. As a minimum, this includes management (participants' supervisor), participants, and all HRD staff.

14. HRD staff should be qualified to do effective needs-analysis and evaluation.

15. Central database for program development to prevent duplication and serve as program resource.

16. Union involvement in total Training and Development plan.

Figure 11-3. Continued

The policy statement addresses critical issues that will influence the effectiveness of the measurement and evaluation process. Typical topics include adopting the five-level model presented in this book, requiring Levels 3 and 4 objectives in some or all programs, and defining responsibilities for training and development.

Policy statements are very important because they provide guidance and direction for the staff and others who work closely with the ROI process. They keep the process clearly on focus and enable the group to establish goals for evaluation. Policy statements also provide an opportunity to communicate basic requirements and fundamental issues regarding performance and accountability. More than anything else, they serve as a learning tool to teach others, especially when they are developed in a collaborative and collective way. If policy statements are developed in isolation and do not have the ownership of the staff and management, they will not be effective or useful.

Guidelines for measurement and evaluation are important to show how to utilize the tools and techniques, guide the design process, provide consistency in the ROI process, ensure that appropriate methods are used, and place the proper emphasis on each of the areas. The guidelines are more technical than policy statements and often contain detailed procedures showing how the process is actually undertaken and developed. They often include specific forms, instruments, and tools necessary to facilitate the process. Figure 11-4 shows the table of contents of evaluation guidelines for a multinational company. As this table of contents reveals, the guidelines are comprehensive and include significant emphasis on ROI and accountability.

Assessing the Climate

As a final step in planning the implementation, some organizations assess the current climate for achieving results. One useful tool, presented in Appendix A, shows a results-based study. This instrument, or some version of it, can serve as an initial assessment of how the HRD staff and managers, whom they support, perceive the status of training and performance improvement. In some organizations, annual assessments are taken to measure progress as this process is implemented. Others take the assessment instrument to the management group to determine the extent managers perceive training and development to be effective. The use of an assessment process provides an excellent understanding of current status. Then the organization can plan for significant changes, pinpointing particular issues which need support as the ROI methodology is implemented.

PREPARING THE HRD STAFF

One group that will often resist the ROI methodology is the HRD staff who must design, develop, deliver, and coordinate training and learning solutions. These staff members often see evaluation as an unnecessary intrusion into their responsibilities, absorbing precious time, and stifling their freedom to be creative. The cartoon character Pogo perhaps characterized it best when he said, "We have met the enemy and he is us." This section outlines some important issues that must be addressed when preparing the staff for the implementation of ROI.

Section 1: Policy
1.1   The Need for Accountability
1.2   The Bottom Line: Linking Training with Business Needs
1.3   Results-Based Approach
1.4   Implications
1.5   Communication
1.6   Payoff
Section 2: Responsibilities
2.1   Training Group Responsibilities: Overall
2.2   Training Group Responsibilities: Specifics for Selected Groups
2.3   The Business Unit Responsibilities
2.4   Participant Manager Responsibilities
2.5   Participants Responsibilities
Section 3: Evaluation Framework
3.1   Purpose of Evaluation
3.2   Levels of Evaluation
3.3   Process Steps for Training Implementation
3.4   Evaluation Model
Section 4: Level 1 Guidelines
4.1   Purpose and Scope
4.2   Areas of Coverage—Standard Form
4.3   Optional Areas of Coverage
4.4   Administrative Issues
4.5   How to Use Level 1 Data
Section 5: Level 2 Guidelines
5.1   Purpose and Scope
5.2   Learning Measurement Issues
5.3   Techniques for Measuring Learning
5.4   Administration
5.5   Using Level 2 Data
Section 6: Level 3 Guidelines
6.1   Purpose and Scope
6.2   Follow-Up Issues
6.3   Types of Follow-Up Techniques
6.4   Administrative Issues
6.5   Using Level 3 Evaluation
Section 7: Levels 4 and 5 Guidelines
7.1   Purpose and Scope
7.2   Business Results and ROI Issues
7.3   Monitoring Performance Data
7.4   Extracting Data from Follow-Up Evaluation
7.5   Isolating the Effects of the Learning Solution
7.6   Converting Data to Monetary Values
7.7   Developing Costs
7.8   Calculating the ROI
7.9   Identifying Intangible Benefits
7.10   Administrative Issues
7.11   Using Business Impact and ROI Data

Figure 11-4. Evaluation guidelines for a multinational company.

Involving the HRD Staff

On each key issue or major decision, the HRD staff should be involved in the process. As policy statements are prepared and evaluation guidelines developed, staff input is absolutely essential. It is difficult for the staff to be critical of something they helped design, develop, and plan. Using meetings, brainstorming sessions, and task forces, the HRD staff should be involved in every phase of developing the framework and supporting documents for ROI. In an ideal situation, the HRD staff can learn the process in a two-day workshop and, at the same time, develop guidelines, policy, and application targets in the session. This approach is very efficient, completing several tasks at the same time.

Using ROI as a Learning Tool—Not a Performance Evaluation Tool

One reason the HRD staff may resist the ROI process is that the effectiveness of their programs will be fully exposed, placing their reputation on the line. They may have a fear of failure. To overcome this, the ROI process should clearly be positioned as a tool for process improvement and not a tool to evaluate HRD staff performance, at least during its early years of implementation. HRD staff members will not be interested in developing a tool that will be used to expose their shortcomings and failures.

Evaluators can learn more from failures than from successes. If the program is not working, it is best to find out quickly and understand the issues first hand—not from others. If a program is ineffective and not producing the desired results, it will eventually be known to clients and/or the management group, if they are not aware of it already. A lack of result will cause managers to become less supportive of training. Dwindling support appears in many forms, ranging from budget reductions to refusing to let participants be involved in programs. If the weaknesses of programs are identified and adjustments are made quickly, not only will effective programs be developed, but also the credibility and respect for the function and HRD staff will be enhanced.

Removing Obstacles to Implementation

Several obstacles to the implementation of the ROI methodology will usually be encouraged. Some of these are realistic barriers, while others are often based on misconceptions. The majority of them were presented and analyzed in the first chapter. The most common barriers involving the HRD staff are reviewed here.

☐ **ROI is a complex process.** Many of the HRD staff will perceive ROI as too complex a process to implement. To counter this, the staff must understand that by breaking the process down into individual components and steps, it can be simplified. A variety of tools, templates, and software is available to simplify the use of the ROI methodology. (The resources listed in Appendix A contains many of these tools.)

☐ **HRD staff members often feel they do not have time for evaluation.** The HRD staff need to understand that evaluation efforts can save time in the future. An ROI impact study may show that the program should be changed, modified, or even eliminated. Also, up front planning with evaluation strategy can save additional follow-up time.

☐ **The HRD staff must be motivated to pursue evaluations, even when senior executives are not requiring it.** Most staff member, will know when top managers are pushing the accountability issue. If they do not see that push, they are reluctant to take the time to make it work. They must see the benefits of pursuing the process even if not required or encouraged at the top. The staff should see the ROI methodology as a preventive strategy or a leading edge strategy. The payoff of implementation should be underscored.

☐ **The HRD staff may be concerned that ROI results will lead to criticism.** Many staff members will be concerned about the use of ROI impact study information. If the results are used to criticize or reflect the performance of program designers or facilitators, there will be a reluctance to embrace the concept. ROI should be considered as a learning process, at least in the early stages of implementation.

These and other obstacles can thwart an otherwise successful implementation. Each must be removed or reduced to a manageable issue.

Teaching the Staff

The HRD staff will usually have inadequate skills in measurement and evaluation and thus will need to develop some expertise in the process. Measurement and evaluation is not always a formal part of preparing to become a facilitator, instructional designer, or performance analyst.

Consequently, each staff member must be provided training on the ROI process to learn how the methodology is implemented, step-by-step. In addition, staff members must know how to develop plans to collect and analyze data, and interpret results from data analysis. Sometimes a one- or two-day workshop is needed to build adequate skills and knowledge to understand the process, appreciate what it can accomplish for the organization, see the necessity for it, and participate in a successful implementation. (A list of the public 2-day workshops is available from the author or at www.ASTD.org.) Each staff member should know how to understand, utilize, and support the ROI methodology. Teaching materials, outlines, slides, workbooks, and other support materials for workshops are available in a special ROI field book available from Butterworth–Heinemann.

INITIATING THE ROI PROCESS

The first tangible evidence of the ROI process may be initiation of the first project in which the ROI is calculated. This section outlines some of the key issues involved in identifying the projects and keeping them on track.

Selecting Programs for ROI Evaluation

Selecting a program for ROI analysis is an important issue. Ideally, certain types of programs should be selected for comprehensive, detailed analysis. As briefly discussed in Chapter 7, the typical approach for identifying programs for ROI evaluation is to select those that are expensive, strategic, and highly visible. Figure 11-5 lists six of the common criteria often used to select programs for this level of evaluation. The process for selection is simple. Using this or a more detailed list, each program is rated, based on the criteria. A typical rating scale uses 1–5. All programs are rated and the program with the highest number is the best candidate for ROI consideration. This process only identifies the best candidates. The actual number evaluated may depend on other factors, such as the resources available to conduct the studies.

Additional criteria should be considered when selecting initial programs for ROI evaluation. For example, the initial program should be as simple as possible. Complex programs should be reserved for the time frame after ROI skills have been mastered. Also, the program should be one that is considered successful now (i.e., all the current feedback data suggest that the program is adding significant value). This helps to avoid

Selecting Programs for ROI Evaluation

Criteria	#1	#2	#3	#4	etc
			Programs		
1. Life Cycle					
2. Company Objectives					
3. Costs					
4. Audience Size					
5. Visibility					
6. Management Interest					
Total					

Rating Scale	
1. Life Cycle	5 = Long life cycle 1 = Very short life cycle
2. Company Objectives	5 = Closely related to company objectives 1 = Not directly related to company objectives
3. Costs	5 = Very expensive 1 = Very inexpensive
4. Audience Size	5 = Very large audience 1 = Very small audience
5. Visibility	5 = High visibility 1 = Low visibility
6. Management Interest	5 = High level of interest in evaluation 1 = Low level of interest in evaluation

Figure 11-5. Selecting programs for ROI evaluation.

having a negative ROI study on the first use of the ROI methodology. Still another criteria is to select a program that is void of strong political issues or biases. While these programs can be tackled very effectively with the ROI methodology, it may be too much of a challenge for an early application.

These are only the basic criteria; the list can be extended as necessary to bring the organization's particular issues into focus. Some large organizations with hundreds of programs use as many as 15 criteria and the corporate university staff rates programs based on these criteria. The most important issue is to select those programs that are designed to make a difference and represent tremendous investments by the organization. Also, programs that command much attention from management are ideal candidates for an ROI evaluation. Almost any senior management group will have a perception about the effectiveness of a particular program. For some, they want to know the impact it is having; for others, they are not very concerned. Thus, management interest may drive the selection of many of the impact studies.

The next major step is to determine how many projects to undertake initially and in which particular areas. A small number of initial projects are recommended, perhaps two or three programs. The selected programs may represent the functional areas of the business such as operations, sales, finance, engineering, and information systems. Another approach is to select programs representing functional areas of training such as sales training, management and supervisor training, computer-based training, and technical training. It is important to select a manageable number so the process will be implemented.

Ultimately, the number of programs tackled will depend on the resources available to conduct the studies, as well as the internal need for accountability. The percentage of programs evaluated at each level, indicated in Table 11-5, can be accomplished within 3–5% of the total training and performance improvement budget. For an organization with 200 programs, this would mean that 5% (10) of the programs will have ROI impact studies conducted annually, and at least 30% (60) will have some type of follow-up (Level 3). All of this can be accomplished with less than 5% of the total training and performance improvement budget. The costs of the ROI methodology do not necessarily drain the resources of the organization. At the same time, the programs selected for this level of analysis is limited and should be carefully selected.

Reporting Progress

As the projects are developed and the ROI implementation is underway, status meetings should be conducted to report progress and discuss critical issues with appropriate team members. For example, if a leadership program is selected as one of the ROI projects, all of the key staff involved in the program (design, development, and delivery) should meet regularly to discuss the status of the project. This keeps the project team focused on the critical issues, generates the best ideas to tackle particular problems and barriers, and builds a knowledge base to implement evaluation in future programs. Sometimes this group is facilitated by an external consultant, an expert in the ROI process. In other cases, the internal ROI leader may facilitate the group.

These meetings serve three major purposes: reporting progress, learning, and planning. The meeting usually begins with a status report on each ROI project, describing what has been accomplished since the previous meeting. Next, the specific barriers and problems encountered are discussed. During the discussions, new issues are interjected in terms of possible tactics, techniques, or tools. Also, the entire group discusses how to remove barriers to success and focuses on suggestions and recommendations for next steps, including developing specific plans. Finally, the next steps are developed, discussed, and configured.

PREPARING THE MANAGEMENT TEAM

Perhaps no group is more important to the ROI process than the management team who must allocate resources for training and development and support the programs. In addition, they often provide input and assistance in the ROI process. Specific actions to train and develop the management team should be carefully planned and executed.

A critical issue that must be addressed before training the managers is the relationship between the training and development staff and key managers. A productive partnership is needed that requires each party to understand the concerns, problems, and opportunities of the other. Developing this type of relationship is a long-term process that must be deliberately planned and initiated by key HRD staff members (Bell and Shea, 1998). Sometimes the decision to commit resources and support for training is often based on the effectiveness of this relationship.

Workshop for Managers

One effective approach to prepare managers for the ROI process is to conduct a workshop for managers, "Manager's Role in Learning and Performance." Varying in duration from one half to two days, this practical workshop shapes critical skills and changes perceptions to enhance the support of the ROI process. Managers leave the workshop with an improved perception of the impact of learning and a clearer understanding of their roles in the training and performance improvement process. More important, they often have a renewed commitment to make training work in their organization.

Due to the critical need for this topic in management training, this workshop should be required for all managers, unless they have previously demonstrated strong support for the training function. Because of this requirement, it is essential for top executives to be supportive of this workshop and, in some cases, take an active role in conducting it. To tailor the program to specific organizational needs, a brief needs assessment may be necessary to determine the specific focus and areas of emphasis for the program.

TARGET AUDIENCES

While the target audience for this program is usually middle-level managers, the target group may vary with different organizations. In some organizations, the target may be first-level managers and in others, the target may begin with second-level managers. Three important questions help determine the proper audience are:

- ☐ Which group has the most direct influence on the training and development function?
- ☐ Which management group is causing serious problems with lack of management support?
- ☐ Which group has the need to understand the ROI process so they can influence training transfer?

The answer to each question is often the middle-level manager.

TIMING

This workshop should be conducted early in the management development process before nonsupportive habits are developed. When this program is implemented throughout the organization, it is best to start with higher level managers and more down the organization. If possible, a version of the program should be a part of a traditional management training program provided to new managers when they are promoted into managerial positions.

SELLING TOP MANAGEMENT

Because convincing top management to require this program may be a difficult task, three approaches should be considered:

1. Discuss and illustrate the consequences of inadequate management support for training, learning, and performance. For example, the statistics are staggering in wasted time and money.
2. Show how current support is lacking. An evaluation of an internal training program will often reveal the barriers to successful application of training. Lack of management support is often the main reason, which brings the issue close to home.
3. Demonstrate how money can be saved and results can be achieved with the ROI process.

The endorsement of the top management group is very important. In some organizations, top managers actually attend the program to explore first hand what is involved and what they must do to make the process work. At a minimum, top management should support the program by signing memos describing the program or by approving policy statements. They should also ask thought-provoking questions in their staff meetings from time to time. This will not happen by chance. The HRD manager must tactfully coach top executives.

Workshop Content

The program will usually cover the topics outlined next. The time allotted for each topic and specific focus will depend on the organization, the experience and needs of the managers, and the preparation of the management group. The program can be developed in separate modules where managers can be exempt from certain modules based on their previous knowledge or experience with the topic. This module concept is recommended.

The Overall Importance of Training

Managers need to be convinced that training and development is a mainstream responsibility that is gaining in importance and influence in the organizations. They need to understand the results-based approach of today's progressive HRD organizations. After completing this module, managers should perceive training as a critical process in their organization and be able to describe how the process contributes to strategic and operational objectives. Data from the organization are presented to show the full scope of training in the organization. Tangible evidence of top management commitment should be presented in a form such as memos, directives, and policies signed by the CEO or another appropriate top executive. In some organizations, the invitation to attend the program comes from the CEO, a gesture which shows strong top management commitment. Also, external data should be included to illustrate the growth of training budgets and the increasing importance of training and development. Perhaps a case showing the linkage between HRD and strategy would be helpful.

The Impact of Training

Too often, managers are unsure about the success of training. After completing this module, managers will be able to identify the steps to measure the impact of training on important output variables. Reports and studies should be presented showing the impact of training using measures such as productivity, quality, cost, response times, and customer satisfaction. Internal evaluation reports, if available, are presented to managers, showing convincing evidence that training is making a significant difference in the organization. If internal reports are not available, other success stories or case studies from other organizations can be utilized (Phillips, 2002). Managers need to be convinced that training is a successful, results-based tool, not only to help with change, but also to meet critical organizational goals and objectives.

THE TRAINING AND PERFORMANCE IMPROVEMENT PROCESS

Managers usually will not support activities or processes that they do not fully understand. After completing this module, managers should be able to describe how the training process works in their organization and understand each critical step from needs assessment to ROI calculation. Managers need to be aware of the effort that goes into developing a training program and their role in each step of the process. A short case, illustrating all the steps, is helpful in this module. This discussion also reveals various areas of the potential impact of training and development.

RESPONSIBILITY FOR HRD

Defining who is responsible for training is important to the success of training. After completing this module, managers should be able to list their specific responsibilities for training and development. Managers must see how they can influence training and the degree of responsibility they must assume in the future. Multiple responsibilities for training are advocated, including managers, participants, participant managers, trainers, developers, and facilitators. Case studies are appropriate in this module to illustrate the consequences when responsibilities are neglected or when there is failure to follow-up by managers. One specific case is available that was designed for this purpose (Phillips, 2002). In some organizations, job descriptions are revised to reflect training responsibility. In other organizations, major job-related goals are established to highlight management responsibility for training. Overall, this session leaves participants with a clear understanding of how their responsibility is linked to the success of training and development.

Table 11-7. Management Involvement in Training and Education

The following are areas for present and future involvement in the Training and Education Process. Please check your areas of planned involvement.

	In Your Area	Outside Your Area
☐ Attend a Program Designed for Your Staff	☐	☐
☐ Provide Input on a Needs Analysis	☐	☐
☐ Serve on an HRD Advisory Committee	☐	☐
☐ Provide Input on a Program Design	☐	☐
☐ Serve as a Subject Matter Expert	☐	☐
☐ Serve on a Task Force to Develop a Program	☐	☐
☐ Volunteer to Evaluate an External T&E Program	☐	☐
☐ Assist in the selection of a Vendor Supplied T&E Program	☐	☐
☐ Provide Reinforcement to Your Employees After They Attend Training	☐	☐
☐ Coordinate an T&E Program	☐	☐
☐ Assist in Program Evaluation or Follow-Up	☐	☐
☐ Conduct a Portion of the Program, as a Facilitator	☐	☐

ACTIVE INVOLVEMENT

One of the most important ways to enhance manager support for HRD is to get them actively involved in the process. After completing this module, managers will actually commit to one or more ways of active involvement in the future. Table 11-7 shows twelve ways for manager involvement identified for one company. The information in the table was presented to managers in the workshop with a request for them to commit to at least one area of involvement. After these areas are fully explained and discussed, each manager is asked to select one or more ways in which he or she will be involved in training and development in the future. A commitment to sign up for at least one involvement role is required. If used properly, these commitments are a rich source of input and assistance from the management group. There will be many offers for involvement, and the training and development department must follow through with the offers. A quick follow-up on all offers is recommended.

MONITORING PROGRESS AND COMMUNICATING RESULTS

A final part of the implementation process is to monitor the overall progress made and communicate the results of specific ROI projects. Although it is an often overlooked part of the process, an effective communication plan can help keep the implementation on target and let others know what the ROI process is accomplishing for the organization.

Communication must be an ongoing, critical part of the process to ensure that all stakeholders are aware of their various responsibilities, understand the progress made and barriers confronted, and develop insight into the results and successes achieved. Because of the importance of communication as part of the ROI methodology, this topic was explored in a separate chapter. Chapter 10 provides a comprehensive coverage of all the issues involved in communicating the results from programs as well as providing routine feedback to make decisions and enhance processes. Detailed information on how to develop and present an impact study is also included in that chapter.

COST SAVINGS APPROACHES

One of the most significant barriers to the implementation of the ROI methodology is the potential time and cost involved in implementing the process. Sometimes, the perception of excessive time and cost is only a myth; at other times it is a reality. As discussed earlier, the methodology can be implemented for about 3–5% of the training and performance improvement budget. However, this is still a significant expense and represents additional time requirements. It is fitting to end this book with 14 steps that can be utilized to keep the costs and time commitment to a minimum. These cost savings approaches have commanded much attention recently and represent an important part of the implementation strategy (Phillips and Burkett, 2001).

☐ **Take shortcuts at lower levels.** When resources are a primary concern and shortcuts need to be taken, it is best to take them at lower levels in the evaluation scheme. This leads to another guiding principle.

Guiding Principle #2
When an evaluation is planned for a higher level, the previous level
does not have to be comprehensive.

This is a resource allocation issue. For example, if a Level 4
evaluation is conducted, Levels 1–3 do not have to be as comprehensive. This requires the evaluator to place most of the emphasis on the highest level of the evaluation.

☐ **Fund measurement and evaluation with the savings from the ROI
methodology.** Almost every ROI impact study will generate data
from which to make improvements. Results at different levels
often show how the program can be altered to make it more effective and efficient. Sometimes, the data suggest that the program
can be modified, adjusted, or completely redesigned. All of those
actions can result in cost savings. In a few cases, the program may
have to be eliminated because it is not adding the value and adjustments will not necessarily improve it (i.e., it was not needed). In
this case, a tremendous cost savings is realized as the program is
eliminated. A logical argument can be made to shift a portion of
these savings to fund additional measurement and evaluation.
Some organizations gradually migrate to the 5% of budget target
for expenditures for measurement and evaluation by utilizing
the savings generated from the use of the ROI methodology. This
provides a disciplined and conservative approach to additional
funding.

☐ **Plan early and thoroughly.** One of the most critical, cost-saving
steps to evaluation is to develop program objectives and plan early
for the evaluation. Evaluations often succeed because of proper
planning. The best way to conserve time and resources is to know
what must be done at what time. This prevents unnecessary analysis, data collection after the appropriate time, and the task of
having to reconstruct events and issues because they were not
planned in advance.

☐ **Integrate evaluation into training.** To the extent possible, evaluation should be built in to the training and performance improvement program. Data collection tools should be considered part of
the program. If possible, these tools should be positioned as application tools and not necessarily evaluation tools. This removes
the stigma of providing data to an evaluator, but instead enables
the participant or others to capture data to clearly understand the

success of the program on the job. Part of this issue is to build in expectations for stakeholders to provide the appropriate data.

☐ **Share the responsibilities.** Defining specific responsibilities for all the stakeholders involved in training and performance improvement is critical to the successful streamlining of the evaluation process. Many individuals should play an active role in measurement and evaluation. These include performance consultants, designers, developers, facilitators, participants, participants' managers, and internal subject matter experts. These individuals can share much of the load that had previously been part of the evaluator's responsibility. This not only has a value of saving time, but also enriches the success of the process by having the active involvement of all stakeholders.

☐ **Involve participants in the process.** One of the most effective cost savings approaches is to have participants conduct major steps of the process. Participants are the primary source for understanding the degree to which learning is applied and has driven success on the job. The responsibilities for the participants should be expanded from the traditional requirement of involvement in learning processes and application of new skills. Now they must be asked to show the impact of those new skills and provide data as a routine part of the process. Consequently, the role of the participant has expanded from learning and application to measuring the impact and communicating information.

☐ **Use shortcut methods.** Almost every step of the ROI model contains shortcut methods—a particular method that represents a shortcut, but has proven to be an effective process. For example, in data collection, the simple questionnaire is a shortcut method that can be used to generate powerful and convincing data, if it is administered properly. This inexpensive time savings data collection process can be used in many evaluations. Other short cut methods are available in isolation and conversion of data steps.

☐ **Use sampling.** Not all programs should require a comprehensive evaluation, nor should all participants necessarily be evaluated in a planned follow-up scenario. Thus, sampling can be used in two ways. First, as described earlier, only a few programs are selected for Levels 3, 4, and 5 evaluation. Those programs should be selected based on the criteria described early in the chapter. Next, when a particular program is evaluated, in most cases, only a sample of participants should be evaluated. This keeps costs and time to a minimum.

☐ **Use estimates.** Estimates are a very important part of the process. They are also the least expensive way to arrive at an issue. Whether isolating the effects of training or converting data to monetary value, estimates can be a routine and credible part of the process. The important point is to make sure the estimate is as credible as possible and that the process used to collect the estimate follows systematic, logical, and consistent steps.

☐ **Use internal resources.** An organization does not necessarily have to employ consultants to develop impact studies and address other measurement and evaluation issues. Internal capability can be developed, eliminating the need to depend on consultants. There are many opportunities to build skills and become certified in ROI Implemention. This approach is perhaps one of the most significant time savers. The difference in using internal resources versus external consultants can save as much as 50% of the costs of a specific project.

☐ **Streamline reporting processing.** When management understands the evaluation process, a streamlined approach to communication may be more appropriate and less time consuming. The streamline report (usually one page) is a high-level summary of the impact of the program, covering the results at various levels. A sample of this kind of document was shown in Chapter 10.

☐ **Use web-based software.** Because this process is sequential and methodical, it is ideal for software application. Comprehensive software has been developed to process data at Levels 1 through 5. Additional information on available software and how it can be used can be obtained directly from the author.

☐ **Use the ROI field book.** A time saving companion field book has been developed as a complement to this book. The field book contains a variety of tools, templates, checklists, and job aids to assist the HRD staff with implementation, it should be an indispensable guide for the HRD staff involved in assisting with implementation. For more information on the field book, see Appendix A.

☐ **Build on the work of others.** There is no time to reinvent the wheel. One of the most important cost savings approaches is to learn from others and build on their work. There are three primary ways to accomplish this:
   1. Use networking opportunities internally, locally, and globally (this issue was described earlier in the chapter).
   2. Read and dissect a published case study. Over one hundred cases have been published (see resources in Appendix).

3. Locate a similar case study in a database of completed case studies (contact the author for information).

These shortcuts are important to weave throughout the ROI methodology to ensure that ROI does not drain the budgets and resources unnecessarily. Other shortcuts can be developed, but a word of caution is in order: shortcuts often compromise the process. When a comprehensive, valid, and reliable study is needed, it will be time consuming and expensive—there is no way around it. The good news is that many shortcuts can be taken to supply the data necessary for the audience and manage the process in an efficient way.

FINAL THOUGHTS

In summary, the implementation of the ROI methodology is a very critical part of the process. If not approached in a systematic, logical, and planned way, the ROI process will not become an integral part of training and development and, consequently, the accountability of the programs will be lacking. This final chapter presented the different elements that must be considered and issues that must be addressed to ensure that implementation is smooth and uneventful. The result would be a complete integration of the ROI methodology as a mainstream activity in the training and performance improvement process.

CASE STUDY—PART J, LINEAR NETWORK SYSTEMS

Implementation Issues

A variety of implementation issues emerged at LNS:

☐ The HRD staff at LNS used the results of this study to make a request for additional funding for measurement and evaluation in the future. In essence, the plan is to use the savings generated from the studies to drive additional funding for measurement and evaluation.

☐ One individual was appointed as coordinator for measurement and evaluation and was asked to lead the process. Appointing a champion and a leader to implement the ROI methodology ensures that the process works properly, is executed timely, and is supported appropriately.

☐ To ensure that the study can be replicated, the internal leader participated in all phases of ROI Implemention. The consulting firm worked closely with this individual to ensure that each step of the ROI methodology was understood and could be applied in other situations.

☐ To help accomplish the transfer of capability, the consulting firm organized additional training for the evaluation leader to develop skills in the ROI methodology and provide additional practice with ROI calculations.

☐ To help improve management support, a 2½-hour briefing was scheduled with the management team (department managers and above) at the next quarterly meeting to discuss the results of this study, and the potential opportunity for significant returns from training. The program also underscored the manager's responsibility to make training effective in the company.

☐ Specific targets were set where a few programs were identified for planned ROI calculations. This provided some guidance for the HRD director to focus on high priority programs.

☐ A policy statement was developed to capture the basic requirements for measurement and evaluation. This document described the responsibilities for all stakeholders, outlined how ROI studies would be conducted, and indicated how the results would be communicated.

Collectively, these seven actions provided adequate support to implement the ROI methodology internally and make it a routine activity at LNS.

REFERENCES

Bell, C.R., and H. Shea. *Dance Lessons: Six Steps to Great Partnerships in Business & Life*. San Francisco, CA: Berrett-Koehler Publishers, Inc., 1998.

Phillips, J.J. *International Electric*. P.O. Box 380637, Birmingham, AL: Accountability Press, 2002.

Phillips, J.J., and P.F. Pullam. "Level 5 Evaluation: Mastering ROI," *Info-line*. Alexandria, VA: American Society for Training and Development, 1999.

Phillips, P.P., and H. Burkett. "Managing Evaluation Shortcuts," *Info-line*. Alexandria, VA: American Society for Training and Development, 2001.

Phillips, P.P., and J.J. Phillips. "Building a Global Consulting Practice in a Niche Market," *In Action: Building a Successful Consulting Practice*. Alexandria, VA: American Society for Training and Development, 2002. pp. 25–42.

FURTHER READING

Dent, S.M. *Partnering Intelligence: Creating Value for Your Business by Building Strong Alliances*. Palo Alto, CA: Davies-Black Publishing, 1999.

Doz, Y.L., and G. Hamel. *Alliance Advantage: The Art of Creating Value through Partnering*. Boston, MA: Harvard Business School Press, 1998.

Fritts, P.J. *The New Managerial Mentor: Becoming a Learning Leader to Build Communities of Purpose*. Palo Alto, CA: Davies-Black Publishing, 1998.

Phillips, J.J. (Ed.). *Implementing Evaluation Systems and Processes*. Alexandria, VA: American Society for Training and Development, 1998.

Phillips, P.P. (Ed.). *Measuring Return on Investment*, vol 3. Alexandria, VA: American Society for Training and Development, 2001.

APPENDIX A

Resources

Many additional resources have been developed to assist with the understanding, utilization, and implementation of the ROI methodology. A brief description of these items is included here. More detail can be obtained directly from the author at the following address:

350 Crossbrook Drive
Chelsea, Alabama 35043
roiresearch@mindspring.com or serieseditor@aol.com

The materials listed below are available directly from the publishers or can be purchased at www.amazon.com.

OTHER ROI BOOKS

The Human Resources Scorecard: Measuring the Return on Investment
Jack J. Phillips, Ron D. Stone, and Patricia P. Phillips
Butterworth–Heinemann (2001), ISBN 0-877-19367-3, 518 pages
200 Wheeler Road, 6th Floor
Burlington, MA 01803

This is the HR version for ROI and shows how the ROI methodology has been applied in a variety of human resources settings. Beginning with a description of 12 possible approaches to measurement, the book makes a strong case for the ROI methodology being a part of the mix. The last third of the book contains detailed case studies and ROI applications for a variety of HR programs. In essence, this is two books in one.

The Consultant's Scorecard: Tracking Results and Bottom-Line Impact of Consulting Projects
Jack J. Phillips
McGraw-Hill (2000), ISBN 0-07-134816-6, 392 pages
Two Penn Plaza
New York, NY 10121-2298

Recognizing that consulting assignments need to be subjected to accountability issues, this book applies the ROI methodology to consulting interventions. This book is appropriate for internal and external consultants involved in large-scale projects, organization development and change programs, as well as technology implementation. Many examples and details from a consulting setting are featured in this unique publication.

Project Management Scorecard: Measuring the Success of Project Management Solutions
Jack J. Phillips, Timothy W. Bothell, and G. Lynne Snead
Butterworth–Heinemann (2002), ISBN 0-7506-7449-0, 353 pages

The book shows how the ROI methodology is applied to the implementation and use of project management solutions. Utilizing the six measures, the book shows how a project management solution, such as training and technology processes, can be measured, along with the success of a variety of approaches to improve project management.

The Bottoms Line on ROI
Patricia P. Phillips
The Center for Effective Performance (2002), ISBN 1-879618-25-7, 117 pages
2300 Peachford Road, Suite 2000
Atlanta, GA 30338
www.ceppress.com

The brief presentation on ROI shows the basics, benefits, and barriers to implementive ROI methodology. It is intended for managers and professionals who are interested in the ROI methodology—but not convinced that it's feasible.

This is the first book in a new series for the Center for Effective Performance and the International Society for Performance Improvement. *Measurement in Action* is designed to present basic tools, templates, and techniques to practitioners.

Implementation Books

ROI Fieldbook
Patricia P. Patti and Holly Burkett
Butterworth–Heinemann (In press 2004), 500 pages

Featuring tools, templates, checklists, flow processes, and a variety of job aids, this detailed guide shows how the ROI methodology can be implemented efficiently and effectively. This is a must-have reference for those involved in any phase of implementation. The book is based on actual practices and experiences of hundreds of organizations implementing the ROI methodology. A CD-ROM is included.

The Handbook of Training Evaluation and Measurement Methods,
    3rd ed.
Jack J. Phillips
Butterworth–Heinemann (1997), ISBN 0-88415-387-8, 420 pages

This is the standard reference and college text for measurement and evaluation, detailing design issues and steps to improve measurement and evaluation. This book contains 23 chapters of information to assist in organizing, developing, implementing, supporting, and maintaining measurement and evaluation systems in an organization. This was the first major evaluation book published in the United States. An instructor's manual is available.

In Action: Implementing Evaluation Systems and Processes
Jack J. Phillips, Series Editor
American Society for Training and Development (1998), ISBN 1-56286-
    101-8, 18 case studies, 306 pages
1640 King Street
Alexandria, VA 22313–2043

This book addresses the challenges organizations face as the ROI methodology is implemented. The first half shows cases of successful integration of the ROI methodology throughout the systems, while the second half shows how the ROI methodology has been utilized with specific programs or divisions. In all, the studies detail the implementation issues confronting organizations and how they were resolved.

Case Studies

In Action: Measuring Return on Investment, vol. 1
Jack J. Phillips, Series Editor

American Society for Training and Development (1994), ISBN 1-56286-008-9, 18 case studies, 271 pages

This initial volume presents case studies from the real world. Each study details how the ROI methodology was applied, with particular focus on lessons learned throughout the process. This book has become the all-time best seller at ASTD and is still in great demand.

In Action: Measuring Return on Investment, vol. 2
Jack J. Phillips, Series Editor
American Society for Training and Development (1997), ISBN 1-56286-065-8, 17 case studies, 282 pages

This follow-up volume expands the traditional training coverage to other issues, including human resources and technology. This book has become the second all-time best seller at ASTD.

In Action: Measuring Return on Investment, vol. 3
Patricia P. Phillips, Editor; Jack J. Phillips, Series Editor
American Society for Training and Development (2001), ISBN 1-56286-288-X, 11 case studies, 254 pages

This third volume builds on the success of the previous volumes. In great detail, this book presents some of the best case studies available on the use of the ROI methodology in a variety of human resources and performance improvement settings.

In Action: Measuring ROI in the Public Sector
Patricia P. Phillips, Editor; Jack J. Phillips, Series Editor
American Society for Training and Development (2002), ISBN 1-56286-325-8, 10 case studies, 240 pages

This book addresses a critical need to bring additional accountability to the public sector with the use of the ROI methodology. This book contains case studies from the variety of settings in the public sector, with most of them involved in workforce development, training and learning, and human resources. The public sector settings vary from the federal, state, and local governments in the United States to governments outside the United States. This book is published jointly with the International Personnel Management Association.

In Action: Measuring Learning and Performance
Toni K. Hodges, Editor; Jack J. Phillips, Series Editor

American Society for Training and Development (1999), ISBN 1-56286-123-9, 16 case studies, 302 pages

Because of the interest in measuring learning and behavior change, this book focuses directly on these two important levels of evaluation. Learning (Level 2) and Application and Implementation (Level 3) case studies are featured in this unique publication. Each study shows what was accomplished, why, and the lessons learned.

In Action: Transferring Learning to the Workplace
Mary L. Broad, Editor; Jack J. Phillips, Series Editor
American Society for Training and Development (1997), ISBN 1-56286-059-3, 16 case studies, 331 pages

Research studies show that up to 90% of what is learned in formal training is not applied to the job. This unique book focuses directly on this problem—how learning can be transferred to the workplace. Many successful models and practices are explored, presenting the very best approaches to ensure that learning is actually utilized.

In Action: Measuring Intellectual Capital
Patricia P. Phillips, Editor; Jack J. Phillips, Series Editor
American Society for Training and Development (2002), ISBN 1-56286-295-2, 12 case studies, 218 pages

Measuring and monitoring intellectual capital is a critical challenge for organizations. These case studies show how organizations have implemented measurement systems to monitor and understand the current status and identify areas for improvement in this area. Common organizational measures are discussed as well as specific programs and processes utilized to measure intellectual capital.

In Action: Conducting Needs Assessment
Jack J. Phillips and Elwood F. Holton, III, Editors
American Society for Training and Development (1995), ISBN 1-56286-117-8, 17 case studies, 312 pages

The initial assessment is very critical to the success of training and development. This case study book shows studies on how organizations have tackled needs assessment, showing a variety of processes in different settings.

In Action: Performance Analysis and Consulting
Jack J. Phillips, Series Editor

American Society for Training and Development (2000), ISBN 1-56286-134-4, 18 case studies, 223 pages

Recognizing that the front-end analysis is elevated from needs assessment to performance analysis, this book focuses directly on case studies involving a detailed, up-front performance analysis. Cases are presented to show how the business needs are developed, job performance needs are analyzed, knowledge deficiencies are uncovered, and preferences are identified. The premise of each study is that a major business problem or opportunity is the driver for intervention and the studies illustrate how analysis is conducted to uncover the linkage to business need.

In-Action: Implementing E-Learning Solutions
Christine Pope, Editor; Jack J. Phillips, Series Editor
American Society for Training and Development (2001), ISBN 1-56286-292-8, 12 case studies, 200 pages

This casebook focuses on implementation of e-learning, primarily from the accountability perspective. The studies detail how e-learning is implemented and compared to other types of delivery processes. Specific ROI case studies are included in this unique publication.

INFO-LINE: THE HOW-TO REFERENCE TOOL FOR TRAINING AND PERFORMANCE PROFESSIONALS

The Info-line series from ASTD offers a variety of brief publications with tools, templates, and job aids included. The following Info-lines have been developed to support the ROI process.

The following Info-lines focus on each of the five levels of evaluation discussed in this book. Each issue shows examples, tools, techniques, tips, and templates needed to tackle the level.

Issue 9813: Level 1 Evaluation: Reaction and Planned Action (1999)
             Jack Phillips, Author; Cat Sharpe, Editor
Issue 9814: Level 2 Evaluation: Learning (1999)
             Jack Phillips, Author; Cat Sharpe, Editor
Issue 9815: Level 3 Evaluation: Application (1999)
             Jack Phillips, Author; Cat Sharpe, Editor
Issue 9816: Level 4 Evaluation: Business Results (1999)
             Jack Phillips and Ron Stone, Authors; Cat Sharpe, Editor
Issue 9805: Level 5 Evaluation: Mastering ROI (1998, 2000)
             Jack Phillips and Patricia Pulliam, Authors; Cat Sharpe, Editor

Issue 0111: Managing Evaluation Shortcuts (November 2001)
        Patricia Phillips and Holly Burkett, Authors

This issue presents a variety of shortcuts for measurement and evaluation that can save time and costs. Each shortcut is examined in terms of its usefulness, while at the same time, keeping in check the credibility.

Planning Evaluation (In press 2003)
Patricia Phillips, Cyndi Gaudet, and Jack Phillips, Authors

This useful guide outlines how evaluation is planned, showing the different forms, processes, tips, checks, steps, and guidelines.

SOFTWARE

Software has been developed to support the ROI methodology described in this book and is available in two different options. The first option is a complete system of measurement for all the different levels, which cuts across a variety of programs, providing various ways to analyze data at Levels 1 through 5. Using a process called Metrics that Matter, this is a comprehensive measurement tool to bring accountability to the overall training and learning function.

The other option is a variety of routines and features to develop specific ROI impact studies. This ROI methodology version can also be used for ROI studies as a stand-alone product. Both products are available on a subscription basis. Additional details can be obtained from the author or directly from Knowledge Advisors (www.knowledgeadvisors.com).

How Results-Based Are Your Training and Development Programs?

ASSESSMENT SURVEY FOR MANAGERS

Overview

The amount of management support needed for organization development, training and development, and human resource development programs are critical to their success. In most situations the amount and quality of support managers are willing to provide is directly linked to their perception of the effectiveness of the programs. If the programs are achieving results and helping the organization reach its goals, managers are often willing to support the programs, provide resources to make them successful, reinforce specific behavioral objectives, and become more actively involved in the process.

The following instrument provides an assessment of the extent to which managers perceive that programs are achieving results. It provides the organization with an assessment of the effectiveness of training and development, human resource development, and organization development as perceived by the managers.

Use

The instrument can be used in the following ways:

☐ It can serve as a benchmark for specific efforts, events, and activities aimed at enhancing the level of support.

363

- [ ] In efforts to increase the effectiveness of programs, this instrument will serve as a periodic assessment of the progress made.
- [ ] It can serve as a useful discussion tool in workshops for managers where the goal is to enhance their support for the training or organization development (OD) function. It is a recommended instrument for a program, *Manager's Role in Training and Development*, where the role of training is discussed, the importance of training is highlighted, the steps of the training process are outlined, and the results of training are underscored.
- [ ] It is a helpful tool to compare one group of managers in a division, plant, region, or subsidiary company with others to determine where specific attention may be needed.

Target Audience

The target audience for the instrument is middle and upper managers who are in the position to provide significant support to the training and development and organization development function. These are the key managers in the organization who can influence the success of those efforts.

Administration

The instrument should be administered without discussion. Participants and managers should be instructed to provide very candid responses. The results should be quickly tabulated by the respondents and discussed and interpreted in group discussion.

TRAINING AND DEVELOPMENT PROGRAMS ASSESSMENT: A SURVEY FOR MANAGERS

Instructions. For each of the following statements, please circle the response that best matches the Training and Development function at your organization. If none of the answers describe the situation, select the one that best fits. Please be candid with your responses.

1. The direction of the Training and Development function at your organization:
   a) Shifts with requests, problems, and changes as they occur.
   b) Is determined by Human Resources and adjusted as needed.
   c) Is based on a mission and a strategic plan for the function.

2. The primary mode of operation of the Training and Development function is:
   a) To respond to requests by managers and other employees to deliver training programs and services.
   b) To help management react to crisis situations and reach solutions through training programs and services.
   c) To implement many training programs in collaboration with management to prevent problems and crisis situations.
3. The goals of the Training and Development function are:
   a) Set by the training staff based on perceived demand for programs.
   b) Developed consistent with human resources plans and goals.
   c) Developed to integrate with operating goals and strategic plans of the organization.
4. Most new programs are initiated:
   a) By request of top management.
   b) When a program appears to be successful in another organization.
   c) After a needs analysis has indicated that the program is needed.
5. When a major organizational change is made:
   a) We decide only which presentations are needed, not which skills are needed.
   b) We occasionally assess what new skills and knowledge are needed.
   c) We systematically evaluate what skills and knowledge are needed.
6. To define training plans:
   a) Management is asked to choose training from a list of canned, existing courses.
   b) Employees are asked about their training needs.
   c) Training needs are systematically derived from a thorough analysis of performance problems.
7. When determining the timing of training and the target audiences:
   a) We have lengthy, nonspecific training courses for large audiences.
   b) We tie specific training needs to specific individuals and groups.
   c) We deliver training almost immediately before its use, and it is given only to those people who need it.
8. The responsibility for results from training:
   a) Rests primarily with the training staff to ensure that the programs are successful.

    b) Is a responsibility of the training staff and line managers, who jointly ensure that results are obtained.

    c) Is a shared responsibility of the training staff, participants, and managers all working together to ensure success.

9. Systematic, objective evaluation, designed to ensure that trainees are performing appropriately on the job:

    a) Is never accomplished. The only evaluations are during the program and they focus on how much the participants enjoyed the program.

    b) Is occasionally accomplished. Participants are asked if the training was effective on the job.

    c) Is frequently and systematically pursued. Performance is evaluated after training is completed.

10. New programs are developed:

    a) Internally, using a staff of instructional designers and specialists.

    b) By vendors. We usually purchase programs modified to meet the organization's needs.

    c) In the most economical and practical way to meet deadlines and cost objectives, using internal staff and vendors.

11. Costs for training and OD are accumulated:

    a) On a total aggregate basis only.

    b) On a program-by-program basis.

    c) By specific process components such as development and delivery, in addition to a specific program.

12. Management involvement in the training process is:

    a) Very low with only occasional input.

    b) Moderate, usually by request, or on an as needed basis.

    c) Deliberately planned for all major training activities, to ensure a partnership arrangement.

13. To ensure that training is transferred into performance on the job, we:

    a) Encourage participants to apply what they have learned and report results.

    b) Ask managers to support and reinforce training and report results.

    c) Utilize a variety of training transfer strategies appropriate for each situation.

14. The training staff's interaction with operating management is:

    a) Rare, we almost never discuss issues with them.

    b) Occasional, during activities such as needs analysis or program coordination.

c) Regular, to build relationships, as well as to develop and deliver programs.

15. Training and Development's role in major change efforts is:
   a) To conduct training to support the project, as required.
   b) To provide administrative support for the program, including training.
   c) To initiate the program, coordinate the overall effort, and measure its progress in addition to providing training.

16. Most managers view the Training and Development function as:
   a) A questionable function that wastes too much time of employees.
   b) A necessary function that probably cannot be eliminated.
   c) An important resource that can be used to improve the organization.

17. Training and Development programs are:
   a) Activity-oriented (all supervisors attend the "Performance Appraisal Workshop").
   b) Individual results-based (the participant will reduce his or her error rate by at least 20%).
   c) Organizational results-based (the cost of quality will decrease by 25%).

18. The investment in Training and Development is measured primarily by:
   a) Subjective opinions.
   b) Observations by management, reactions from participants.
   c) Dollar return through improved productivity, cost savings, or better quality.

19. The Training and Development effort consists of:
   a) Usually one-shot, seminar-type approaches.
   b) A full array of courses to meet individual needs.
   c) A variety of training and development programs implemented to bring about change in the organization.

20. New Training and Development programs, without some formal method of evaluation, are implemented at my organization:
   a) Regularly.
   b) Seldom.
   c) Never.

21. The results of training programs are communicated:
   a) When requested, to those who have a need to know.
   b) Occasionally, to members of management only.
   c) Routinely, to a variety of selected target audiences.

22. Management involvement in training evaluation:
   a) Is minor, with no specific responsibilities and few requests.
   b) Consists of informal responsibilities for evaluation, with some requests for formal training.
   c) Very specific. All managers have some responsibilities in evaluation.
23. During a business decline at my organization, the training function will:
   a) Be the first to have its staff reduced.
   b) Be retained at the same staffing level.
   c) Go untouched in staff reductions and possibly beefed up.
24. Budgeting for training and development is based on:
   a) Last year's budget.
   b) Whatever the training department can "sell."
   c) A zero-based system.
25. The principal group that must justify Training and Development expenditures is:
   a) The Training and Development department.
   b) The human resources or administrative function.
   c) Line management.
26. Over the last two years, the Training and Development budget as a percent of operating expenses has:
   a) Decreased.
   b) Remained stable.
   c) Increased.
27. Top management's involvement in the implementation of Training and Development programs:
   a) Is limited to sending invitations, extending congratulations, passing out certificates, etc.
   b) Includes monitoring progress, opening/closing speeches, presentation on the outlook of the organization, etc.
   c) Includes program participation to see what's covered, conducting major segments of the program, requiring key executives to be involved, etc.
28. Operating management involvement in conducting training and development programs is:
   a) Very minor; only HRD specialists conduct programs.
   b) Limited to a few specialists conducting programs in their area of expertise.
   c) Significant. On the average, over half of the programs are conducted by key line managers.

29. When an employee completes a training program and returns to the job, his or her supervisor is likely to:
   a) Make no reference to the program.
   b) Ask questions about the program and encourage the use of the material.
   c) Require use of the program material and give positive rewards when the material is used successfully.
30. When an employee attends an outside seminar, upon return, he or she is required to:
   a) Do nothing.
   b) Submit a report summarizing the program.
   c) Evaluate the seminar, outline plans for implementing the material covered, and estimate the value of the program.

INTERPRETING THE TRAINING AND DEVELOPMENT PROGRAM'S ASSESSMENT

Score the assessment instrument as follows. Allow:

1 point for each (a) response
3 points for each (b) response
5 points for each (c) response

The total will be between 30 and 150 points.
The interpretation of scoring is provided below. The explanation is based on the input from dozens of organizations and hundreds of managers.

Score Range	Analysis of Score
120–150	**Outstanding Environment** for achieving results with Training and Development. Great management support. A truly successful example of results-based Training and Development.
90–119	**Above Average** in achieving results with Training and Development. Good management support. A solid and methodical approach to results-based Training and Development.
60–89	**Needs Improvement** to achieve desired results with Training and Development. Management support is ineffective. Training and Development programs do not usually focus on results.
30–59	**Serious Problems** with the success and status of Training and Development. Management support is nonexistent. Training and Development programs are not producing results.

Index

About the Author

Jack J. Phillips, Ph.D.

As a world-renowned expert on measurement and evaluation, Dr. Jack J. Phillips provides consulting services for Fortune 500 companies and workshops for major conference providers throughout the world. Phillips is author or editor of more than 40 books—12 about measurement and evaluation—and more than 150 articles.

His expertise in measurement and evaluation is based on more than twenty-seven years of corporate experience in five industries (aerospace, textiles, metals, construction materials, and banking). Phillips has served as training and development manager at two Fortune 500 firms, senior HR officer at two firms, president of a regional federal savings bank, and management professor at a major state university.

His background in training and HR led Phillips to develop the ROI Methodology—a revolutionary process that provides bottom-line figures and accountability for all types of training, performance improvement, human resources, and technology programs. Phillips has received numerous awards for his books and work.

Phillips regularly consults with clients in manufacturing, service, and government organizations in 36 countries in North and South America, Europe, Africa, and Asia.

Books most recently authored by Phillips include *Managing Retention*, Butterworth-Heinemann 2003: *The Project Management Scorecard*, Butterworth-Heinemann 2002; *How to Measure Training Results*, McGraw-Hill, 2002; *The Human Resources Scorecard: Measuring the Return on Investment*, Butterworth-Heinemann, 2001; *The Consultant's Scorecard*, McGraw-Hill, NY, 2000; *HRD Trends Worldwide: Shared Solutions to Compete in a Global Economy*, Butterworth-Heinemann, 1999; *Handbook of Training Evaluation and Measurement Methods*, 3rd edition, Butterworth-Heinemann, Boston, MA, 1997; and *Accountability in Human Resource Management*, Butterworth-Heinemann, Boston, MA, 1996. Phillips served as series editor for the In Action casebook series, which became the most ambitious publishing project of the American Society for Training and Development and includes 30 titles. He currently serves as series editor for Butterworth-Heinemann's Improving Human Performance series, and serves as editor for the Measurement in Action series published by the Center for Effective Performance.

Phillips has undergraduate degrees in electrical engineering, physics, and mathematics from Southern Polytechnic State University and Oglethorpe University, a master's degree in decision sciences from Georgia State University, and a Ph.D. in human resource management from the University of Alabama.

Jack Phillips can be reached at PO Box 380637, Birmingham, AL 35238-0637, 205-678-0176 (phone), 205-678-0177 (fax), or roiresearch@mindspring.com.

Special Offer from Jack Phillips for ROI Readers

Send for your own ROI Process model, an indispensable aid to implementing and presenting ROI in your organization . . .

Jack Phillips is offering an exclusive gift to readers of Return on Investment in Training and Development Programs. This 11″ × 25″ multi-color foldout shows the ROI methodology flow model and the key issues surrounding the implementation of the ROI methodology. This easy to understand overview of the ROI methodology has proven invaluable to countless trainers and HR executives in presenting and implementing ROI programs in their organizations. Please return this page or email your information to the address below to receive your free foldout (a $6.00 value). Please check the area(s) of interest in ROI.

Please send me the ROI model described in the book. I am interested in learning more about the following ROI materials and services:

❏ Workshops and briefings on ROI   ❏ Books and support materials on ROI
❏ Certification in the ROI methodology   ❏ ROI software
❏ ROI Consulting Services   ❏ ROI Network information
❏ ROI Benchmarking   ❏ ROI research

Name _____

Title_____

Organization _____

Address_____
_____

Phone _____

E-mail address_____

Functional area of interest:

❏ Organizational Development   ❏ Training and Learning   ❏ Quality/Six Sigma
❏ Human Resource/Human Capital   ❏ Consulting   ❏ Technology
❏ Performance Improvement   ❏ Change   ❏ Other (Please list)

Organizational Level: ❏ student   ❏ trainer   ❏ consultant   ❏ management
                          ❏ executive

<u>Return this form or contact</u> Jack Phillips

P. O. Box 380637
Birmingham, AL 35238-0637
Or e-mail information to *roiresearch@mindspring.com*
Please allow 4-6 weeks for delivery.

The Value of Belonging

ASTD membership keeps you up to date on the latest developments in your field, and provides top-quality, *practical* information to help you stay ahead of trends, polish your skills, measure your progress, demonstrate your effectiveness, and advance your career.

We give you what you need most from the entire scope of workplace learning and performance:

Information
We're your best resource for research, best practices, and background support materials – the data you need for your projects to excel.

Networking
We're the facilitator who puts you in touch with colleagues, experts, field specialists, and industry leaders – the people you need to know to succeed.

Technology
We're the clearinghouse for new technologies in training, learning, and knowledge management in the workplace – the background you need to stay ahead.

Analysis
We look at cutting-edge practices and programs and give you a balanced view of the latest tools and techniques – the understanding you need on what works and what doesn't.

Competitive Edge
ASTD is your leading resource on the issues and topics that are important to you. That's the value of belonging!

For more information, or to become a member, please call 1.800.628.2783 (U.S.) or +1.703.683.8100; visit our Website at www.astd.org; or send an email to customercare@astd.org.

ASTD
Linking People,
Learning & Performance

900-31410